A TASTE OF CÔTE D'AZUR

IDEA
ROBIN LEACH
RICHARD HÄGGLÖF

TEXT & PHOTO
RICHARD HÄGGLÖF

EDITING
INGER LISE EISENHOUR

ILLUSTRATIONS
LENNART NYSTRÖM

GRAPHIC FORM
LARS MODIN

A TASTE OF CÔTE D'AZUR IS PRODUCED BY TOPSPOT PRODUCTION, TEXBARTER AG, ZUGERSTRASSE 45, CH-6330 CHAM, SWITZERLAND

COPYRIGHT ©1993 TOPSPOT PRODUCTION, TEXBARTER AG, CHAM, SWITZERLAND

ISBN 3-9520562-1-9
PRINTED IN MALAYSIA BY TIMES OFFSET (M) SDN BHD.
A TOPSPOT PRODUCTION

A TASTE OF CÔTE D'AZUR

CONTENTS

Previous page: M/Y Maridome, ex. Stepharen anchored outside Hotel du Cap on Cap d'Antibes

Above: Terrace chairs at an outdoor café in front of the light house on Cap d'Antibes, shaded by an umbrella pine tree

OUR TASTE

The star spangled Côte d'Azur - sparkling brilliantly as
the Mediterranean shimmers in the summer sun...

The enchantment of the Côte d'Azur does not come to an end when its well publicized summer season is over. New seasons begin, filling the air with charm, beauty and options of their own. Whatever the experience you are looking for - be it cultural or a luxurious extravaganza; or may be the simplicity of exercise in nature, mingled with privacy relaxation and fresh air - all of it exists along this benevolent coast.

When it all started, more than a century ago, it was wintertime. The Mediterranean climate was soft and alluring compared to the harsh winter weather of the rest of the "civilized" world; a fact that is still as true today as it was back then. The French Riviera was one of the only spots in the world that combined a semi-tropical holiday climate with decent living, luxurious accommodations and easy access.

In the 1920s fashion, trends, tans and bikinis turned the Riviera holiday season upside down and over the past 40 years most tourist related investments have focused on summer, palm fringed beaches and the sun. Today, these are still important attractions to the Côte d'Azur, but they only represent a fraction as to what the region has to offer. Especially the beaches in July and August, when not even exorbitant entry fees can stop the invasion that leaves tourists lying crushed shoulder to shoulder, splattered with the sand of passing feet.

It's better then to be at sea, in a quiet unspoiled bay, only accessible by a private yacht. Or in the countryside behind the beaches, discovering vineyards, small auberges, fields of wild flowers, lakes, rivers, canyons, mountains and snow covered alps. For many, these are unmapped territories - with endless possibilities.

A TASTE OF CÔTE D'AZUR will guide and assist you in planning your next trip, always sensitive to your interests and your preferred travel style. It share with you the best kept secrets of the Côte d'Azur - how to find the best beaches, tour the vineyards of St Tropez on horseback, hike in the back country mountains, go river rafting in the immense Grand Canyon of Verdon, stroll through ancient hilltop villages or cruise the coast aboard a private yacht.

This is what A TASTE OF CÔTE D'AZUR is all about.....

RICHARD HÄGGLÖF

American poetess Sylvia Plath in a letter
to her Mother in January 1956

How can I describe the beauty of the country? Everything is so small, close, exquisite, and fertile. Terraced gardens on steep slopes of rich, red earth, orange and lemon trees, olive orchards, tiny pink and peach houses.

To Vence - small, on a sun-warmed hill, uncommercial, slow, peaceful. Walked to Matisse Cathedral - small, pure, clean-cut. White, with blue-tile roof sparkling in the sun. But shut! only open to public two days a week.

A kindly talkative peasant told me stories of how rich people came daily in large cars from Italy, Germany, Sweden, etc., and were not admitted, even for large sums of money.

I was desolate and wandered to the back of the old nunnery, where I could see a corner of a chapel and sketched it, feeling like Alice outside the garden, watching the white doves and orange trees. Then I went back to the front and stared with my face through the barred gate. I began to cry. I knew it was so lovely inside, pure white with the sun through blue, yellow and green stained windows.

Then I heard a voice. "Ne pleurez plus, entrez," and the Mother Superior let me in , after denying all the wealthy people in cars. I just knelt in the heart of the sun and the colors of sky, sea and sun, in the pure white heart of the chapel. "Vous êtes si gentille, I stammered. The nun smiled. "C'est la misericorde de Dieu." It was!

Sylvia Plath, Letter Home: Correspondence, 1950-63, ed Aurelia Schober Plath, Faber & Faber, 1976

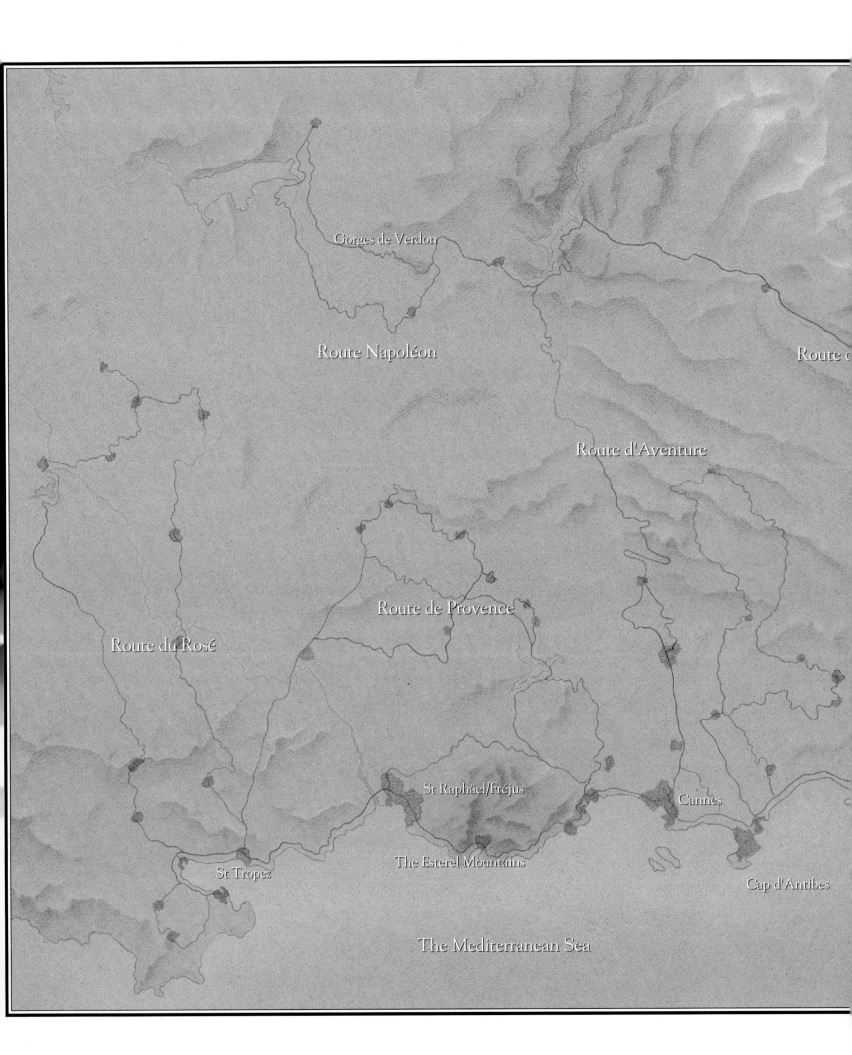

Gorges de Verdon

Route Napoléon

Route d'Aventure

Route d'

Route de Provence

Route du Rosé

St Raphäel/Fréjus

Cannes

The Esterel Mountains

St Tropez

Cap d'Antibes

The Mediterranean Sea

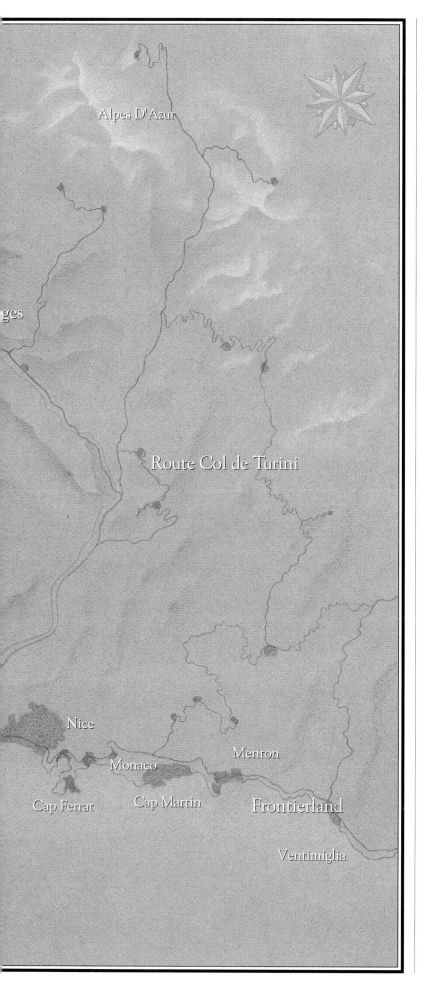

 TASTE OF
CÔTE D'AZUR

An introduction

TASTE OF CÔTE D'AZUR is the first ever complete traveller's book to one of the most enchanted and many-faceted vacation regions on earth. Like never before, the French Riviera is revealed as a whole - not regionalized as in other books - to encompass the magic and mystery of all five departments spanning 80 km (50 miles) of Nice.

A TASTE OF CÔTE D'AZUR proudly presents the best of everything in this southeast corner of France - from hotels to restaurants, to chic cafés, nightlife and shopping. It also points the way to the very finest in sport - golf, skiing, horseback riding, even hang-gliding. Best of all, excellence is judged on merit- the single criteria rated above repute, popularity and price.

Because the past explains so much of the present, the region's elegant evolution is explained from Belle Epoque Grandeur, the 1930's extravaganza to 60's chic and into the no-nonsense 90's where cost is always a consideration. With this knowledge, the reader is then invited to stray from the usual tourist haunts to rediscover the secret hideaways of Fitzgerald, Garbo and Bardot.

First-timers perhaps intimidated by the Riviera's swanky reputation, will discover a solid, practical book to enjoying the region. For them the emphasis is knowing where to go, when to go, how to get there and what they will find once they arrive.

Veteran travellers perhaps blasé about the Côte d'Azur will discover a deeper understanding of a vacation destination they only thought they knew. A plate of *moules* and watching a game of *boules* will be all the more enriching for knowing even the quirkiest local customs.

A TASTE OF CÔTE D'AZUR - an up-to-the-minute focus on luxury you can put a price on.

Previous page: Natural setting near Gordon,
only 16 km (10 miles) from Nice

Above: Château Eza, built by the Ligurians thousands of years
ago, it has today been transformed into a four star hotel

The columns of the Alpine Trophy in La Turbie, a monument erected to the glory of Emperor Augustus

CÔTE D'AZUR

A piece of history

Who discovered the French Riviera, the Côte d'Azur? If you ask an Englishman, his answer would be; Lord Brougham, who settled in Cannes. Many Englishmen followed suit and the Riviera became their fashionable winter residence with it's mild climate and charm.

History is subjective and sometimes it can be turned upside down; for example, stating that Columbus first discovered America or Colonel Spears the sources of the Nile. For there were others on the scene before them.

THE FIRST INHABITANTS

The first inhabitants of the Riviera are housed in the Prehistoric Anthropology Museum of Monaco along with their skeletons and stone tools. Judging from their diet (bones left behind of elephants and hippopotami), the climate was milder in those days even than today. And you may wonder: how did these people manage to triumph over a hippopotami with only the help of a stone axe? Perhaps the hippopotamus was more docile in those days than today?

We now jump forward in time, almost a million years to find the Riviera inhabited by a fairly peaceful people today known as the Ligurians. They had the habit of decorating the enclosures around their settlements with the skulls of their vanquished enemies.

As time passed, a few centuries before Christ, tradesmen came sailing from the East, from Greek settlements in Asia Minor and from Phoenician seaports in Syria. They set up small colonies along the coast of Provence where they were able to barter goods from the Rhone River area in exchange for products from their homelands. They brought grapevines, orange and olive plants. The Phoenicians brought something of equal value: their own great invention, the alphabet, the ability to write words by putting one letter after the other. Culture came to the Côte d'Azur from the East. From the North came the immigrants, the invasions. There were tribes from France, from Germany, and from the British Isles. These "Barbarians" were attracted by the warmth and riches of the Mediterranean coast land.

THE ROMAN EMPIRE

Time passed, and as the Greek colonies expanded and prospered - Marseille, Toulon, Antibes, Nice - they felt the need for protection from the north. What was more natural than to turn to Rome, the new world power which from the Appenine peninsula was extending its might around the Mediterranean? The protection led to domination and Provence soon became a province of the Roman Empire and remained so for nearly half a millennium.

Once the Romans conquered Spain, a safe road link along the coast was needed. This led to the construction of the "Via Aurelia," still recognizable today as our Route National 7. From Provence, the armies of Julius Caesar marched out to conquer France, Gallia in those days. At Fréjus, near St. Raphaël, anyone interested in archaeology can study the excavated garrison town and naval base of the Roman Emperors, its arena, theater, and lighthouse. When you turn the tap on in your hotel, the water streaming into the bathtub is most likely running through remnants of a Roman aqueduct. Above Monaco, at La Turbie, in addition to the splendid panorama, you can admire the columns of the Alpine Trophy, a monument erected to the glory of Emperor Augustus and his generals who had defeated a number of bellicose tribes in the Alps. The trophy has been restored thanks to a generous American patron.

PROVENCE SPLITS BETWEEN INDIVIDUAL BARONS AND COUNTS

In recent times, Empires have broken up within a few decades. In those times, it took centuries. As Barbarians, coming from the north conquered the provinces and towns of Southern Europe, they tried to imitate the Roman way of life, impressed by its refinement and splendor. Meanwhile, in the centuries after Christ, a new cultural influence made itself known, permeating the minds, doubling the civilian administration, establishing churches, parishes, and cloisters. The bishop had his seat at Aix en Provence. A monastery on the islands of Lérins outside Cannes grew in fame and spread it's disciples and teachings around southern Europe. The civilization became Roman-Catholic.

But the imperial link loosened more and more and Provence split into small principalities, each governed by its own local baron or count, most of the time fighting amongst themselves, much to the detriment of the population.

THE SARACENS

Then the Saracens made their entry. The Arabs had conquered North Africa and Spain by the 8th century and in the following century, bands of brigands from across the sea set foot on the "Côte d'Azur" and ran over the countryside, robbing and pillaging, taking prisoners and hostages. The intrusion of these Saracens went on for centuries. They used the mountains and dense cork forests of the *Maures Massif* close to St. Tropez as their hideout. There, they built and held, for a hundred years a strong fortress, the remnants of which can be seen at the pretty village of La Garde Freinet. The inhabitants of the Riviera, harassed by the Saracens, had to withdraw from the shore up into the hills. The hill villages, perched like eagle's nests on the hilltops, still bear witness of those troubled times. To fight the Saracens, to liberate the country from their piracy, became a common task for the barons and counts. During a fight against the Saracens, one of the feudal families, the Counts of Arles, proved their ability as leaders and in the end, became the recognized lords and masters of Provence. They remained the Counts of Provence for the next 500 years.

PROVENCE AND THE CÔTE D'AZUR WERE NOT PART OF FRANCE

Today we think of Provence as a part of France and of the coast as the French Riviera. There was nothing of the sort in those days. France was far away, a loose state in the making. The French kings were busy defending their realm against

Untouched, unbeaten, and endless - was this the vista seen by the first invaders?

the British, the Burgundians, and the Flemish. The counts of Provence, for their part, had their eyes on the Mediterranean, their traders filling the sea to Spain, Italy, and Sicily. They fought wars, concluded alliances, and married their daughters to princes of Toulose, Barcelona, and even Naples. Their people did not speak French, but *provençal*, a Latin dialect. This went on for hundreds of years.

To the east, the border of Provence fluctuated somewhat. The city of Nice was Italian most of the time. As a part of Piedmont it belonged to the dukes of Savoy. Further to the east, Monaco belonged to the Italian city of Genoa until, in medieval times, the Grimaldis, a powerful Genoese family, succeeded in holding and defending Monaco as an independent principality of their own. So it still remains today with a ruling Grimaldi prince.

PROVENCE AND PARTS OF THE CÔTE D'AZUR BECOME PART OF FRANCE

Towards the end of the Middle Ages, France had grown in power, French kings succeeded in consolidating and extending their control through war, alliance, and marriage. The Count of Provence now looked to France for support and protection. In 1481, Charles III, Count of Provence, dictated on his deathbed his testament which made Louis XI, King of France, his sole heir. Thus, Provence became part of France.

The kings of France respected the institutions, laws, and customs of Provence, but as time passed discipline tightened. The *province* was governed by lieutenants representing the king. The French language, by decree from Paris, was to replace the *provençal* in administration and in the courts. French armies, time and again, marched through on the way to Italy, always a coveted target of France.

As century followed century and as France grew to become the mightiest and most populous nation on the European continent, power and political life were more concentrated to Paris, where revolution replaced monarchy and emperors were succeeded by republics. Meanwhile, the Côte d'Azur was a distant and rural corner of the French realm, still half Italian in temperament and style, a calm, lush land with its forests, olive groves, and orange orchards. How lovely it must have appeared as the first "tourists," following in the footsteps of Lord Brougham, came to visit the Riviera.

The railway reached Toulon in 1856 and Nice in 1860. Nice became French in 1860, ceded by the King of Piedmont to Napoleon III as a reward for his help in making him sovereign ruler of a united Italy. And the railroad brought new life to the French Riviera.

Casino domes in Monte-Carlo - the epitome of Belle Epoque architecture

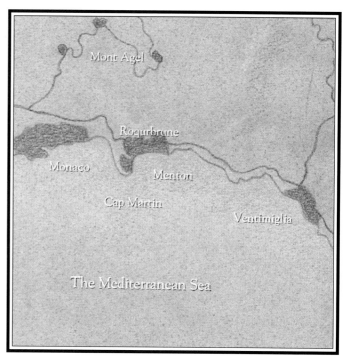

LA BELLE EPOQUE

Moves on to the no-nonsense jet-age

The winters in the north of Europe were cold and long, so the Côte d'Azur became a perfect escape. For extended winter sessions, aristocrats, the rich, titled, and artistic could socialize in the proximity of Kings and Queens, without ever being invited to a real palace. The Mediterranean sun smoothed out differences and the climate was for one and all. The train provided an easy and comfortable ride to the luxury that seemed to sprout overnight along the Côte d'Azur and the palace hotels of the Belle Epoque recreated the grandeur of the finest salons "back home" - Noblesse oblige!

Such was the start of the Riviera, and the modern lifestyle of the Côte d'Azur is directly descended from the giddy show of wealth and position so fashionable during the Belle Epoque. At this time visitors were advised never to stroll in the sun without a parasol and swimming was considered a medical treatment, to last no more than ten minutes and only in wintertime. Women were carried down to the water fully dressed by strong *maitre baignants* to be lowered once into the water, before being carried back to their private cabins. Maybe this is a reason for the bad reputation that modern swimming instructors have to live with.

THE TRAIN OF PARADISE - *LE TRAIN BLEU*

The train was the link between the two worlds, the officiousness of the north and the frivolity of the south. Its construction was nothing short of a technological masterpiece - hung onto the cliff walls, framed in golden sunlight. From St Raphaël to Ventimiglia it was strung across the coastline, every station a pearl of Mediterranean beauty.

In the early days traveling by train was stylish and elegant. If you were royalty or very rich, you had your own custom-built carriage - as you would have a private jet or a yacht today. If not, you used the legendary *Train Bleu*, one of the most culturally significant trains of all time, that still evokes nostalgia in those who relish the lazy, lavish kind of travel enjoyed when getting there was still part of the pleasure. Painted blue with gold stripes it soon became known as the Train of Paradise.

The archetypical passenger brought to the Riviera by the train was a middle-aged gentleman, who arrived early in January with his wife, friends, and private servants. He was either wealthy or *nouveau riche*. The group would settle into one of the luxury hotels for about three months, or until the weather up north became decent, at which time they would travel back to meet the spring and spend summer with their children at home.

A SIMPLE BUT STRICT FORMULA OF LIVING

His formula of southern living was simple: after a long relaxed morning with precious little to do, it was always nice to take a shady rest in the afternoon with even less to do, without a worry in the world.

But his time table was always very strict, as read in an old diary: an early wake-up call by his butler at 7:30 a.m. was followed by breakfast and the newspapers at 8:00 a.m. in the breakfast room, without his wife. Then he would head back to the room for a bath and dress properly for the morning activities, while his wife was still having breakfast in her room.

The hours before lunch were spent strolling up and down one of the seaside promenades arm-in-arm with his wife, shaded by a small umbrella or a big hat against the soft winter sun. They would sit for awhile on a bench gazing out to the Mediterranean before eating their lunch, which was always taken outside the hotel at the same restaurant, the same table, and the same time every day.

The two of them would then return to the hotel about 3:00 p.m. for a two hour rest after their "busy" morning. Then he would take a short swim in the sea, without his wife. At 6:00 p.m. the men would meet at the highly polished wooden bar for a couple of drinks before dining at the hotel, with their wives.

A game of cards was played in the salon after dinner and at 9:00 p.m. the gentlemen left the hotel for some fashion-able nightspot, preferably the Casino or wherever the roy-als decided to show up. The wives went to sleep. At two in the morning he would break up and return to the hotel, go to his bedroom, smoke a cigar, and order a bottle of Per-rier before going to sleep.

THE TRANSFORMATION FROM A WINTER ESCAPE TO A SUMMER RESORT

The Belle Epoque hotels with their sumptuous salons and their seaside placement were built to accommodate such a lifestyle. Nearly a century later, these same winter palaces still exist - their impressive facades still looking out to the sea. You can still be seated in their bars, their dining rooms or on the elegantly romantic terraces and recapture lingering memories of the halcyon days that reached their apogee in 1914, before they abruptly vanished.

When holiday life on the Côte d'Azur started to change after World War I, there were just a few places to go if you were looking for sun, beaches or a touch of extravaganza. It was the "lost generation" of Americans, like Scott Fitzgerald and Ernest Hemingway, who discovered Juan-les-Pins and Cap d'Antibes in the mid 20s. And when the hotels in Cannes first opened for the summer due to rainy summers up north, they instantly attracted thousands of visitors - a new season had begun - the Côte d'Azur suddenly became a summer resort.

The soldiers and officers who had freed Europe by a brave invasion needed time to forget the war and relax. It was during this period that people started to undress and enjoy life again. This "new generation" realized that a refreshing summer swim in the sea was neither dangerous to one's life, nor bad for morals.

THE AMERICAN INFLUENCE: BIKINIS, CHEWING GUM, COCA-COLA & COCKTAILS

In gratitude for American participation in World War I, on January 26, 1918, the mayor of Nice officially renamed the Quai du Midi at the end of Promenade des Anglais to Quai des Etats-Unis and by October the same year 1,200 "Sammies" per week were showing up in the city for leave. Within 6 months 40,000 Americans left the fronts for the "Nice Leave Area" to benefit from the Mediterranean climate.

In just a few years, the Côte d'Azur started to party summertime and the Americans brought lasting fashions: bikinis, chewing gum, sun bathing, Coca-Cola and cocktails!

THE PALATIAL HOTELS STILL STAND - IMPOSSIBLE TO REBUILT

The interiors of the grand palaces have successively been changed and modernized with disparate success to catch up with the current demands of a spoiled generation of the no-nonsense jet age, accustomed to waking up in New York and boarding an afternoon flight to the Côte d'Azur for a couple of days of sunshine, before shooting off to Tokyo. The Côte d'Azur is no longer considered a winter resort, although most of the palatial hotels stay open and the winter climate remains much the same as it was during the Belle Epoque. As a matter of fact, the best season on the Côte d'Azur for those not dreaming of endless southern beaches is the quiet and mild period between October and Easter, when the sun is gentle, the air crisp, and vast stretches of beach vacant - while the rest of the northern hemisphere is grey, cold, and dull.

A MODERN JET-AGED "BLUE TRAIN" FLYING LOW THROUGH FRANCE

The *Train Bleu* lives on and leaves Gare de Lyon in Paris every day, but it might have lost some of its former poshness. However old fashioned, train travel is still appealing, even adventurous and in the last years, it has been revitalized. Today there is an atmospheric alternative that you can climb aboard - the shark snouted TGV (*Train Grande Vitesse*) - the fastest and most advanced high-tech train in the world. While the airlines continue to discover new ways to shoe-horn people into less space, the TGV is doing the opposite. It provides large comfortable first class seats, wide aisles to stretch your legs, a cheery bar, and a restaurant for social-izing with fellow passengers. You avoid the long transporta-tion to airports and crowded check-ins. The TGV leaves Gare de Lyon several times a day, reaching Nice in less than 7 hours. At Gare de Lyon, before boarding, dip into the past by enjoying a meal in the restaurant LE TRAIN BLEU. While

the facade of this old station bears features of La Belle Epoque, the most striking manifestation of the era has been preserved inside the dining room. The decor overwhelms with 41 paintings in all, each portraying a euphoric scene along the classic railway network. The huge painting on the ceiling in the main dining room, the Gold Room, is "Nice - the Battle of Flowers" painted by Henri Gervex, a close friend of Renoir. On the surrounding walls you'll find paintings of Villefranche, Monaco, etc.

The ride is smooth and quiet; the windows large and clean. As you "fly" safely and glibly through the French countryside at 260 km/hour (160 miles/hour), instead of looking down at clouds, you'll know that you are approach-ing the next village when the top of a church steeple rises slowly on the horizon. You'll be reminded of the days before the skyscraper, when the tallest structures around were spires and ship masts. The TGV will not slow down until it reaches Avignon close to Marseille. At that point it will proceed at a slower speed, but remains faster and quieter than any other train as it continues along the coast.

THE MÉTRAZUR - A UNIQUE OPPORTUNITY TO TRAVEL IN COMFORT ALONG THE CÔTE D'AZUR

Along the coast you can still take advantage of the railroad; another modern "Blue Train" serves every day of the year. It is nicknamed the MétrAzur. The Côte d'Azur's own version of a Métro stops at 31 stations, including all the famous coastal resorts. It runs from St Raphaël to Ventimiglia, Italy, in less than 2 hours. Welcome to the discovery of a modern jet-aged Côte d'Azur.

Belle Epoque facade of the Hermitage in Monte-Carlo

A fairy-tale palace on top of a rock - the Principality of Monaco

Monaco Harbor - encircled by the Rock and Monte-Carlo

MONACO

A safe world of its own

A fairy-tale palace, complete with princes and princesses, pomp and tragedy; the playground of the chic; the haunt of countless multi-millionaires. The independent and sovereign state of Monaco is smaller than half of New York's Central Park, which makes it the world's tiniest country after the Vatican and San Marino. Squeezed into this little world of its own, Monaco offers all the ingredients of "the good life." It all began nearly 700 years ago.

The Principality has been in the hands of the ruling family, the Grimaldis, since the beginning of the 14th century. Its history is turbulent and sometimes very violent. The old town of Monaco is located on the Rock with its palace which is ringed by towers and bastions. It was originally built by the Genoese in the 12th century, but taken by the supporters of the Grimaldi family when Francesco Grimaldi made his way into the fortress disguised as a monk in 1297 (the Monegasque emblem consists of two monks with knives

in their hands). Until the middle of the 19th century, Monaco was just a tiny, poor village of little importance. But its location has always been unique - on a rock overhanging the Mediterranean against a backdrop of impressive mountains.

THE MODERN HISTORY OF MONACO CASINOS AND *DE LUXE* HOTELS

Monaco's modern history begins when it gained independence in 1861. At that time, elegant villas and palaces dotted the neighboring countrysides. Only Monaco, very hard to access, remained poor and forgotten. Prince Charles III of Monaco realized that his country possessed an enormous asset - its independence. Since gambling had long been forbidden in France, he decided to build a casino; the first gambling license was granted in 1856. But Monaco had a transportation problem. The daily coach from Nice took over 4 hours of dangerous driving, plus a mule ride down the steep descent from La Turbie. It's hardly sur-

The official Monegasque emblem: two monks with knives in their hand

prising that only one gambler entered the first casino in November, 1858. He won 2 francs, but the journey had cost him 50 francs. The casino soon went bankrupt.

Two years later Francois Blanc, a Frenchman who had successfully brought casinos and beautiful hotels to Bad-Homburg in Germany, was given a fifty years concession to build a casino and luxury hotels in Monaco by Charles III. The location was the top of the hill opposite Monaco village, soon to be named Monte-Carlo and the standards; better than in Bad-Homburg.

He knew he had a gold mine in his hands ... if only there was transportation! The French government had promised to improve the roads, but that was not enough. Francois Blanc lent the French government the enormous sum of FF 4.8 million at low interest to complete the Opera in Paris - in exchange the French government extended the railway along the steep cliffs to Monaco.

This time the casino project was a success, and only a few years later Europe's most luxurious hotel, the HÔTEL DE PARIS, opened next door. Monaco became the playground of the rich and royal society of Europe.

A FAVORITE REFUGE FOR THE DISCREET AND ONE OF THE SAFEST PLACES ON EARTH

Since then Monaco has evolved into a favorite international haven of refuge for the "discreet." Among its 36,000 residents, as many as 30,000 are foreigners, vastly outnumbering the 6000 Monegasque citizens. In addition to a favorable tax situation, the security and political stability offered are considered significant assets, rare in the modern world. There is one proper, politely dressed policeman for every 80 inhabitants, plus surveillance cameras at every main intersection and public area. Furthermore, Monaco is accessible by only a few roads, making it easy to seal off. There are stories of people who have left valuables in open convertibles only to find a friendly note from a police officer stating that the property is at the police station.

Apart from being one of the safest places on earth, Monaco is also one of the cleanest. It almost looks like a movie set with its orderly appearance swept by the pure fresh air of the Mediterranean. Bus loads of tourists arrive, but visitors are mannerly and clean-cut. Tourists are informed by prominent signs that in Monaco there is a dress code - shoes must be worn, bathing suits are to remain on the beaches and a proper shirt is a must!

Monaco taxi cabs are shiny, first-class vehicles in mint condition! Buses are washed and polished every day and drivers wear white uniforms with an embroidered Monegasque emblem. Each company and store displays a gold framed picture of their beloved royal family.

The mini-paradise itself is draped in the Monegasque colors of red and white. Poverty and homeless people are virtually non-existent. Such a combination of advantages makes the sovereign state of Monaco one of the most sought after homes for millionaires, international celebrities, fashion tycoons, artists, and sports figures.

TOURING MONACO AND HOW TO GET THERE

To get to Monaco, regulars know the stylish way to arrive - by sea aboard a private yacht or cruise ship. The quickest route is by HELIAIR MONACO, a helicopter shuttle from Nice Airport, offering a beautiful approach after only 5 minutes in the air. Otherwise, there are a number of roads. The fastest is the new tunnel from the Autoroute de l'Esterel, a shortcut slashed through the mountain which joins the Moyenne Corniche straight into Monaco.

Squeezed into this little world of its own, Monaco provides everything "the good life" can offer: gourmet restaurants, first-class hotels, elegant boutiques, international banking, casinos, and all kinds of sporting facilities. Parking, on the other hand, in the streets of Monaco is very restricted, contrary to what you'll get used to in neighboring France. If you don't want to find your car impounded and subject to a hefty fine, leave it in one of the elegant parking garages.

THE ROCK - MONACO VILLE

Start your visit by climbing the long ramp which begins near the harbor and winds all the way up to Place d'Armes, the square in front of the pretty beige palace, home of Prince Rainier and his family. Every day at noon the "Changing of the Guards" takes place on this square, a popular and very tourist-oriented ceremony. From the parapets sidling the palace, the vistas of sea and mountain and Monaco are spectacular, especially after sunset when the entire country twinkles with light.

With its tidy, quaint little streets, the Rock is in some ways reminiscent of the tiny medieval villages in the hinterland. The cobblestone streets run parallel to each other, connected by vaulted passages called *carrugieti*, carved and sculpted to the delight of those who stroll by.

After meandering through the narrow alleys of the old town, Monaco Ville, a visit to the Oceanographic Museum is recommended. The most pleasant route is along the western side of the Rock, through *Les Jardins St.Martin*, where nice shady walks wind through tropical vegetation with exuberant blossoms, past pine trees, ponds and fountains to a beautiful belvedere atop the cliffs which looks out over the coastline to Cap Ferrat. The museum itself is in an impressive building cut into the sheer white cliff that ascends dramatically out of the sea. This landmark was built early in the century by Prince Albert I, an oceanographic explorer himself.

While winding your way down the serpentine stairs, you will pass the *Theatre du Fort Antoine*, formerly an old fortress facing the entrance of the harbor, now a small amphitheater for summertime entertainment.

MONACO HARBOR - ENCIRCLED BY THE ROCK AND MONTE-CARLO

Between Monaco Ville on the Rock and Monte-Carlo, the Principality circles around the sheltered harbor and La Condamine, a shopping area and the center of Monaco's administration. Though not quite as sophisticated as the exclusive boutiques by the casino, there are pleasant shops

The Royal palace in Monaco where the touristic "changing of the guards" takes place every day at noon

The Rock - Monaco Village, perched on a cliff that forms an isolated peninsula. In the foreground the royal palace and on the western side the spectacular Oceanographic Museum

The Oceanographic Museum cut into the rock

EXOTIC GARDENS, AN OLYMPIC STADIUM AND INTERNATIONAL BUSINESS

The *JARDIN EXOTIQUE* and the observatory cave are located high in the northern extremity of the Principality. During excavation of this rocky terrain, an immense cavern was discovered more than 300 feet below the surface by a croupier of the Casino. The grotto contains stalagmites and stalactites, as well as evidence that prehistoric man once lived there.

But Monaco is more than pretty Belle Epoque facades, a medieval old town, flowers, and manicured gardens. It's also modern, business-minded and efficient. Touring Monaco, don't hesitate to use the comfortable buses and don't be surprised if you hear a phone ring. No, it won't be the driver's intercom, it's your fellow passenger, the guy dressed in an Italian suit who is traveling between meetings and has just received a business call from New York or Tokyo. International banks and holding companies thrive.

Fontvieille, a recently developed area built out of land reclaimed from the sea, is now part of Monaco. A sophisticated industrial zone surrounds the Louis II stadium, host to such events as the Special Olympic Games and where international soccer matches are played on the 8th floor roof. A modern residential area looks up at the Rock and palace, and residents are within walking distance of the heliport, the Princess Grace Rose garden, the Chapiteau permanent circus tent, and a large shopping mall with treacherously shiny marble-tiled floors and an exquisitely decorated MacDonalds restaurant, from where you can eye both the palace and the new luxury yacht harbor while chomping down on your favorite BigMac! Don't ever blame Monaco for not keeping up with modern world standards.

WHAT'S TO COME NEXT?

While much of the world is more or less neglecting pollution, noise, and traffic as important urban problems to tackle, Monaco is acting. All non-residents will soon have to park their cars at new parking garages being built at both ends of Monaco, which will be serviced by a frequent bus shuttle into town. There are even plans of making a subway! More streets are to become pedestrian zones and everyone is being encouraged to "ride, not drive."

Because of its land limitations Monaco spent years spreading upwards in the shape of huge skyscrapers before it spread outwards by creating new land from the sea. Now it will spread inwards, into the rocks. The railway will be moved into the mountain and go underground with a new shopping center to make room for additional skyscrapers on the valuable land now occupied by the railway. Extensive plans have also been laid out to dramatically extend the harbor into the sea, adding two large piers which will be able to host up to six cruise ships and protect the harbor from strong easterly winds. There are also murmurs of an un-

reflecting the daily life of Monaco's inhabitants. The harbor, planned by Prince Albert, docks huge cruise ships and private mega-yachts.

Continue along the eastern side of the harbor until you reach the tunnel that runs underneath the Convention Center. From a marble "public lobby" infiltrated with soft music, elevators will bring you straight up into Monte-Carlo, a majestic setting of palaces, gardens, rich villas, elegant shops, flowered terraces and open-air displays of modern art. The HÔTEL DE PARIS and the Casino are both well worth a visit, even if you do not intend to overnight at the hotel or play the tables at the Casino. The overwhelming beauty of the Belle Epoque architecture is unforgettable. The well-manicured gardens and fountains in front of the Casino create a somewhat artificial scene. The streets are filled with fairy lights and the shops decorated in tinsel, and as you stroll along wisps of music from hidden speakers waft through the air.

derwater walkway between the Rock and Monte-Carlo, where you'll be able to walk at the bottom of the sea through a glass tunnel and watch the marine life at the bottom of the Mediterranean Sea.

EATING IN MONACO
STARS AND PRIMA PASTA

Unless you prefer MacDonalds and the view it offers, there is a rich variety of restaurants in Monaco, ranging from the very best to the most Italian. Steadily Monaco has been receiving new stars for its gastronomical efforts and is already a threat to Mougins in the culinary star-spangled sky of Michelin.

In the old town just a minute's walk from the palace, you'll find PINOCCIO, a casual restaurant full of Italian charm, with entrances on both sides, a front door and back door that will take you through the kitchen. There are only a few tables but a very chic clientele, including local princesses and princes. Reservations are a must, since strangers of the street will rarely find space. During the summer, tables are scattered outside on the narrow pavement. The restaurant specializes in Italian food, obviously with a great variety

With restricted space, houses are almost built on top of each other

Always busy - Café de Paris on the Casino square with Hôtel de Paris in the background

of pasta dishes and a superb carpaccio.

In Condamine, or the district around the harbor, *al fresco* luncheons are good on the sunny terrace of RESTAURANT DU PORT, once again very Italian with excellent pastas and a ringside seat on the harbor. Monaco's most popular restaurant is THE TEXAN, next door to the Ferrari dealer up from the port. It's trendy and always crowded, not for its location or view, because there is none. This is hot, noisy dining where young internationals gather with barons and baronesses; it was opened by a dear friend of Grace Kelly. The chicken nachos, brownies and peanut butter ice cream are delicious, and the Alamo bar a scream. It's the only place on the coast where American-style TV monitors can show you action movies, Presidential debates or American football while you're downing a tequila.

AND IN MONTE-CARLO...

Monte-Carlo also has plenty of choices, all depend on your taste and on how deeply into your pocket you are willing to dig. For *al fresco* luncheons or an afternoon tea, CAFÉ DE PARIS facing the Casino is a must. It offers a *brasserie* variety of dishes, seafood platters and oysters in a turn of the century Monegasque setting. On the sidewalk café, you can watch a continuous stream of shiny red Italian sports cars, Rolls Royces, elegant residents in expensive furs, inspite of the mild climate, and tourists with video cameras hoping to get a scoop.

Across Place du Casino in HÔTEL DU PARIS, you'll find the most flamboyant restaurant and innovative gastronomic experience on the Côte d'Azur - the LOUIS XV, where Super Chef Alain Ducasse presides over the grand dining room. The cuisine has been awarded all the highest tributes, including 3 stars from the gastronome's Bible - the Michelin Guide. In a pompous setting of white linen, delightful ceiling frescoes, gilt mirrors, and crystal chandeliers, the menu reflects the seasons with a penchant for *provençal* and Italian-style dishes. Perfection with a touch of rustic simplicity. The international jet-set goes into ecstasy over the finer points of his remarkable repertoire and over the antique wines from the cellars of the HÔTEL DE PARIS, where over 300,000 bottles are stocked in the rock beneath the hotel. The table of the royal family always stands ready and the rest of the restaurant is booked up to 6 weeks in advance, not necessarily by the Monegasque, so don't forget to make a reservation well ahead for a dressy gourmet evening.

In the same building on the top floor, there is more of Alain Ducasse at THE GRILL. The uninterrupted view of Monaco and the coastline is magnificent. The food is cooked over a wood fire, hence the restaurant's name, and on a pleasantly sunny day the roof slides open.

Around the corner from the Place du Casino is the ever so popular "in-place" RAMPOLDI, another excellent choice for a good Italian dinner, chic and trendy. Once after a Nureyev Ballet in the tiny Royal Theater at the Casino, the doors of this restaurant were flung open and in walked Nureyev himself for a late dinner. The guests gave him warm applaude. A young American girl visiting Monaco on her honeymoon called for the waiter and asked him, "*Who's that?*," in a loud Southern accent.

The waiter politely told her that it was the famous ballet dancer Nureyev. Seconds later the door opened again and Princess Caroline gracefully entered the restaurant to join Nureyev for dinner. The guests stood up and applauded her. The American bride looked confused about the obviously famous newcomer. Again, she called the waiter and almost yelled at him. "*Waiter, waiter! Who's that famous model?*" The waiter, somewhat humiliated, bent over the American couple and asked them quietly and politely to lower their voices when her highness, the Princess of Monaco entered the restaurant.

ONLY STEPS FROM THE CASINO, BUT MORE CASUAL WITH VALUE-FOR-MONEY

Moving a little further away from the Casino through the park and uphill, the restaurant POLPETTA is hidden on a side street. Even though it's open for lunch, this is a dinner spot - casual and fun, in a lively Italian ambience. The owner, one of the Guasco brothers, will rush to greet the men welcome before he gives the ladies his attention and compliments and an Italian gentlemanly kiss on the hand. As the evening gets later, one party of diners might start to sing in Italian,

Previous page: Large cruise ships and private yachts fill up Monacos harbor

accompanied by a guitarist, and soon all the other nationalities will join in, until the place turns into a kindergarten for adults. Don't be surprised if you find yourself seated between a tennis star and a Formula 1 race car driver loudly talking across the tables. In Monaco everyone seems to know each other as equal children.

The best value-for-your-money restaurant is PULCINELLA, only a 2-minute walk from the casino. Make sure you have your reservation because even with the best will in the world, it's not possible to squeeze in another table and this restaurant is always full. PULCINELLA is as Italian as can be, a place where 8 easily fit at a table set for 4 and where cars have to give room for tables when the sidewalk is full. Once again you'll notice how everyone seems to know each other like a big *famiglia* in any small village - even the cats and dogs seem to be old pals.

Eating first class Italian food in a casual setting is as easy as it can be... just add four P's to your list of favorite restaurants: PINOCCIO, PORT, POLPETTA and PULCINELLA

MONACO'S LIMITED NUMBER OF HOTELS TEND TO BE EITHER 5-STAR *DE LUXE* OR NOT TERRIBLY WELL-RECOMMENDED

The grand history of the Côte d'Azur's Belle Epoque hotels and sites is an integral part of the region's folklore, and it started in Monaco. Where else in the world can you find such gorgeous palaces lined up along a short coastline, ready to welcome you to the "high life" of the Belle Epoque, starting let's say with Caviar and Champagne at the HÔTEL DE PARIS!

The legend of Monte-Carlo is a story in itself, but it's closely linked to the HÔTEL DE PARIS, which has played an important role in Monaco since it opened in 1862. When the HÔTEL DE PARIS was being built, Francois Blanc ordered his collaborators to "*spend freely ... economize on nothing.*" His wife Marie had a taste for sumptuous extravagance and played the role of interior designer, ordering an abundance of antique furniture, rich carpets, ornate mirrors, paintings, sculptures, crystal chandeliers, and gleaming silverware. Though this was just the beginning, important French newspapers already hailed Monaco as an "earthly paradise," creating a veritable California gold rush among English Lords, Russian Grand Dukes, and other high ranking aristocrats, who were joined by *nouveaux riches* business tycoons.

The first dinner served, on opening day, naturally included Caviar and Champagne in the magnificent *Salle Empire* and was celebrated by European Royalty and Noblesse. Only a few years later, the hotel became too small. Extensive developments over the years have enlarged it into a 300-bedroom hotel with balconies and frescoed loggias. For over a century the HÔTEL DE PARIS has never ceased to adapt itself to the times, while always blending luxury and tradition.

THE HERMITAGE

In the shadow of the grandiose HÔTEL DE PARIS, there was an old inn, once the Chapel l'Hermitage, which stood at the edge of the cliffs above the harbor, in groves of olive and orange trees, facing the old village of Monaco. In 1889, an Englishman bought it and decided to turn it into another luxury establishment. Ten years later a new hotel stood on the spot, its decoration and facade inspired by the Palace of the Prince of Monaco.

At first, the restaurant and the hotel were separate entities and clients who wished to go from one to the other often covered the short distance between the two in a horse drawn carriage. A glass covered passageway closed this gap and connected the two buildings. A splendid Winter Garden was created, its entrance illuminated by an artistic glass dome designed by Gustave Eiffel. From the beginning the HERMITAGE became a serious rival of the HÔTEL DE PARIS. Influenced by the Russian Grand Dukes who moved in, its faithful clientele became more and more numerous, charmed by the beauty of its decor and the magnificent view of the harbor and the Rock which the galleries and balconies provided.

In 1928, the *Societe des Bains de Mer* or SBM, the owners of the HÔTEL DE PARIS, brought this new jewel into its possession and all competition abruptly ended as they became sisters. THE BELLE EPOQUE, the original dining

A little corner of paradise. The Monte-Carlo Beach Hotel, located by a private beach at the eastern end of Monaco Bay, with a magnificent view of Monaco

The Hermitage decked out for the evening and the main road leading to the Casino square

room, was recreated and is considered today to be one of the most beautiful dining rooms in Europe.

The two hotels are connected by an underground tunnel which also leads to a recently built fitness center and a seawater swimming pool, heated all year round so jet-setting visitors to Monaco can sunbathe and keep themselves fit in any season. From the magnificent entrance hall at the HÔTEL DE PARIS, there is also a tunnel to the casino, for the discretion of guests, that was ordered by Aristotle Onassis, who also had his own suite built at the hotel to entertain private house guests, the most famous being Winston Churchill and his parrot.

BEACH PLAZA

Less sophisticated and not even remotely similar in style to the Belle Epoque, the BEACH PLAZA is also less expensive. It's a modern seaside hotel and the only one in Monte-Carlo to possess a private beach. The rooms are bright and comfortable and of a good size considering European standards. Make sure you ask for a room with a sea view and you will get a private terrace as well.

Neither the rooms nor the architecture are the main attractions here, instead it's the setting. You are only a few minute's walk from the Casino, but still very peacefully located in a small cove by the Sporting Club. In addition to the private beach, there are three swimming pools, both fresh water and sea water, on the sunny terraces by the sea.

A LITTLE CORNER OF PARADISE

At the turn of the century, the beach which marks the eastern end of Monaco Bay was visited only by fishermen. When the Côte d'Azur first started to become a summer resort in the 1920s and the young generation of Scott Fitzgerald discovered the charms of Juan-les-Pins, setting a new tone on the Riviera, Monaco decided to build a summer hotel to add to the Belle Epoque palaces targeting the winter guests. The hotel opened in 1928, hidden at the foot of the rocks of *Pointe de la Veille*. A talented entertainer, Elsa Maxwell, who was also a famous American journalist and the queen of organizing receptions for the rich and famous, was asked to host the opening of the establishment. From the early morning onwards on opening day, vessels strange to the local fisherman made their appearances - yachts showed up with beautiful young women in bathing costumes lounging nonchalantly on thick cushions, while motorboats towed athletes on water skis. The event was a complete success and Monaco managed to demonstrate its supremacy in the realm of summer holiday entertaining. With The Old Beach a new era started for Monaco!

Today the MONTE-CARLO BEACH HOTEL is still as much a summer place as it was back then. It's built on three levels and each room has its own loggia facing a fantastic panorama of sea, Monaco, and soaring cliffs. The heated Olympic-sized pool is where Monegasque elite meet on hot summer days. Down on the beach, activities include water skiing and jet skiing, and white cabanas line the sand. Reservations are a must. Staying at the MONTE-CARLO BEACH HOTEL in the summer feels like living offshore on a secret and romantic island, while the pleasures of Monte-Carlo and an exciting night life are within easy reach.

EVENTS IN MONACO - STARTING WITH THE MONTE-CARLO RALLY

The calendar of events starts in January, when the world's fastest rally drivers meet in Monaco for the first race of the Championship. For almost a week all the tiny roads above Monaco up to the Turini Pass become a race track for these dare-devil drivers and co-drivers who balance their saloon cars on the edge of steep ravines day and night, at speeds of over 200 km/h (130 miles/h).

Only days after the winner has crossed the finish line in the harbor and opened his traditional bottle of champagne, it's time for the next important event: the Circus Festival that started in 1974, when Princess Stephanie got it for her birthday present. Lucky her! Since then the festival has developed into a major circus event televised around the globe. Winners of the *Clown d'Or* will be seen at the best circuses worldwide for the coming years. For acrobats and clowns, the festival is equivalent to the Oscar ceremonies that honor movie stars. Don't think of this as an ordinary circus show. Think of it as a prestigious cultural event, when all of Monaco's social elite dress up in fancy clothes, covering their shoulders in red and white scarves. A posh dinner is served in a nearby tent before the show. Then everyone is obliged to be present and seated in the big tent 5 minutes prior to show-time. The M.C. asks for silence and everyone stands up as he announces the arrival of the Royal Family and their friends. The show can begin!

Next on the agenda ... In February, Monaco hosts the International TV Show Festival that each year attracts a number of international TV superstars, which means the Tourist Office can add new names to its long list of celebrities spending time in its microworld.

In April, the Grand Prix of Tennis moves to the Country Club of Monaco as the outdoor season opens. Once again the streets of Monaco fill with celebrities, this time from the tennis world. For many of them, Monaco is the home that they so seldom have the opportunity to visit.

Shortly after the tennis, it's time for the big boys of golf to show up at the Professional Golf Tournament, and then attention turns to the important annual social event, the *Bal de Rose*. It's a boon to international gossip magazines, who want to know which of the two ever so popular Princesses, Caroline or Stephanie, will be allowed to represent Monaco, depending on their previous behavior, and to find out whom Prince Albert will be seen with at his table, the date always a prime candidate for fairytale princess bride.

While shifting gears each 4th second for two hours, the drivers have to maneuver around narrow streets and sharp corners

THE MONACO GRAND PRIX

In May, it's time for the Event of Events - the Monaco Grand Prix - when Monaco becomes the focus of approximately 500 million TV viewers all over the world. For more than two months, hundreds of workers transform the town to a modern race track. Massive grandstands are built, the park in the harbor becomes a pit lane, and the narrow streets are fenced off by enormous metal anti-shock barriers. Monegasques flee their country, as a mass invasion of racing fans, race-groupies, stars, celebrities, royals and *Tifosis*, the Italian Ferrari supporters, assail the Principality for a few hectic days. The hotels are fully booked years in advance, so if you're not a regular client forget about this for a moment. If you still want to join the party and not stay an hour's drive from Monaco - here's the formula:

Rent a private yacht in the harbor and you'll be in the middle of the action, seated front row in full comfort! Or, some hotels offer special Grand Prix "week rates." They dictate the conditions and it won't be a room with a view!

* book at least 6 months in advance
* prices are doubled
* full payment (non-refundable) upon booking
* minimum one week with full board only
* personal check-in on day one, and they will kindly take care of your passport. No show, no room.

Four days prior to the race, huge shiny buses and motorhomes covered with colorful Marlboro or Camel signs roll into Monaco and unload state-of-the-art, high-tech F1 racing cars, computers, spare parts, racing tires, engineers, and mechanics in parking garages that have temporarily been converted into laboratories ready to build a modern race car. At Nice airport, a line of private jets belong to the super star drivers, and a specially chartered Concorde flies in more VIPs. After two days of practicing, testing, and partying in the streets, the big event, the Grand Prix, shouts off at 3:30 PM sharp Sunday afternoon, just like it has since it started in 1929. If you don't have a private balcony or a front row table at LOUIS XV, the best place to catch the action in comfort is at the RESTAURANT LE PORT, seated with a good pasta and a bottle of rose next to the track. Reservations have to be made at least 3 months in advance, and as the restaurant knows its value - it will be the most expensive pasta you've ever eaten. The harbor is full of yachts and everyone seems to be partying. The grandstands are full, the slopes of the Rock are covered with *Tifiosi* waving huge Ferrari flags. Every apartment and balcony with a view of the track is full of spectators and around the track there are more than 600 highly-trained security men, rescue teams, doctors, and nurses. In the grid the cars are lined up, the drivers are getting ready. Photographers and camera teams are running around in illogical patterns. Celebrities and racing-groupies are posing in front of the drivers, while mechanics are preheating the tyres and making last minute adjustments. The computers are linked up with foreign countries, so that the performance of the engines can be monitored continuously throughout the race. The atmosphere is tense, everyone is waiting for the arrival of His Highness Prince Rainier and the green light.

Minutes before the race, the cars and drivers are left alone and the engines are started. The sound reverberates between the buildings that form an amphitheater around the harbor and reach a crescendo when 28 cars release close to 20,000 units of horsepower. They set off towards the Casino just as coffee is being served at the elegant 3-star LOUIS XV, converted for the day into a royal box seat. The show takes 2 hours, as drivers maneuver their cars at speeds exceeding 250 km/h (160 miles/h) through the small streets, shifting gears each 4th second. When the show is over, the racing cars are disassembled and moved to the next Grand Prix and Monaco quickly returns to "normal" again.

Also in May, Rock Music invades Monaco for a long night at the Sporting Club when the annual World Music Awards are distributed in the *Salle d'Etoiles*, so named because the impressive roof slides open to the starry sky. The best selling popular music artists from a host of countries around the world arrive to perform their mega-hits before receiving awards from previous superstar winners of the Rock Music Industry. The event is presided over by Prince Albert, in person, and keeps swinging late into the night at Jimmy'z disco two floors down.

During summer there are several musical events including evenings when the Prince opens up the gates of his Royal Castle and classical music is performed live on the inner courtyard. In August the sky is lit by spectacular fireworks when Monaco hosts an international fireworks competition.

It's true that Monaco is one of the smallest countries in the world but when it comes to happenings and events everyone knows about Monaco! And if ever anyone should get bored with the ongoing activity, Monaco is surrounded by an easy accessible countryside. Whether you walk or take the MétrAzur, you will discover the mountains, the villages, and seaside walks of Frontierland.

The harbor of Monaco is filled with yachts, racing-flags and spectators every year in May during the Monaco Grand Prix

*Monaco Ville and the yacht harbor of Fontvieille
as seen from the vertical rocks of Tête de Chien*

The MétrAzur skirts the entire Côte d'Azur from Ventimiglia to St Raphäel

FRONTIERLAND

To the market in Ventimiglia

Monaco's unique location - squashed between the southern Alps and the sea, with Italy only 5 km (3 miles) to the east, and the plunging coastal mountains of the Riviera corniches to the west - makes the principality a special place for all kinds of excursions: long coastal walks or hilltop golfing; visiting Roman monuments and medieval villages; or taking a train ride on the Côte d'Azur's own convenient metro, the MétrAzur, to the market in Ventimiglia - Italy.

LONG COASTAL SEASIDE WALKWAYS CAP D'AIL & CAP MARTIN

Staying on the coast, you have a choice of two walkways along cliffs at the edge of the sea. The shorter takes less than an hour and leads to Cap d'Ail, west of Monaco. The longer leading to Italy takes about two hours.

From Fontvieille and the Marquet beach, there is a walking path that skirts the sea drenched rocks at the foot of Cap d'Ail. The 45 minute walk leads you past breathtaking villas and properties dating back to the golden days of the Riviera and opens up magnificent views of the Principality, the steep corniches, and Cap Ferrat. At the edge of Cap d'Ail you pass a beautiful house which once belonged to the late Swedish actress Greta Garbo, nowadays rumored to be the French summer hideaway of Colonel Kadaffi. Cap d'Ail is sheltered by pine, palm, and cypress trees and has a small and very secluded sandy beach, a favorite escape for the *Monegasque*, with its restaurant LA PINEDE. Behind this restaurant steep stairs lead up to Cap d'Ail's train station where you can catch the MétrAzur back to Monaco, only one station away.

CAP MARTIN - *LA PROMENADE LE CORBUSIER*

Starting at the elegant Casino square in Monaco, another walk leads along the entire, well-prepared, coastal path *La Promenade le Corbusier*. This path first follows the seaside

Skyline of Monaco and silhouette of Tête de Chien seen from Cap Martin

through the fashionable residential areas of Monte-Carlo until it reaches the Monte-Carlo beach and the BEACH HOTEL after half an hour.

If this is enough of a walk, stop for lunch at the poolside restaurant. If not, descend the steps behind the hotel and you'll leave the Sovereign Principality of Monaco behind, and enter the resort of Roquebrune, with its long beach bedecked by villas built on terraced balconies over the sea.

The walkway continues all the way around Cap Martin over the seaside rocks in a series of stairs and slopes skirting the grounds of enormous private properties. The vegetation is wild and abundant and the views wonderful of Monaco and its impressive natural setting.

One of the magnificent estates you might catch a glimpse of is one of the many second homes belonging to President Mobuto. This $50 million estate makes headlines each year in the local newspaper *Nice Matin*, when the President arrives in style to the coast in his private Boeing 747 with bodyguards, servants, and friends for one of his rare and short visits to see his dentist.

As you pass the southernmost point of the Cap, you'll arrive at a great spot for an *al fresco* lunch, the excellent fish restaurant ROQUE MARTIN. Situated by the water with views of Menton and the Italian Alps, its terrace is well-protected by glass wind breakers, allowing it to be used in winter as well.

The trail continues on the eastern side of Cap Martin shaded by huge pine trees, until it reaches a sea resort unique in the world, with two claims to fame: its elderly population and a Lemon Festival that takes place annually in February to March. Like many towns along the Côte d'Azur, Menton also has a nice seafront walk, Promenade de Soleil that makes a natural prolongation to the walk from Monte-Carlo. It leads along the shoreline passing many cafés and restaurants, the old town, a small harbor, and a pretty beach, until it finally reaches the Italian border, the eastern corner of the Côte d'Azur, where life instantly and abruptly becomes 100% Italian and hardly anyone speaks a word of French or English anymore. Jump back on the MétrAzur in Menton and Monaco is only 3 minutes away!

MENTON - THE AGED CITRUS

Menton claims to be the warmest resort in France, encircled by high cliffs and protected by Cap St Martin against the Mistral winds. Officials deny the reputation that the mild winter attracts mostly an elderly generation, as just another myth of the Côte d'Azur, but they admit that the lemon and orange trees and the *Fête de Citron* is the highlight of the year that brings tens of thousands of people to the town each winter.

A true *mentonnais* even claims that the citrus in Menton has its origins in a much more distant past. The Bible overlooks the incident: As Adam and Eve fled the wrath of God, Eve, conspicuously fond of fruit, snatched a lemon from a tree. Adam urged her to drop it at once, but stubborn as she was, she held on to it. Later when they came to Menton, Eve was overwhelmed by its beauty, the closest place to paradise she had seen since Eden, and she dropped the lemon. Long before tourism got underway, citrus fruits were the staple of the local economy. Then a local genius in the early 1930s got the obvious idea of creating a lemon festival and that's the way it's been since. The recipe is simple: you take 120 tons of citrus fruits and turn them into decorative art - citrus sculptures and floats - then you parade up and down the Promenade de Soleil for two weeks.

THE BEAUTIFUL GARDENS OF MENTON

The architecture in Menton differs from what you see along the rest of the Côte d'Azur, having a variety of splendid villas overlooking the Mediterranean Sea and wonderful gardens, most bordered by palm and lemon trees, with colorful flowers and ornamental fountains and statues.

The gardens of Menton represent an age-old passion, usually associated with the British, who were indeed largely responsible for turning their Riviera properties into a delightful middle-ground between their beloved gardens back home and the lush, tropical jungles of India and Africa. For many of them, the gardens became their life's work and a truly artistic endeavor. Their vegetation has been nurtured in an extraordinary natural greenhouse: a warm, humid climate, a geographic rarity formed by the soaring cliffs surrounding Menton. Each garden is special, reflecting its creator's taste and temperament, his favorite colors and scents and his favorite season.

THE ITALIAN STYLED OLD TOWN...

... a maze of narrow streets stands majestically against a mountainous backdrop. At the top of the steps leading from the beach you'll reach Parvis St Michel, an Italian-styled square overlooking the coast towards Italy. It is paved with

Fête de Citron

Hotel des Ambassadeurs in Menton

handsome mosaics and surrounded by old houses and the facade of St Michel, the largest Baroque church in the region. At *Place aux Herbes*, between the old town and the sea, you'll find an attractive market open every morning. Opposite the market there is a small fish restaurant L'OURSIN, decorated simply and offering delicious seafood! From the old town and its pedestrian zone, continue along the main shopping street, Rue St Michel, lined with citrus trees and many boutiques. HOTEL DES AMBASSADEURS in midtown has a touch of the Belle Epoque and is the choice to make if you want to stay longer and discover more of Menton's secrets.

ONCE IN A LIFETIME - A CRAZY NIGHT AT LE PIRATE

For funseekers the restaurant LE PIRATE, located by the sea on the western end of the Bay of Menton, is worth a dinner excursion on its own once in a lifetime.

Preferably don't bring a car, make sure you and your friends are in the mood and do negotiate the price of the dinner before starting or you will realize at the end that they actually were real pirates! The chief pirate greets you welcome with a toast of something he "calls" sangria, then he throws his glass at the wall - and the fiesta can start.

Expect anything to happen and let the child within

LE PIRATE by the water with snow covered peaks as a backdrop

you loose. Everything is allowed for a few hours. You might end up bare breasted with a bandana on your head singing with pirates and the *chef.* Or seated out of reach in the trees or on the roof spraying foam at other guests. If there isn't enough wood in the open fire, the furniture in the restaurant will do and when you've finished your food, throw away your plate to make room for more. When dinner is done, a donkey might come to clear what's left-over at the table - do we need to tell more!

Much more tranquil, BAIA BENIAMIN is a hideaway at the other end of the bay, just across the Italian border. It is the ultimate contrast to Caribbean pirates, situated on a secluded beach that you will share only with the local fishermen. Like a cabana on a South Seas island, it has the feel of real paradise. With few walls and comfortable chairs, the terraces on the water are shaded under a lush vegetation. This is an excellent restaurant, lunch or dinner. Or breakfast, if you prefer to stay overnight in one of the few rooms. Almost directly across the coastal road from Baia Beniamin, BALZI ROSSI is another treasure that will make your dreams of Italy come true. In an exquisite setting in the private villa of owner Giuseppina Beglia, the restaurant will offer you the best an Italian kitchen can produce and more.

THE CLIFFS ABOVE MONACO
TÊTE DU CHIEN

While the coast permits nice walks or a smooth ride with the MétrAzur, going uphill you'll need a car. Leave Monaco by climbing the steep and winding road towards La Turbie, the same road where Princess Grace had her tragic accident. In the Roman stronghold of La Turbie, you might take a quick look at the Baroque Church or at the *TROPHÉE DES ALPES,* a 50 meter (165 ft) high monument that is regarded as a symbol of peace and built to honor Octavius Augustus, Caesar's nephew, for his victory over the Gauls. Louis XIV did what he could as King of France to blow it up, but today the remains have been beautifully restored thanks to the generosity of an American gentleman, Mr. Edward Tuck. Most impressive however is the magnificent view over Monaco and the coast from the nearby cliff *Tête du Chien.*

Follow the signs for *les Hauts de Monaco,* an old fortress on top of a rock with a panoramic view of the entire Côte d'Azur. On a clear day you can see far into Italy to the east and beyond St Tropez to the west, while almost 1600

Menton and St Michel - the largest Baroque church in the region

View from Tête de Chien of Monaco, Cap Martin, and the coastline towards Italy

feet directly below the sheer cliffs, the Principality of Monaco opens up like a map. These heights are also a center for mountaineering. Climbing the steep vertical rocks, using only hands and feet, no ropes, has become a popular adventure. Para-sailing and hang-gliding are also favorites. The brave jump out from the rocks and glide like colorful birds over Monaco, using the strong winds from the sea and mountains to stay up in the air for hours, smoothly touching down on one of the beaches east of Monaco.

From La Turbie continue up towards Mont Agel and at an altitude of approximately 800 meters (2600 ft), you'll find the most spectacular golf course the region has to offer, the MONTE-CARLO GOLF CLUB. It is also, by far , the most demanding, as it sits on a cliff offering grandiose views of the Côte d'Azur and the Alpes d'Azur. A truly inspiring challenge for dedicated golf enthusiasts! The club is open only to members and guests, and has a restaurant and typical golf bar. For golfers, electric buggies are not allowed except if you are playing in the same party as HSH Prince Rainier of Monaco.

ROQUEBRUNE - THE OLDEST FEUDAL CASTLE IN FRANCE

From the plateau of Mt Agel, the road serpentines down towards the coast with new birds-eye views of Monaco. After you've completed this trip, you might almost feel like a bird or one of the brave hang gliders circling Monaco after a jump from Mt Agel, who knows exactly what Monaco looks like from above. Before reaching the coast, a minor detour back to the Middle Ages might be a good excuse for dinner or lunch in the old village of Roquebrune, nestled on a hillside with its medieval fortress.

To savour its charm, stroll through the covered streets, all very steep or formed as stairways. At the central square *Place des Deux Frères* a flower enclosure marks the entrance to The Keep - the well preserved and oldest feudal castle in France. The walls are an impressive 2-4 meters (7-13 ft) thick and the fortress has every form of medieval defense system: cannon embrasures, machicolatiations, battlements and loopholes, etc. It was built at the end of the 10th century by Conrad I, Count of Ventimiglia, to stop the Saracens from establishing themselves in the area. For several centuries it belonged to the Grimaldi family, like everything else in the region it seems.

Back to the Place des Deux Frères and its vista of Monaco from yet another angle, and it's time for lunch or dinner. HOTEL LES DEUX FRÈRES on the square has a few comfortable rooms, if you intend to stay overnight, but make sure yours faces Monaco, so you don't forget how it looks. The hotel also has a small restaurant with a nice open fire. Take a two-minute walk to the left, down the main street which leads from the square, and you'll find the small Italian restaurant PICOLO MONDO, where the owner/chef

A secluded fisherman's bay across the border from Menton - the idyllic location of BAIA BENIAMIN

proudly displays fresh vegetables and other "pick of the day." Let him make the selection for you and you will appreciate the meaning of the word "fresh." If it gets too crowded or hot at the few small tables inside, he spreads tables the entire length of the narrow cobblestone street, providing he has enough food for all of his guests. Quality of the cuisine is generally very high, but as experienced Monegmque gourmands put it: the chef has an Italian temperament and the food very much depends on his mood!

DAME JEANNE is the place if you want to stay with an ambience of the Middle Ages. The ground floor resembles a vaulted cellar, great for a winter dinner. You will be well taken care of by Mme Nobbio and the food is absolutely excellent.

VENTIMIGLIA OR XX-MIGLIA JUST ACROSS THE BORDER TO ITALY

To complete a visit to Monaco or the Côte d'Azur, an outing to Italy and the market is a must, since it is an integral part of life on the coast. From the train station in Monaco board the MétrAzur in the direction of Italy to the end-station XX-miglia, as locals spell it out.

Located only 10 minutes across the Franco-Italian border, the train station is conveniently close to the market held each Friday. Everything can be purchased here: Rolex watches, Cartier jewelry, Louis Vuitton bags and other high class fashion wear at prices much more reasonable than elsewhere, but with origins far from the proper design houses, and probably copied in some small unknown Italian village.

Unfortunately, apart from the market, XX-miglia has little charm and you'll feel very far from what you've experienced and seen on the Côte d'Azur - yet it's so close. Even

restaurants might disappoint you and sometimes you could believe the expression, "The best Italian food is to be eaten outside of Italy!" Along the coast road, you won't find fine sandy beaches or palm-lined elegant promenades. The stony beaches are filled with fishing boats just like along the Côte d'Azur 150 years ago.

The town is divided in two by the Roya River which flows down from Tende up in the Alps. The modern town is on the eastern bank, while the old medieval village of XX-miglia tumbles down the slopes of the western bank. Instead of being abandoned or transformed into a showplace of the past with boutiques, galleries and cozy small restaurants, the village continues to be lived in, much as it was centuries ago.

As you drive uphill to the top of the old town, modern civilization is replaced by an older urbanism, mixed with a world of small peasant farmers. The road narrows and winds itself up between greenhouses and vegetable gardens. It's a two-way road but if you meet another car, the problem has to be solved the Italian way - with a long discussion. There are no fences, no barriers as you look down at the sea far beneath. Once you've reached the top, you will be greeted by the sight of a modern and first-class hotel - Italian standards - LA RISERVA. This eagle's nest is perched on a balcony 350 meters (1200 ft) above sea-level with a panorama of two different worlds: Monaco and the Côte d'Azur to the west and XX-miglia and the Italian coast to the east. The hotel has rooms facing either direction, as you prefer, plus a pool, tennis courts, and a very nice *ristorante* open only in the summer.

XX-miglia and its surrounding countryside is the place to choose for those who pretend that life was much better before!

Next page; The sun streams into the narrow streets of Ventimiglia's Old Town

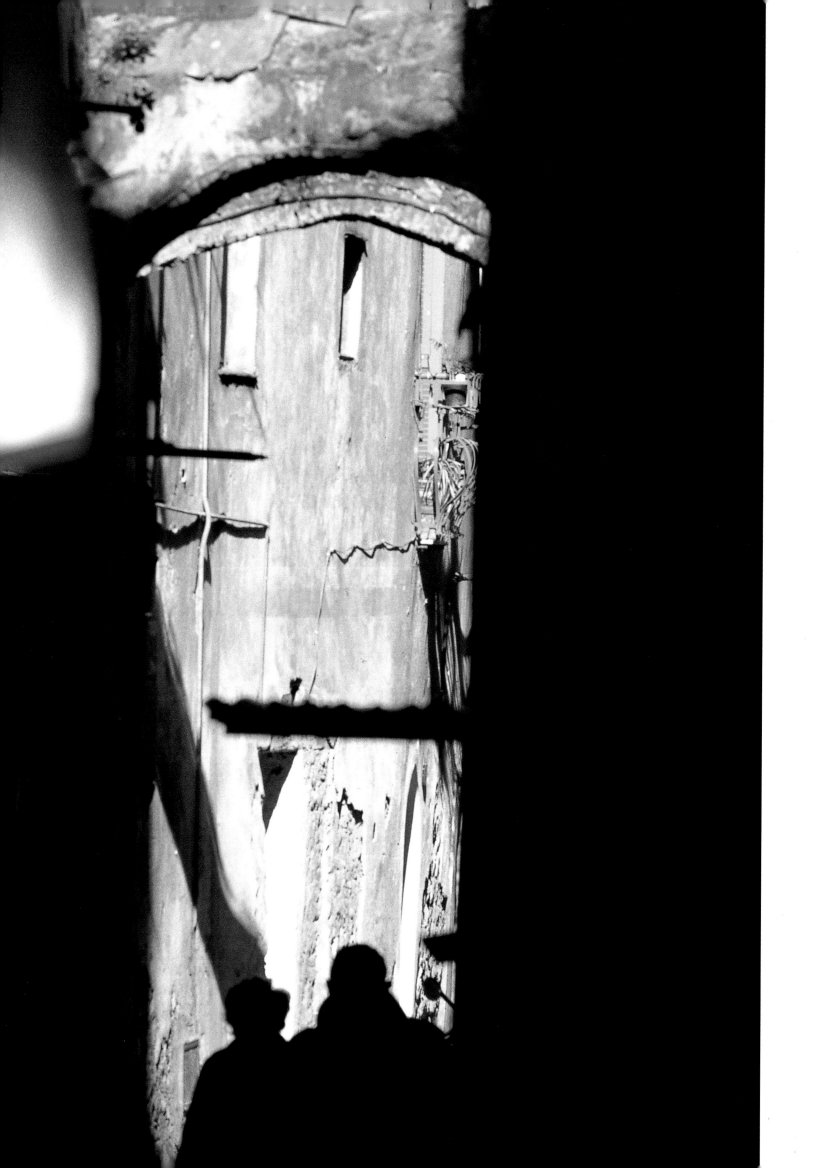

Previous page: Action and close racing
on the streets of Monaco during the
Grand Prix

Above: The MétrAzur offers a spectacular panorama as it clings to the rocky cliffs between
Monaco and Beaulieu

View of Cap Ferrat and Beaulieu-sur-Mer from the Moyenne Corniche

CAP FERRAT

The golden triangle - a club for the impossibly rich

Cap Ferrat, discovered by King Leopold II of Belgium, is still a unique hideaway on the Côte d'Azur, quiet and elegant, not the least bit touristy, and preserved as a heritage of the "golden years" of the Riviera. It is essentially a private club for the very rich. Nearly every square foot of this rugged pine-wooded peninsula is occupied by private château-sized mansions ensconced in vast, bougainvillea-clad parks.

Driving from Monaco towards Nice along the Basse Corniche coast road could easily be described as a beautiful, but sometimes hair-rising experience. In the summer, the road is invariably choked with traffic, as it winds its way above the sea, clinging to the sheer cliffs and occasionally going straight through them. The view of the Mediterranean, dotted with white sails and the silhouettes of luxurious private yachts, is truly a sight to be seen - by passenger eyes only! Unless you have chosen to travel by the MétrAzur, which offers an equally spectacular panorama, but allows you to bypass the traffic quickly and smoothly, seated front row. Between Monaco and Beaulieu there are only two stations and the ride takes only 10 minutes, while it can easily take a long hour by car.

Shortly before Beaulieu on the rocky shoreline at Eze-sur-Mer, the CAP ESTEL was built as a private villa by Prince Stroganoff in 1882, but was later transformed into a first class hotel. From the coastal road you'll see only a big iron gate. Inside the gates a private, rocky peninsula opens up. In a dreamlike romantic setting and far away from the madding crowd, this is a world on it's own, commanding a serene view across the Mediterranean from Cap d'Ail to Cap Ferrat. The many amenities include an outdoor and indoor pool, both continuously filled by refreshing sea-water. There is a sauna, solarium, a private beach, and a beautiful well maintained garden where lunch and dinner are served in the shade off by huge trees. The rooms in the main building are comfortable with large terraces offering spectacular views. But there are also a few private cabanas by the water, where guests will experience total privacy.

Hotel Cap d'Estel - private and romantic on its rocky peninsula

BEAULIEU-SUR-MER - "LITTLE AFRICA"

Located at the foot of towering cliffs, in a bay protected by most winds, this ancient fishing village is blessed, just like Menton, with the warmest climate in France - a prime asset, especially in winter. Beaulieu-sur-Mer has long been known as "Little Africa," so named by its large population of ex-colonial Brits, who brought along exotic vegetation to be planted in their coastal gardens. It's also an oasis of peace and quietness, with its own casino discreetly poised in the palms of the seaside promenade. The English and Russian gentry were the first on stage here, followed closely by an American clientele led by Gordon Benett, the eccentric owner of The Herald Tribune.

LA RÉSERVE DE BEAULIEU opened its doors in 1883 and has since conserved its timeless charm and hosted more celebrities than most other 4-star hotels in the world. Originally LA RÉSERVE was a restaurant on the rock above a fish reservoir. Its superb seafood and stunning elegance made lunch at its tables "a must" for the royal, wealth and otherwise famous visitors to the Côte d'Azur and LA RÉSERVE soon became... "the king of restaurants and the restaurant of kings."

LA RÉSERVE played a leading role in the golden legend of the Riviera. Its pure and genuine elegance has an atmosphere of hushed calm, as if protected from all the hustle and bustle of the outside world. In a fairytale setting of pink and white, it stands at the edge of the sea, woven into a timeless suspension of beauty between soaring cliffs and the shimmering Mediterranean. Each room has a view of the sea and there are four superb round rooms in the tower above the central patio with balustrade balconies, ideal for a long and lazy breakfast. The swimming pool is filled with the Mediterranean itself. Each day before lunchtime a local fisherman arrives at the hotel with his morning catch. He sails into the hotel's private little harbor below the pool deck in his *pointu*, a boat used by fishermen for centuries. The crowded deck is a hodge-podge of wet nets, bouys and tubs full of deep-water rock fish, shiny sea-bass, lobster and wriggling squid. Fresher fare than this is hard to find.

The neighboring METROPOLE also had its fair share of glory in the golden days and remains one of the last bastions of discreet and nostalgic elegance, built in the style of an Italian palace with a large garden and a setting equal to LA RÉSERVE.

THE VILLA KERYLOS - A UNIQUE RECREATION OF AN ANCIENT GREEK HOME

Thanks to Greek scholar and archaeologist Baron Theodore Reinach, there is no need to travel as far as Athens to recapture the beauty of centuries-old Greek culture. This Greek villa, neighbor to the METROPOLE, is a splendid reconstruction of the pure, classical architecture that marked ancient Greece. The Reinachs went so far as to recreate Greek daily life that went on in such a villa. They dressed in Greek gowns, slept on the ancient Greek cots, and Baron Reinach even ate dinner lying on his Greek lounge in front of guests seated at small three legged tables. The house is situated dramatically at the very edge of the sea, and surrounded by gardens filled with rare flowers, wild plants, cypress and pine trees. The symbol throughout the mosaic floors is the heart-shaped ivy leaf. Unlike Italian or French architecture, the VILLA KERYLOS is completely open - to the sea, the mountains, and the sun. The interior is a harmonious blend of marble, stone, ivory, exquisite mosaics, frescoes, and a pillared courtyard which serves as an ideal setting for a magnificent collection of antiques.

THE IDYLLIC FISHING VILLAGE ST JEAN-CAP-FERRAT

From VILLA KERYLOS a lovely path, *Promenade M. Rouvier*, traces the water's edge to St Jean-Cap-Ferrat, the picturesque fishing village tucked into an eastern harbor of Cap Ferrat. The peninsula has long been the privileged retreat of many distinguished residents. Most of the land still belongs to wealthy individuals who appreciate the tranquillity, natural beauty, and relative isolation of the peninsula. At the turn of the century, property could still be had for next to nothing, but that was before foreigners such as King Leopold II of Belgium, King Umberto II of Italy, Charlie Chaplin, Somerset Maugham, and David Niven (a longtime resident, much loved by the locals and remembered as the real English gentleman he was) transformed the *Cap* into a billionaire's paradise - and so it has remained.

In the harbor of St Jean, there are several restaurants to choose between. LE PROVENÇAL is famed for its excellent cuisine and elegant *rustique provençal* ambience. Along the dockside LE CALABU is in a much more modern setting but highly recommended.

Built on a rock overlooking the village with small fishing boats tossing in the waves at its feet, the VOILE D'OR is an elegant and expensive first class hotel with an excellent restaurant. A little further away nestled quietly between some rather large estates, the BRISE MARINE is a pearl - less expensive and with no pool, but it has a nice garden and a superb view of the sea and the rocky coast.

TOURING THE CAP

Only a few minutes' walk from St Jean and its snug little harbor, you'll come to a pine forest and a tranquil Mediterranean cove, PALOMA BEACH, in a pretty bay facing Monaco and the Alps. This is one of the few beaches where even in summer you can spend a quiet day relaxing on the beach, since the cove is off the usual tourist route. Daytime rentals include water-skiing and windsurfing or less energetic activities such as paddle boats or beach mattresses for a snooze in the sun. If watersports or lazy sunbathing don't thrill you, one of the most enchanting seaside walks in the area starts here. The St Hospice Point walk winds along the shore of the peninsula with great views of the Mediterranean, the mountains, Monaco, and Cap Martin. Around the point there is an 18th century prison tower, a chapel, and a path which skirts Le Colombier Point and Les Fosettes Bay, before heading back along the rocks around the very tip of Cap Ferrat to the Bay of Villefranche and PLAGE PASSABLE on the western side of the Cap facing Villefranche.

VILLA EPHRUSSI DE ROTHSCHILD

For art enthusiasts, Cap Ferrat offers a rare insight to one of the wealthy homes of the Belle Epoch era. Villa Ephrussi de Rothschild is a pink palace built early this century in the style of the magnificent Italian Renaissance *palazzinos* and symbolizes the extravagant wealth and passion for beauty that absorbed society prior to World War I. The Baroness de Rothschild spent 7 years building her home on the narrowest slip of land on the peninsula. From here she could see water on three sides of her property, which she named the *Ile de France*, after the great ocean liner of the same name. She flattened the formal garden in front of the house to create the shape of a ship's deck. Six other gardens, each with a geographic theme, grow from the craggy cliffs below. The home was bequeathed to the Academy of Beaux-Arts in 1934 following the death of the Baroness and now houses her exceptional private collection of porcelain, 16th century furniture, tapistries, and paintings by Fragonard and Tiepolo - all exhibited in the style of a home, often as it was when the Baroness lived here.

GRAND HOTEL DU CAP
THE BEL-AIR OF CAP FERRAT

The fabulous GRAND HOTEL DU CAP FERRAT was inaugurated in 1905 and soon became one of the most fashionable rendez-vous spots on the Côte d'Azur. It is set in a garden of Eden - majestically poised atop a craggy cliff at the very southernmost tip of the Cape. The opening of the 1991 season marked a new era in the hotel's history. Refurbished by its new owners it became HOTEL BEL-AIR CAP FERRAT, twinned with the fabled Bel-Air of Los Angeles.

The hotel opened its doors in 1908 and attracted royals early on, including Queen Victoria's daughter and the Duke of Connaught. The hotel is situated in 14 acres of private park, its atmosphere of a grand villa, as envisioned by King Leopold II of Belgium, has been kept - to create an intimate hideaway.

The vista as seen from the sumptuous rooftop penthouse is grandiose. Across the shady patio of century-old

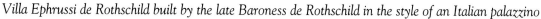

Villa Ephrussi de Rothschild built by the late Baroness de Rothschild in the style of an Italian palazzino

HOTEL DU CAP - BEL AIR, *twinned with the famous Bel Air in Los Angeles,*
located on the tip of Cap Ferrat in 14 acres of private park

pine trees and immaculate green lawns, a balustraded belvedere seems to teeter in the distance on the brink of Land's End, with sweeping views of the Mediterranean beyond. Also facing seaward, the superb dining room LE CAP is resplendent in its new tropical exuberance. Classical Greek mosaic floors are complemented by bright murals of peacocks in still-lifes of pineapples and oranges. Chef Jean-Claude Guillon has been with the hotel since 1970 and his cuisine has been awarded gourmet distinctions, bringing not only hotel guests to his table, but people from all over the coast. A rugged path twists down from the look-out point at the end of the garden through terraces of bright pink and yellow rock-flowers to the seaside pool area below, LE CLUB

The "Golden Book" of Pierre Grünberger contains
priceless signatures and drawings by some of the
worlds most famous individuals

DAUPHIN, home of one of the most famous swimming instructors in the world, Pierre Grünberger, who has been with the hotel since he arrived as a poor student looking to earn some money in 1949. He guarantees to teach any one of any age to swim in three days. Don't be surprised, while enjoying your poolside lunch, to find young and old singing loudly with transparent salad bowls over their heads. They are simply Pierre's students practicing their breathing exercises before he allows them in the deep end of the pool, where he will guide them with a pole like a farmer herding his charges. Pierre's private "Golden Book" is full of thanks from the world of the rich and famous he taught to swim and includes drawings from Picasso and Cocteau and words of praise from the Beatles, Charlie Chaplin and Onassis to name a few.

Breathe deeply and enjoy the splendor of the BEL-AIR DE CAP FERRAT. Seated by the pool of your Shangri-La, you are surrounded by exquisite natural beauty. The sea sparkles through your champagne glass. Experience the tranquillity of nature from your private cabana: hear the lapping of the waves, the wind on the awnings, maybe some laughter in the distance. A rare and enchanting hideaway for the lucky few.

VILLEFRANCHE - THE MOST PICTURESQUE WATERFRONT ON THE CÔTE D'AZUR

Opposite Cap Ferrat in the northwestern corner of the Bay of Villefranche, you'll find a charming little seaside village with a history that dates back to the 14th century, when it was founded as a customs-free port by Charles II of Anjou.

A sleepy tranquil haven in the winter, it comes alive as a colorful resort in the summer. Boasting one of the world's deepest natural harbors, it's a favored anchorage for the biggest cruise ships. Clinging to the steep cliffside, the old town consists of a maze of dark, winding streets and stairways which descend to the quayside of the bay, also known as La Rade. Lined with tall, *Italiante* houses painted in ochre and pretty pastel shades, the waterfront offers a good selection of restaurants and cafés from which to soak up the atmosphere and the warmth of the sun. The most famous and "the best" is ST PIERRE in the WELCOME HOTEL just opposite the jetty used to shuttle in guests from cruise ships or private yachts. The shaded square next to the harbor also has a nice café, LES PALMIERS.

On Sundays the antique market is a popular rendez-vous. The 14th century St Peter's Chapel, *Chapelle St Pierre*, stands opposite the main square where the antique market is held, at the entrance of the fishing harbor. For many years, it was used by the fishermen of Villefranche to store their nets. In 1957 the artist-poet Jean Cocteau, who had spent his childhood in this village, completely redecorated the chapel in his own distinctive style.

Walk up the stairs from La Rade and you'll find a nice little station from where you can board the MétrAzur before it enters a long tunnel under Mount Alban. Once you see light again 3 minutes later, a completely different world will open up: the capital of the region, Nice. Or you can discover the hinterland by driving up to the Moyenne Corniche to the medieval village of Eze. For nature lovers, Eze can also be reached in one hour by a well-marked hike.

Pierre Grünberger, swimming instructor of celebrities, young and old, at the trompe l'œil poolside of the CLUB DAUPHIN at the HOTEL DU CAP - BEL AIR

The seaside walk, La Rade, in Villefrance, lined with restaurants and Italian-styled private homes

*View from La Grande Corniche of the medieval village
of Eze towering over Cap Ferrat*

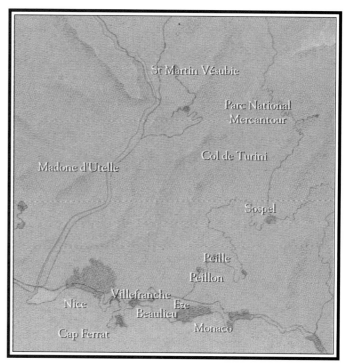

ALPES D'AZUR

The rugged Hinterland of Nice

ne of the best kept secrets of the Côte d'Azur is hidden from most visitors by the summer heat haze that rises from the coast. Located just a few miles from the coast, but light years away from the hectic bustle and activity, the Alpes d'Azur present a total contrast to the chic, fastpace of the sun-&-sand set. The Hinterland - so accessible, yet so often overlooked by visitors - is secluded and left to the chirping of its birds, the splashing of waterfalls and the foot-steps of contented nature lovers.

In less than an hour's drive you will ascend from sea level to over 3,000 meters (10,000 feet). Destination? A world so far from sun oil and deck chairs that you might wonder if it's possible you're in the same country! It's a world where chamois and mouflon run wild in forests of larch, where waterfalls cascade into clear mountain lakes, and sheep studiously ignore the occasional alpine hikers. It's also where ski resorts nestle between snow-covered peaks in meadows of wild flowers.

More than a winter sport playground, the Alpes d'Azur are home to over 50 enchanting little villages perched on hilltops or hidden in wild gorges cut into the red earth. Though each is an unsung jewel of the Riviera that retains both character and integrity, three are particularly

* More than 320 km (200 miles) of rivers navigable by kayak or other crafts
* 200 listed caves for the adventurous
* 180 km (110 miles) of cross country skiing
* Over 480 km (300 miles) of down-hill skiing
* Over 5600 km (3,500 miles) of marked hiking paths

THE MERCANTOUR NATIONAL PARK AND A MARVELOUS VALLEY

The Mercantour National Park is a 270 square mile wonderland that was once the private hunting ground of the King of Italy. Reclaimed by France after World War II, it was made a national park in 1979.

Beneath towering snow-capped mountains are lush, glacier-hewn valleys containing such wildlife as chamois, ibex, wild sheep, marmots, partridges, and the white hare. Botanists have thus far counted only 2,000 species of wild flowers in the park, half the total in all of France. The park is a paradise for fishing and hiking, with 1900 km (1,200 miles) of rivers and over 1,600 acres of lakes. It's considered the lifeblood of the Côte d'Azur, because the origins of all rivers that flow through the region to the Mediterranean Sea are found here. It also boasts the famed *Vallée des Merveilles* - the Valley of Marvels - home of several thousand Bronze Age stone engravings.

TRAVELING THE HINTERLAND

The Hinterland can be explored by car, by train, on a mountain bike, or on foot. A hiker's favorite is the glorious coastal path called *Sentier des Balcons de la Côte d'Azur* and designated trail GR 51.

The GR 52 takes four to five days and leads straight up from Menton to the Mercantor Park and the Valley of Marvels. Another famed walking path is *La Grande Randonnée* - GR 5 which begins in Nice and doesn't end until it reaches Amsterdam, Holland!

Motorists will find that the roads are mostly excellent, exciting, and well maintained, although they can be narrow and winding at times on steep mountainsides.

A LAID BACK LIFE

Our suggested tour - ROUTE COL DE TURINI - gives a good understanding of the area and will work as an introduction to further excursions. As soon as you leave the coastline behind, it's not only the landscape that changes character, but also the quality of life. Everything gets simpler and more laid back. Restaurant tables no longer have fancy settings, waiters are not in white. There are no more 4 star hotel suites with private terraces and 24 hour room service. Life is casual, food might come from the backyard and the scattered *auberges* provide comfortable accommodation but nothing more.

Next page: The medieval village of Roubion perched on a hillside below snow covered Alps

Numerous brown signs along the roads of the hinterland point out hikes

recommended. St Martin-du-Var offers a unique alpine, almost Swiss landscape. Eze offers spectacular views of the sea and some unique places to stay. Ste-Agnès - located 750 meters (2,300 feet) above Menton and the sea - stands majestically as Europe's highest coastal village.

THE ALPES D'AZUR - FOUR FULL SEASONS AND PLENTY TO OFFER THE ENTIRE FAMILY

The Hinterland, a true paradise for nature and sport enthusiasts, enjoys the pleasant coastal climate, but unlike the coast it offers four full seasons. Among its natural attractions are:

The medieval village of Peille, less than 9 km (5 miles) from the famous coast, but in a completely different world

The narrow switch back roads in the Alpes d'Azur wind their way along steep gorges

ROUTE COL DE TURINI

Touring the Hinterland

A hazy curtain drops between the glamorous coast, where the razza-ma-tazz of gold and glitter glistens in the limelight of an exquisite sun, and the wilderness that lies in the Maritime Alps, the *Alpes d'Azur*. Backstage behind the curtain there is less hustle, the lights are softer, the backdrops and dramatic scenery of Mediterranean forests and mountains are in place for a spectacle of nature to be played out. And here for those who love nature pure and clean, the coast will be upstaged.

The curtain falls behind the Corniche roads, mere shelves that shimmy across the sheer cliffs as they plunge to the Mediterranean between Nice and the Italian border. Three famous roads, the movie sets of Cary Grant and Grace Kelly's 1950s film "It Takes A Thief:" the Grande Corniche, the Moyenne Corniche and the forever delightful Basse Corniche which sprints along the azur sea slipping into all the coastal resorts.

Move inland behind them and the decor sets you in mountain valleys, pastures, and tranquillity - to the tune of silence, brooks, and birds. The *Alpes d'Azur* are a back garden to the Côte d'Azur, reachable only by a number of narrow switch back roads. The isolated villages, sometimes more or less abandoned, still serve as a reminder of the history and culture of the region.

TRAVELING ALONG THE EDGE OF THE STAGE

Traveling along the edge of the stage on the Grand Corniche, from Nice to La Turbie, you'll be snapping some unforgettable scenes into your mind. Looking south, breathtaking vistas of coastline trace the star-studded silhouettes of Cap Ferrat and the Bay of Villefranche into the azure blue waters. Looking north, the snow covered Alps.

At Col d'Eze gaze down on medieval Eze, perched divinely in the dizzy heights straight above the sea and Cap Ferrat.

THE MOST FAMOUS PERCHED VILLAGE IN THE WORLD - EZE-VILLAGE

The village of Eze is impaled on a rocky spike like an eagle's nest 400m (1300 ft) right above the Mediterranean. The strategic skills of the architects who could build such a place are to be revered! The present structure of the village goes back to the Middle Ages, but Eze has been occupied since the Bronze Age. The Ligurians made a *castellara* out of Eze: a living place enclosed by huge rocks to protect men and cattle. Before the Greek occupation, legend tells that the Phoenicians had a temple built to Isis. After the collapse of the Roman Empire, the area underwent several invasions, most were Saracen. Then Eze belonged to Monaco for a long period and it wasn't until 1860 that the inhabitants of Eze voted for their annexation to France.

Today Eze is a favorite tourist site, maybe because its location allows easy access from the crowded coast. Walk through the small archway that leads into the village; streets become narrow and intimate, sometimes twisting upward in a series of steps, other times running smoothly along carefully restored houses in small passages where you must shoulder your way through the tight crowds that arrive throughout the summer months in a never ending stream of buses. Every house seems to have its own "smart" boutique or artist's studio selling a hodge podge of "typical" Eze souvenirs. Don't be put off yet. There are still a few spots left

Luggage heading to CHÂTEAU D'EZA is brought up by mule-pack

A spectacular view from the terrace of CHÂTEAU CHEVRE D'OR, overlooking Eze Bord-du-Mer and Cap Ferrat in the distance

worth visiting, where life can be enjoyed to its utmost! CHÂTEAU CHEVRE D'OR and CHÂTEAU EZA both have the ambience of romantic havens, with heavenly food, beautiful antique rooms, and breathtaking vistas of the coast from towering heights that match their prices.

CHÂTEAU EZA was formerly the residence of Prince William of Sweden. This unforgettable thousand-year-old *bastion* clings to a cliff overlooking 160 miles of coast; it was restored only few years ago into a first class, 4-star hotel. There are only eight rooms and suites, all fully equipped with the modern comforts you would expect from an exceptional hotel, but the furnishings are well beyond the realm of expectation. You'll find Oriental rugs, beautiful antique furniture, and rooms with a romantic fireplace facing the *grand lit*. The reception is near the entrance of the village next to a mule stable. Once you have checked in your luggage will be loaded on a mule and brought to your room along a steep path in this old-fashioned way.

In 1924, the famous American violinist Balakovic and his wife Joyce, who both loved to spend a lot of their time in Eze, discovered the ruins of an old *bastide* on the edge of high cliffs between the sky and the sea. They had followed a goat to the ruins. An old legend exists that since ancient times a golden goat would appear in Eze at this spot. The Americans bought the old *bastide* ruins that dated back to the 12th century and named it in honor of the golden goat, CHÂTEAU CHEVRE D'OR. In 1953 it became a restaurant with a gourmet reputation that it has kept ever since. Between 1959 and 1989 a Swiss gentleman took on the painstaking work of transforming this medieval site into an intimate luxury hotel, its few rooms restored with sophisticated decor. It's a unique place in a unique location, literally hanging 427 meters (1,400 feet) above the Mediterranean Sea. The bar is located in a vaulted stone room with delicate Gothic windows facing the open southern horizon. The violinist once practiced his music in this room and it has remained the same since Balakovic and his wife moved out.

Walking the village streets, you will come across many restaurants with both pleasing locations and good food, although not up to the standards you have already discovered at CHÂTEAU EZA or CHEVRE D'OR. A good choice for reasonably priced food is the tiny AUBERGE TROUBADOUR. It only has a few tables, so make a reservation.

From Eze drive straight up to the Grand Corniche and continue on the road built into the steep mountainside towards La Turbie. The panoramas of the Mediterranean are superb! On a clear day you might catch a glimpse of Corsica in the hazy distance. Shortly after Col d'Eze a modest sign on your left announces LA BERGERIE which is hidden in the forest behind the road. This old stone farmhouse has been nicely converted to a restaurant with a warm, relaxed atmosphere. On the terrace you are seated almost above Eze with a spectacular view of the village and

The streets of Eze form a labyrinth of narrow cobblestone alleys

the sea. Inside there are a couple of huge log-burning fireplaces and the preferred food is meat.

LEAVING THE COAST BEHIND

The road leading to Peille follows the eastern side of Mont Agel. Immediately after leaving La Turbie you will begin to appreciate what the Alpes d'Azur have to offer: the peace and harmony of the stone houses so weathered by time, recalling a distant and glorious past, and the forest of sea pines and oak trees criss-crossed by natural paths scented of thyme, lavender, and sensuous floral fragrances. The road winds gently upward for 9 km (6 miles) with some narrow

Terraced gardens and olive grows, scents of thyme, lavender, and sensuous floral fragrances - a different world than the hectic coast

passages, sometimes on the edge of steep rock formations. Along this road, the FERME DE LA GORRA serves dishes straight from "*mama's* kitchen" made by 2 *mamas*! Louisette et Albane. Their restaurant is far from the luxury of the coast and their old stone house certainly melts easily into the countryside. It's a favored hideaway for the *monegasque* who want a breath of fresh air. There is no formal *entrée*, you come in by the kitchen. The two dining rooms confirm your first impression of country simplicity: white walls, a little fireplace, wooden furniture, and a rustic decor that opens up to a huge terrace. Make sure you have a reservation. Space and tables might not be a limitation, but the mamas have to know how much food to prepare!

PEILLE

Peille is built on terraced slopes above a deep ravine surrounded by a forest full of oak and pine trees. In the Middle Ages, Peille was governed by a municipal magistrate, later it became a *baillage* (seat of the bailiff) consisting of 18 communities. At that time, the higher and lower courts of justice were located on Place de la Colle, the main square. Criminals who had been sentenced to death were hung from the gallows whose foundations are still visible today.

To the right of the Place de la Colle, a small auberge

RESTAURANT ET HOTEL BELVERDE has a terrace that gives a magnificent view. On a clear day you can see all the way to the Esterel Mountains and the peninsula of St. Tropez 80 km (50 miles) away. Peille also offers a couple of nice hikes and excursions ranging from twenty minutes up to three hours, the longest climbing to the top of Mont Ongran. Since Peille isn't a gourmet center of the hinterland and doesn't offer suitable accommodations, a good suggestion is to make a little detour to the neighboring village - there is only a mountain in between - Peillon. To reach it from Peille, you can either return down the D53 all the way into the valley and then rewind your way up on the other side of the mountain or there is a hike of about 1 hour 30 minutes.

PEILLON - THE "INN" VILLAGE OF THE ALPES D'AZUR

Peillon is considered to be one of the most beautiful, well-kept villages in the entire area. It is built on the side of a rocky spur in the midst of magnificent scenery. There are few tourists and the proud "inhabitants," the number swells from its usual 100 to about 1000 in the summertime, have carefully preserved and restored their medieval village. Tall narrow houses form the outer walls, giving the village a rather stark and austere external appearance. Inside the village you will discover a maze of small cobblestone streets that wind their way under stone arcades and vaulted passage ways. Nestled into the scene, as if on a throne, the serene AUBERGE DE LA MADONE offers several very comfortable rooms and a restaurant that is highly recommended! The terrace sits in colorful flower beds right above the village square, and the auberge itself is set in its own little park with a pool and tennis. It is one of the truly unique and tranquil hideaways of the region - and still not more than a 30 minute drive from the coast!

STE-AGNÈS - THE HIGHEST COASTAL VILLAGE IN EUROPE

Go back down the road from Peille towards the coast and La Turbie until you lose sight of Peille and soon there will be a roadsign for Ste-Agnès. Turn left, the road narrows and starts winding gently upwards. You'll have wonderful views down onto Peille until you reach Col de la Madone at 1,000 m (3,300 ft). Here the road gets exciting as it creeps along a sheer ravine in the untouched landscape above radiant glimpses of the azur sea. As you round a bend, Ste-Agnès appears suddenly, perched on top of her cliff over 650 m (2,100 ft) above sea level, less than 1.5 km (3/4 miles) from Menton on the Mediterranean shore. Ste-Agnès is a classified site, the highest "coastal village" in all of Europe and still "undiscovered;" her streets are real and uncluttered by tourists. Towering high in the lovely arid landscape, this tiny village has preserved its rural aspect particularly well. Many of the houses, some dating from the 15th century, have been tastefully restored and the village offers pleasant walks through the nooks of its shady little streets. Panoramic views from the cliff sweep the coastline from San Remo in Italy to St Tropez, and northwards you can see Alpine peaks, some snow covered even in the summer.

The village of Ste-Agnès, perched on top of a cliff 650 meter (2,100 feet) above the sea

In this *village artisan*, plenty of small shops sell fine artwork, handicrafts, and jewelry, as well as souvenirs also found along the coast, but at lower prices. LA VIEILLE AUBERGE has an open fireplace, is small and casual in ambience, with views of the valley from its terrace and main rooms. Choose one of two menus, the most extravagant has 5 dishes and the other has two. Prices are hard to beat. The 5-course lunch goes for what breakfast would cost at any of the lavish palaces along the coast. A 2-hour hike links Ste-Agnès and Menton, excellent for those who prefer to lose some calories after a deliciously filling lunch.

COL DE BRAUS

Leaving for L'Escarène, follow the very narrow V7 which begins near the exit of Ste-Agnès. This road is excellent for bikers and all right for cars, although you may encounter a problem when meeting other vehicles (the road serves two-way traffic with only one lane). When arriving at L'Escarène, continue towards Col de Braus and Sospel. The road starts to climb sharply to the Col de Braus. As it snakes uphill, the view scans the horizon with Mont Gros above Nice, the Cap d'Antibes, and the Esterel Mountains outlined against the sea. The *Col* is located at 1,002 m (3,300 ft). From this point, three different hikes (20 minutes to 2 hours) are possible, as well as a bikepath which gives bikers a shortcut to Sospel through the woods.

SOSPEL

From the Col de Braus, the road descends sharply 700 m (2100 ft) to Sospel 12 km (7.5 miles) further down the valley, offering extensive views of the mountains of the Bevera River Valley. In the lower altitudes, the road swings through large olive groves and skirts the southern side of Mont Barbonnet with its commanding military fort at the top. Sospel is an enchanting mountain resort with old Italian-looking houses built along both sides of the Bevera River. Opposite the main gateway and bridge which lead across the river into the old village, the small Italian restaurant LA TAVERNA TOSCANE, is one of those little places you dream to find. The very few tables are nicely set. The door to the kitchen is always open and you can follow "his" loud efforts as he prepares the excellent food. "She" entertains, creating a wonderful family atmosphere and grandmother sits hunched next to the kitchen watching over the scene. The food in combination with its price makes a journey to Sospel and eating here worth it.

MERCANTOUR NATIONAL PARK AND THE TURINI PASS

From Sospel ROUTE DE TURINI climbs up through the Bevera Valley forest. Over thousands of years, the river has cut a very deep channel through the rocky wooded heights.

Above: Sospel, once an important railway junction and the gateway to Italy and Northern Europe

Below: Pastel colored houses with lots of tradition but most of them abandoned

At higher altitudes, the road runs along the Mercantour National Park with pretty views of the picturesque little village of Moulinet, where guided horseback excursions into the forest are available.

Once you have reached the Turini Pass there are a couple of small auberges and several ski lifts. The auberge LES TROIS VALLÉES is just off the main road when reaching the pass. From this point, many excursions can be taken. Head towards L'Authion, located at 2,100 m (7,000 ft). The road passes through pine and larch woods and the mountain scenery becomes more and more magnificent. At the top, a sensational view sweeps across the entire Côte d'Azur and *Alpes d'Azur*.

You have entered the beautiful, protected terrain of the Mercantour National Park that is the site of the *Vallée des Merveilles*, the Valley of Marvels, a valley that still exercises the same eerie fascination on today's visitors as it did some 4000 years ago upon our ancestors. The indelible imprints constitute one of the region's most remarkable prehistoric legacies. They can only be reached on foot or by horseback, either an exhilarating experience in this remote mountain wilderness. Numerous hikes and trails start from this point, leading into the National Park and to the *Vallée des Merveilles*. Your choices range from a 300 m (1000 ft)

rock climb to a calmer 5-hour hike on a well-marked trail. Mountain guides are available. For experienced mountaineers there are longer excursions lasting up to a week or two into the Mercantour Park with special cabins for rests and overnighting.

COL DE TURINI TOWARDS
LA VALLÉE DU VÉSUBIE

The Col de Turin is the highest point on this route. From here the road winds sharply to the Vésubie Valley. For bikers a separate trail, GR 52, leads through the forest. Located half way down, the pleasant small village of La Bollène-Vésubie stands on a hill in a chestnut forest at the foot of Les Valliers Peak and offers a good view of the Gorges de Vésubie. The GRAND HOTEL DU PARC is the place to choose for a night's rest and a bite to eat. It makes for a charming stopover, quietly situated in a big private park.

After Les Valliers the road continues to wind down to the Vésubie River, where it meets the main road which borders the river all the way through the Vésubie Valley back to the coast. If instead, you head north you will soon reach *La Vallée du Vésubie* and the scenery will change completely as you move into "Little Switzerland." The road continues to run beside the river encircled by lofty alps. The villages and hamlets are sleepy and relaxed, where dogs sometimes nap in the middle of the road and elderly farmers watch the slow traffic move by.

ST MARTIN VÉSUBIE - THE GATEWAY
TO LITTLE SWITZERLAND

Houses suddenly start looking like little Swiss chalets, the fields turn into a Swiss summertime postcard with green grass, flowers and cows, and ever present in the distance are the Alps, especially splendid in their winter white. The area is an important summer mountaineering center and during the winter season, there's plenty of good cross-country skiing. St Martin Vésubie is not the end of the road, but it is a good bet for a stopover, especially for outdoor enthusiasts looking for a long walk or riding excursions along the riverbeds and many small brooks. Perched on a spur at the junction of two rivers, this village was the first in France to install public street lighting. Our only selection for a night's rest or a meal is AUBERGE ST PIERRE in the center of the village. The restaurant has a small shaded terrace, along with a rustic dining room in wood, an open fireplace, and a very Swiss ambience. The chalet-look-alike hotel offers 20 comfortable rooms.

The Vésubie Valley is connected with the upper Tinée Valley above Nice by a road that crosses the St Martin Pass at 1,500 m (5,000 ft) and continues through the Valdeblore countryside, which is still reminiscent of Switzerland with its wooded and grassy slopes and Alpine peaks covered with snow long parts of the year. A couple of the

While passing through the small villages in the Hinterland even dogs look suspiciously at newcomers

local villages are quite pretty, like St.Dalmas-Valdebore with its tiny AUBERGE DES MURS which has only 9 rooms and a good local kitchen. Horses are available for private excursions into the mountains or as part of an organized tour with a guide. The landscape gets rougher when descending towards the steep Tinée Valley, where the sometimes purpled cliffs and rocks begin to drop dramatically into a new gorge.

LA TOUR

Not too far down towards the coast along the Tinée Valley, a roadsign shows the way to La Tour to your left. Once again the road starts to climb sharply and in addition to spectacular views of the valley behind, the landscape ahead soon opens up to another ample view of the mountains. La Tour is only 7 km (4 miles) away, but requires a steep climb of 500 m (1,600 feet). Once again you will be able to "discover" an absolutely unspoiled and charming little hilltop village, located on a platform with beautiful panoramas in all directions. The village is situated at the intersection of 3 "main" mountain roads and at least 10 different hikes. The central square is composed of pretty old village houses and a fountain in the middle where the elderly locals tend to assemble and solve village problems.

Next stop will be Madone d'Utelle, located across a steep valley on another plateau south of La Tour. On a clear day the chapel on top of this plateau can be seen from La Tour. To get there one must deftly negotiate a narrow, rather fascinating mountain road which skirts along the cliffs with sharp drops and rises on both sides, without a single security rail and few embankments for meeting another car. The road is about 18 km (11 miles) long and offers a number of nice

La Madone d'Utelle, located on a platform with a panoramic view of the snow covered Maritimes Alps and the entire coastline

In the area between La Tour and Madone d'Utelle a wide open nature offers numerous hikes

hikes. Halfway up, almost in the middle of nowhere, a wooden stand appears with a sign reading, "Fresh Vegetables for Sale." Looking up behind it, there is a stone house. The little stand turns out to be a bar where hikers and other visitors can have refreshments. Horses can be rented for guided excursions high into the mountains, to areas that would be difficult to reach without a horse.

MADONE D'UTELLE

Utelle is located on a terrace overlooking the Vésubie Valley with a magnificent view over the Turini Forest and Gordolasque Mountains. This tiny village was built in the 14th century and has retained its original character. It has a beautiful church, St.Veran, with Gothic doors and a carved wooden alterpiece. AUBERGE BELLE VUE offers a restaurant and accommodations in relaxed surroundings with a terrace, a pool, and a great view as the name already told you. A short excursion to take from Utelle is to the top of Mt. La Madone, an excellent two hour hike. A plateau 1,154 m (3,786 ft) above the sea, less than 20 km (12.5 miles) from Nice and the Côte d'Azur, hosts the sanctuary Madone d'Utelle. The view is impressive, taking in the entire coastline from the south to west and looking north, wooded mountains and Alpine peaks.

Heading back, the winding D32 swings down to the small village of St Jean la Riviere built on the slopes of the Vésubie River and keeps descending with impressive views over the Vésubie Valley. When reaching the river, follow the D2565 south towards the coast threading through the narrow Gorges de la Vésubie, where you'll find the steep rockwalls to be quite colorful. Before the river, the town *Le Cros d'Utelle* offers a couple of pleasant hikes. The trans-European hike, GR 5, crosses the river here and leads back up to the Madone d'Utelle on one side of the river and up to the charming hilltop village of Levens on the other side.

The last stretch of the Gorges de la Vésubie, before reaching the Var, was created over thousands of years leaving spectacular walls towering 800 m (2600 ft) above the river.

Coming out of the Gorges de la Vésubie to the Var River catapults you back into civilization instantly. The highway N202, known as the *Route des Neiges*, leads along the Var south to Nice and the coast.

The Gorges de la Vésubie where the river has cut its way through the mountain for thousands of years leaving spectacular walls towering 800 meters (2600 feet) above the river

Castle Hill as seen from the harbor

Nice, Promenade des Anglais, and the coastline

NICE

"The Big Olive" - Capital of a privileged region

The rock of Nice was first put on the map over 2000 years ago. Much later it became known as Castle Hill, a stronghold for an ancient tribe known as Ligurians. Fourth century Greeks then renamed it *Nikaia* - "she who gives victory" - and turned the port community into a busy trading post. Always fiercely independent, the inhabitants of Nice spoke their own language, *nissart*, and their Alpine-Piedmont influence lasted until 1860 when, reluctantly, Nice became a part of France.

Traces of prehistoric animals and humans dating back 400,000 years have been found. But it wasn't until the Middle Ages that a turbulent and violent era began, first with various Counts of Provence, who one after the other fought over the land. In the 15th century, what we know today as Old Nice was entrenched in fortifications. The Turks arrived with all their savagery in the 16th century and a laundry woman named Catherine Segurane became Nice's

own Joan of Arc when she tore down the Turkish flag. In the 17th and 18th centuries, the Dukes of Savoy allied themselves with the British to fight Louis XIV - and so it went until a much gentler invasion swept the coast, when British Lords began arriving in their carriages.

AN EARLY INVASION OF ENGLISH NOBLES AND RUSSIAN ARISTOCRACY

Long before Monaco started to "live it up," several thousand wealthy English families made Nice their home away from home, and with the arrival of the railway Russian princes followed in the wake of the Tsar, as did aristocrats and nobles from all over Europe, all headed for Nice and the sun.

The visitor can feel much of the city's history underfoot by walking the picturesque streets of *le vieux* Nice, the old town of Nice, up to the rock atop Castle Hill. Gnarled stairways shaded by huge pine trees climb up to the rock and the medieval ruins so efficiently destroyed by Louis XIV. Today it has been lovingly converted into an elegant park with a huge artificial waterfall, beautifully lit at night, and panoramas of Nice and the coastline.

To the east, there's the harbor, the commercial district, and a century-old pink castle built by an eccentric Englishman, clearly with the Taj Mahal in mind! To the west, a spectacular coastline stretches along the famed Promenade des Anglais to Antibes and the Cap d'Antibes. Directly beneath your feet, the sprawling city of Nice, sheltered from cold northerly winds by a semi-circle of mountains and hills.

With close to a half million inhabitants - including many retirees - Nice is the fifth largest city in France and the undisputed capital of a very privileged region. Though its cultural life spans theaters, museums, and an opera house, most visitors head straight for the seafront and the shops. Nice natives - the *Niçois* - generally turn up their gallic noses at their own pebbled beach and head for the golden sands of Cannes, Juan-les-Pins, and Monte-Carlo. With over 4000 restaurants, Nice could be considered a gourmet's paradise. Incredibly, you can actually eat your way to and through each of its Top Hot Spots: Castle Hill, the market place, the flower market, the quaint old town, and Promenade des Anglais.

THE OLD TOWN AND COURS SALEYA
THE MARKET PLACE

Coming back down, use the winding walkways and stairs at the southernmost point of the rock, Montée du Château. You'll pass the circular Bellanda Tower, a rebuilt 16th century bastion that now serves as the entrance to the Nice Naval Museum. Below is Quai des Etats Unis, a prolongation of Promenades des Anglais bordered on the seaside by a

public beach and to the north by the only existing remnants of the old fortifications, where several archways lead you into the market square, Cours Saleya.

The food and flower market at Cours Saleya is the biggest and most frequently visited market on the Côte d'Azur, a must for all visitors. It's open early every morning until lunch, except Mondays when it turns into a bustling antique market. Long colorful awnings cover the temporary stands from the sun. Farmers from all over the region arrive at dawn to display their comprehensive variety of fresh produce, including live chickens, ducks and fresh olive oil bottled and sold in copper cans and used wine bottles.

Among the visitors, you'll find chefs from the first-class restaurants deciding on the day's menu, housewives eagerly looking for quality and the best deal, plus curious tourists. This square, once the meeting place of Nice's high society, is lined with restaurants and bars, some of them very good, whose pleasant terraces fill up already at breakfast with the first rays of morning sunshine.

Rue Francois-de-Paule, one of the most exciting addresses in Nice, runs from the end of the flower market and creates a western border to the old town. Along this street you'll find the Opera House, many tourist traps, the best hotel in Old Nice, the BEAU RIVAGE, and the very special shop of NICHOLAS ALZIARI. In the small, country-style store, the family sells many regional products: fresh olives by the pound, lavender flavored honey, herbs, handicrafts. But the Alziari family is most famous for its pressed olive oil, classed among the finest available. Three huge copper vats dominate the little shop. Each is filled with a different olive oil - depending on your needs, they range from a good basic quality suitable for frying to the finest gourmet oils for salads.

Cours Saleya in the Old Town

If Provence is known to be a store for the freshest and finest products, then the Côte d'Azur and its markets is the display window

You simply ask for the oil of your preference, and if you haven't brought an empty can of your own, the shop will happily provide you with one.

Old Nice reminds you of Italy, as charming as a stage set, but it is real and criss-crossed with walking streets. It's a compact self-contained world, best explored at an early, unhurried stroll. Here your senses can experience the true sights, sounds, and smells of the region. Pastel colored houses harmonize with the Mediterranean light and along the narrow main street, Rue de Marché, aged Parmesan and assorted local cheeses are stacked outside tiny storefronts. They vie for attention alongside barrels of olives, salted anchovies, emaciated stockfish, and the catch-of-the-day. On each side of Rue de la Marché, a labyrinth of tiny side streets weave past Baroque churches, bistros, boutiques, and street vendors peddling local peasant dishes such as cattle-bone shaped *panisses* or *socca*, both very thick pancakes... and bring you to those other culinary treasures, the genuine *niçois* restaurants.

NIÇOIS RESTAURANTS IN THE OLD TOWN

Old Nice's most exclusive restaurant is MIRENDA. It's always full and getting a table isn't easy, for there is no telephone to call in your reservation! So, after a long wait outside, Christiane, the owner, will inform you - *helas* - the empty tables in front of you are all *réservées*. How then do they fill as if by magic with people who appear to have no reservation at all? Here's the secret: first you must stay at the NEGRESCO and befriend manager Michael Palmer. He may be persuaded to contact the barbershop directly opposite from the MIRENDA, and a discreet reservation can thus be made. The best and most casual restaurant is CHEZ BARAL. Old Madame Baral lives in the house where her mother had a restaurant and where there has always been a restaurant. She is an institution of Nice and links the past and the younger generation together. It's a bar in the morning, a great meeting place for locals where everyone drinks coffee, and the language spoken is still *nissarda*. For dinner Madame prepares one simple menu and you eat what is served! Madame cooks, serves, entertains, and if she is in a good mood, she'll even play piano and make everyone sing about Nice. You must have a reservation and don't be surprised if the temperamental hostess refuses to welcome you!

Or you can save yourself a lot of trouble simply by walking into any of the other excellent restaurants in the market place, not all necessarily serving an original *niçoise* cuisine: SPAGHETTISSIMO is for unrepentant prima pasta

An assortment of olives "sold by the ounce" for sale at Cours Saleya

fans with its terrace on the sunny side of the Cours Saleya. Its casual and lively atmosphere is all-Italian red-white-and-green décor, with giant country hams hanging from the ceiling and bottles of *vino* pegged to the walls to put you in the mood. LE SAFARI next door is for the young *niçois*, the "hip" crowd. LA CIVETTE DU COUP is more like a bistro, where you enjoy a glass of wine while watching the activity on the market place.

On the shady side of the Cours Saleya by the flower market, LES DENTS DE LA MER is a sumptuously decorated seafood restaurant offering amazing value for money. Homesick Americans and the trendy *nicois* gather at the appropriately named FROG for a dinner consisting of *Burgers à la Français* or TexMex food, while listening to live music.

THE PAILLON RIVER SPLITS NICE IN TWO - EACH HALF WITH A DIFFERENT CHARACTER

Nice is split in two by the Paillon, a parched old river bed that only occasionally during extreme weather conditions fills up with water. Nice ex-Mayor Jacques Medecin had the good taste while in office to convert this ugly river bed into a long beautiful park complete with a convention center. Nowadays Mr Medecin is rumored to be a refugee in Uruguay, since he fled Nice in the late 1980s with his American born wife Ilene and certain public funds. Six months before he resigned and left the country, Nice was in a mess. Ilene protected him by saying, "*He's either brilliant or a bullshitter.*"

At a later point from a distant land she corrected herself saying, "*He's brilliant and a bullshitter.*"

Place Massena marks the beginning of the park and is also considered a focal point in Nice, separating Old Nice from Modern Nice. The Promenade du Paillon is a garden of fountains, flowers, and manicured lawns, offering nice walks leading to the Museum of Contemporary Art, the new Theater of Nice and the Acropolis Convention Center.

Modern Nice has little of the charm of Old Nice and it could be anywhere in France, if it weren't for the Promenade des Anglais and the beach around the corner. When shopping here, all roads lead from Place Massena. Avenue Jean Medecin and the adjacent pedestrian zone are treasure troves of chic boutiques and local designer stores. A short walk to Nice Etoile reveals the region's biggest shopping mall - less exclusive, but much less expensive. Rue Longchamp targets a younger generation with the latest fashion trends. The main intersection in the pedestrian zone is a meeting spot for young Nicois, who gather in the modern coffee houses. For non-shoppers TABAC RUE PARADIS is a perfect choice for an afternoon beer or *café noir*, to be enjoyed with a cigar from the café's wide selection, while you sit and watch the crowds.

Close to the shopping area of the pedestrian zone, the world famous Promenade des Anglais stretches almost 7 km (4 miles) along the seafront. It is where David Niven, following in the footsteps of his British heritage, once took his afternoon constitutional walks. It was built in the early 19th century by British nobility longing for a comfortable walkway to fulfill their ritual habits. The magnificent views of the Bay of Angels seen from the Promenade sweep from Cap de Nice to the Fort Carre in Antibes. Elegant facades line the road, most are residential with a smattering of hotels, the most eye-catching being the NEGRESCO with its fine red

Next page: A main street in Nice's Old Town, leading from the market place to Castle Hill

dome. Inside this Belle Epoque hotel, the true gourmet can do no better than the CHANTECLER restaurant, where reservations and fancy dress are required. In a regency-styled dining room of sumptuous wood panelling, the glimmer of fine crystal and silver signal the fanciest restaurant in Nice. Dining here is a privilege and a pleasure to be savored to the fullest. The CHANTECLER'S star chef is Dominique Le Stanc, a young man of cosmic talents, one of the few chefs chosen to prepare the culinary opening of the Olympic games in Albertville. He creates a divine mix of *nouveau* and traditional *niçoise* cuisine and has been honored by the highest awards attainable by a French chef.

Much more casual BRASSERIE FELIX FLO, behind Place Massena in the shopping district, is a most fashionable place - a sister restaurant to world famous La Coupole in Paris - and a favorite among the bourgeois and the bronzed young trendies alike, informal yet terribly self-aware. Located in an old art-deco theatre with an extensive collection of modern art on the walls, the atmosphere is in stark contrast to the haunts of the more laid-back Old Nice.

Likewise, BOCCACCIO in the pedestrian zone offers exquisite dining at a traditional zinc oyster and lobster bar,

Promenade des Anglais, created by British nobles in the early 19th century

but keep in mind that you'll also be paying for its somewhat pompous decor and ambience.

NICE'S HOTELS SPAN FROM SPARTAN TO SUPER *DE LUXE*

The legendary HOTEL NEGRESCO - a gem on the Côte d'Azur - is a prime example of Edwardian *grandeur* from the Belle Epoque. It was built by Henri Negresco at the turn of the century, who dreamed of creating a Palace on the Promenade des Anglais befitting his royal guests. Since its inauguration in 1913, it has played an illustrious role in the star-spangled history of the Côte d'Azur - the lingering scent

of past scandals mingles with priceless art treasures. Today the NEGRESCO is not only a hotel of privilege, it has also become a legend in its own time. In 1974 it was declared a National Historic Monument - a most remarkable private museum! Since 1957, the NEGRESCO has been owned by the Augier family, who in an exceptionally honorable way try to make the legend re-live its former glory for the modern generation. No costs are spared to revive the splendor of the Belle Epoque.

You will be welcomed to the museum-cum-hotel by livery men dressed in the 18th - 19th century garb of aristocratic household staff. Their top hats each sprout a tall red plume that fans up against the pink and green dome, a bit of an anachronism on today's hectic Promenade des Anglais. There is no parking facility, since parking problems did not exist in the Belle Epoque, so the Rolls might do best on the street in front of the hotel. Near the reception, the spacious drawing room Salon Louis XIV has a coffered ceiling from a *château* in the Savoie region where Louis' first love lived. The king-sized fireplace comes from yet another *château* associated with his majesty and on the wall an enormous painting of Louis XIV dressed in his royal mantle stares superciliously down at you. The tableau is from a series of paintings of which only two other known originals exist, both in Paris, one at the Louvre Museum and the other at the Palais de Versailles. The interior of the circular Massena Salon, the banquet hall, has not been touched since the NEGRESCO was built and is decorated in 24-carat gold leafs. Even the English-styled bar looks exactly as it did for the opening in 1913. And the sculpted wooden doors are from the home of the mother of England's Henry the IVth.

Every floor of the hotel has its own character and style and the 150 rooms are individually decorated with astonishing antique furniture and historical paintings collected by the owner Mme Augier, a compassionate dreamer who draws much of her inspiration from the Palais de Versaille. It is important to request a room facing the sea and, unquestionably, the best rooms are those underneath the dome facing both the Alps and the sea. The most lavish of the 9 suites is the Napoleon or Imperial Suite, which has such a splendid theatrical setting of red and gold that you can pretend to be the Imperial couple, Napoleon and Josephine.

Less legendary, much less expensive, but of particular note is the recently restored BEAU RIVAGE opposite the beach, squeezed between the Promenade des Anglais and Old Nice. Once the residence of a Russian prince, it is oozing with *avant garde* elegance and offers bright spacious rooms and several junior suites with views of the sea. Ask for the 3rd floor and above if you require peace and quiet, because nightlife and traffic in Nice are notoriously noisy.

Another find - LA PEROUSE - is located at the foot of Castle Hill facing the sea, offering a fantastic view of the coast, especially from its relaxed rooftop equipped with a private pool. A favorite among visiting artists, it can be noisy far into the night, so make sure you get a room at the highest floor possible.

Quietly situated on the outskirts of downtown, the PALAIS MAETERLINCK is Nice's latest deluxe hotel and one of the most spectacularly placed 4-star establishments on the Côte d'Azur. Set high on a cliff, yet below the Basse Corniche between Nice and Villefranche, it commands a breathtaking view across the sea from Cap Ferrat to Cap d'Antibes. The palace was built between the two World Wars by Maurice Maeterlinck, a Belgian author and recipient of the Nobel Prize for Literature. His home later became a private club and hideaway for an elite membership of multi-millionaires. Its Neo-classic architecture and majestic colonnades around the swimming pool set the tone and its décor reflects the Mediterranean environment, with lavish use of marble and a preference for light colors. The Italian-inspired gardens are filled with lavender and jasmine shaded by rows of noble cypresses. The peaceful restaurant MELISANDE has a beautiful terrace and is delightful for *al fresco* lunches or a romantic dinner. A narrow footpath winds its way down to the private beach and a little harbor where the hotel's private sloop is moored. It also boasts its own helicopter, always ready for a quick jump to Monaco or St Tropez.

"Every day - buy fish directly from the fisherman…"
Along the beach in Nice the fishingboats sometimes outnumbers the sun-worshippers

The Negresco Hotel, a legend and a landmark on Promenade des Anglais

The Negresco Hotel, declared a National Historic Monument in 1974,
is a remarkable "museum" where no costs have been spared to
revive the splendor of the Belle Epoque

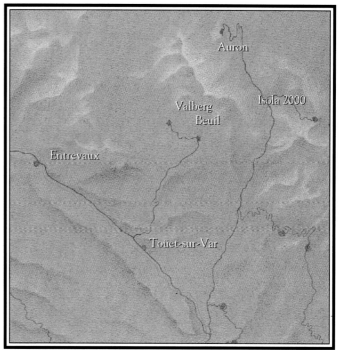

THE MARITIMES ALPS

Golf in the morning and ski in the afternoon

An early round of golf in the morning and skiing in the afternoon - an unbeatable combination possible up to six months a year, only on the Côte d'Azur. The region offers more than its celebrated sunny beaches and scenic mountain roads. It invites you to take advantage of one of the widest ranges of sporting activities in the world. Besides sailing, water-skiing, tennis, and golf along the coast, the Mediterranean Alps play host to skiing in the winter and cater to active outdoor enthusiasts in the summer with hiking, fishing, para-gliding, horseback riding, and much more.

For many people it's a well-kept secret that within 80 km (50 miles) of Nice, or less than a two hour drive from anywhere on the coast! - there are twenty major ski resorts and close to 30 golf courses. It's possible to play an early 18 holes in Monaco or Valbonne, then drive a few miles, enjoy a hearty lunch in one of the Alpine villages - so Swiss in character - then strap your skis on and spend the afternoon swooshing down the snowy slopes above panoramic views of the Alps and the sea. Toss back an expresso or a *vin chaud* to heat up before driving back down to the coast in time for an *al fresco* seafood dinner and some fresh oysters. Then, tired after a busy day, to say the least, you'll have a restful sleep in a quiet

Auron and Isola 2000 are by far the best ski resorts that can be reached within an hour and a half from the coast

provençal auberge gently nestled in the surrounding vineyards. Hard to believe, yes. To make this possible anywhere else in the world would require a helicopter or private jet.

LE PETIT TRAIN DES PIGNES

Most of the ski resorts and villages are located in the Maritimes Alps and accessed by the Route des Neiges, N202, that starts in Nice and tags north along the Var River to Digne 140 km (88 miles) from Nice. The river is also skirted all the way by a "mini" single track railroad, the *Train des Pignes*. The old "one-car" train that looks almost like a tram provides service three times a day. Both the road and the railroad are exciting excursions, even for those who aren't skiers, because it brings you away from the coast into a more rugged, mountainous and remote landscape and through deep impressive gorges. You'll discover historical sites, spectacular panoramas and dramatically narrow roads that climb the steep mountainsides. And you'll pass such picturesque villages as Villar-sur-Var, Puget-Theniers, and Entrevaux - small towns that dish up a wonderful selection of restaurants ranging from first-class gastronomic to traditional, casual and inexpensive places where food is still lovingly prepared.

THE TENDE CONNECTION - REACHING LIMONE ON THE EDGE OF SKI D'AZUR

Even if the *Route des Neiges* provides the easiest access to most ski resorts, there are alternatives, such as Limone in Italy, easily reached by a two hour drive or by the spectacular Tende connection.

Completed in 1928, the quaint, little-known, yet international Tende Alpine railway is as spectacular as many of the more famous Swiss mountain routes. It links Turin, Italy, and the Côte d'Azur, running in and out of France on its way. An engineering *tour de force*, it has scores of bridges, viaducts, and corniches balanced on the edge of

dizzying precipices. Leaving Nice, the train runs along the coast until it reaches Ventimiglia. From there it heads straight north up the Roya River before traversing a series of tunnels and *voilà*, it's back in France. The railroad spirals on and up through more tunnels until it reaches one that burrows for 8 km (5 miles) beneath the Tende Pass, exiting back into Italy and the ski resort of Limone on the outer rim of Ski d'Azur. In less than 20 km (13 miles) this very special railroad has climbed over 1,000 meters (3,300 ft).

SKI D'AZUR - A SKIER'S PARADISE BETWEEN BLUE SKIES AND AZUR SEA

Ski d'Azur and enjoy all the fun while basking in the glorious sunshine of the Alps. Each of the area's ski resorts and villages, boasts its own individual charm, and the sce-nary keeps changing. Over 250 well prepared, marked ski slopes offer a combined length of more than 600 km (375 miles) of runs. They range from the difficult black diamond trails to the less challenging blue circle ones. There's day skiing, night skiing on slopes flooded by light, helicopter skiing with professional guides and, for some real fun, acrobatic skiing. For the brave, there is a flying kilometer in Valberg where you can race against the clock and try to break the local record.

Cross country ski trails extend for more than 400 km (250 miles) and ski hiking, for the adventurous cross country skier, can be done with or without a guide. You can traverse the wilderness on marked, but unprepared ski trails and spend nights in warm mountain huts. This is a sport which is fast becoming popular because of the stable climate and endless possibilities.

SUMMER IN THE MARITIME ALPS

During the summer, the ski resorts stay open catering to sports and backpacking adventures. When the snow melts in late spring, the soft green pastures and spring flowers lure you to the pleasant trails. A myriad of outdoor summer sports becomes available: hiking, mountain climbing, horseback riding, tennis, archery, canoeing, fishing, cross country motorcycling, mountain biking, camping in the wilderness, and swimming in calm, refreshing lakes with crystal clear mountain water.

MUCH OF THE HERITAGE OF THE REGION REMAINS INTACT DESPITE MODERN TOURISM

The traditional wooden houses reflect the past and blend in smoothly with the surrounding landscape. Many of the villages now rely on tourism for income, but they also have centuries of experience in agricultural commerce. Almost every village boasts delightful small restaurants serving the excellent local gastronomy, but in the past few years, under the influence of modern living, some fast food establishments have slowly started to appear.

Next page: There are over 300 ski lifts in the region that quickly and efficiently carry skiers to ski runs ranging from the blackest black to the easiest blue

Beautiful vistas of craggy mountains from one of the regions many ski resorts

A sunny terrace overlooking the ski slopes in Auron

ROUTE DES NEIGES

The best ski resorts in the Alpes d'Azur

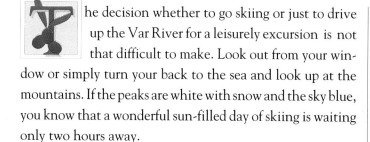he decision whether to go skiing or just to drive up the Var River for a leisurely excursion is not that difficult to make. Look out from your window or simply turn your back to the sea and look up at the mountains. If the peaks are white with snow and the sky blue, you know that a wonderful sun-filled day of skiing is waiting only two hours away.

Leaving Nice, you will travel through one of the most unpleasant areas of the entire region, the industrialized zone of Nice. This once fertile land nourished Nice through both World War I and II, but it has been eaten up today by warehouses and offices.

Don't let this scare you off. It extends only a few miles north and as you approach the small village of St-Martin-du-Var, the coastline and the industries will seem far behind. Here the mountains start to rise just as if you were nearing the Swiss Alps, rather than being 15 minutes away from the Côte d'Azur!

AN AUBERGE IN THE SHADOW OF THE ALPS

Just before entering this mountainous landscape at St-Martin-du-Var you should look out for a sign hidden in the cluster of stucco houses announcing the AUBERGE DE LA BELLE ROUTE, situated in an unpretentious building behind some trees next to the road. Most people pass this restaurant without even taking notice of its existence. Don't do so if you seek a gourmet surprise. Slow down and drive into the backyard parking. This restaurant is "living" proof that you can find top-notch gourmet cuisine in small, unpredictable corners anywhere in France. It has been decorated with the highest awards of the "Gourmet Bibles" - Michelin and Gault Millau - making it comparable to some of the best known restaurants in the world. There are no fancy trappings here, such as a grandiose terrace or a magnificent view. Even the decor is simple. The food is the main attraction, a tantalizing *provençal* cuisine. Chef and owner Jean-Francois Issautiers will welcome you and indulge you with his love of food. If you stop here for lunch and still expect to do some skiing in the afternoon, forget it! Try to visit this restaurant as an excursion on its own, or stop for dinner on your way back after a day in the ski slopes.

As you enter "the Alps" the road makes a couple of treacherous turns through the narrow and impressive gorge where vertical rock formations shoot up to 1000 ft on both sides of the road, before you arrive to a main intersection where the Tinée River floats into the Var River. From this point you can choose to continue along the Var River or to drive north into the Tinée Valley which leads to the best ski resorts. Let's start with some skiing along the Tinée Valley.

PART I - EXPLORING THE TINÉE VALLEY

Only a few miles up the river there will be signs to point you to the first of these coastal ski resorts, La Colmaine located in Little Switzerland. This resort is the closest to the coast, but it's fairly small and situated at a low altitude, which means that snow conditions are not always the best. The area is excellent for cross-country skiing and for excursions up into the wilderness of the Mercantour National Park.

Drive another few miles up the valley along the Tinée and you will arrive at the village of Isola, where signs indicate the road that ascends the mountains to the resort of Isola 2000 - the biggest and the best in the region. Isola 2000 was built in the early 1970s, so it is by far the most efficient and, as the name suggests, the most modern. For those who are anxious to get skiing and don't want to waste time in a car, Isola 2000 can also be reached comfortably by helicopter from the coast in a short 10 minutes ride above stunning vistas of the Alps.

ISOLA 2000 - A PERCHED CONCRETE BUNKER

Located at a level of 1800 m (6000 ft) with ski slopes up to 2600 m (8600 ft) and deep-snow heliskiing up to 3000 m (9850 ft), Isola 2000 is undoubtedly the best skiing in the region and claims to belong to the top 10 ski resorts in France.

If you don't fancy the architecture, remember that Isola 2000 is made for skiing, not to be looked at. It's a huge ultra-modern indoor complex shared by shops, restaurants, apartments, a cinema, bars, nightclubs, and hotels.

A unique feature of Isola is that both snow and sun are guaranteed. If the heliograph of the resort registers over 3 consecutive days of no sunshine on a week's vacation, you will be entitled to one week's ski rental free of charge. If a lack of snow results in your having to walk back to the main complex or that less than half of the ski-lifts were not able to function, you get one daily ski pass free for each day without sufficient snow!

For the adventurous and those seeking something different, Isola has it: an ice driving circuit, snow scooter trails, night skiing on the specially lit Belverde slope and excursions into the mountains at sunset when the ski lifts are closed. Dog sled excursions are available and can last from one hour up to several days in the wilderness, with overnight stays in isolated mountain cabins, although such adventures have to be arranged well in advance.

Considering the stark indoor appearance of the main concrete building that houses most of Isola's inside activities, Hotel LE CHASTILLON comes as a surprise. Its pleasant lobby rises several floors, decorated in natural wood and plants. Well designed and comfortable, this is a first-class hotel right at the ski slopes. After a day in the snow, guests literally ski straight into a reception room connected to the main lobby. The hotel bar is probably the favorite *après-ski* spot, after the less chic LE RENDEZ-VOUS located in the noisy shopping arcade. The rooms are well equipped, each with a balcony facing south towards the slopes and the sun. The hotel restaurant THE EDELWEISS offers excellent food in a warm, cozy atmosphere by a large open fire. This is the place to have dinner if you are not staying at the luxurious LE DIVA.

Separated from the hubbub of the main bunker, this Swiss-styled chalet is situated on a slope above the commercial center of Isola 2000, and overlooks the entire mountain valley. LE DIVA is by far the most exclusive hotel in the Alpes d'Azur. A huge terrace stretches out in front of the English-styled wooden bar and the tastefully decorated gourmet restaurant. Each room and suite has a private balcony facing south. Unfortunately, access from the ski slopes when there is a scarcity of snow is not as simple as "ski in" at LE CHASTILLON, but the hotel offers a chauffeur driven shuttle from the village.

On the slopes, you'll not exactly find any culinary extravaganza, but try LA BERGERIE, a restaurant located in an old stone house in the middle of the lower ski area. Its sunny terrace overlooks the slopes and its rustic interior is warmed by a huge stone fireplace for romantic dinners. Make sure you have a reservation since space is very limited and the demand is high.

AURON - MORE WHAT YOU'D EXPECT A SKI RESORT TO LOOK LIKE

Auron is the second largest ski resort in the region and one of the furthest away from the coast. Instead of turning right for Isola 2000 in Isola village, you continue on the same road along the Tinée River for another half hour and you will reach Auron. This is more what you would imagine a ski resort to look like, with Swiss-styled chalets, an ice skating rink in the central square and a proper cable car to transport you up into the ski areas. To avoid parking problems and long lines by the cable car, it is advisable to pass through the village, continuing on the short road leading to an ample parking lot next to the ski area, Chastellares, where most of the lifts take off.

Auron village is located at an altitude of 1600 m (5300 ft) and has skiing up to 2450 m (8100 ft). The highest point Cime de Chavalet is reached by a long chairlift *télésiège*. Here you will find long fairly easy slopes and beautiful panoramas over the mountain scenery. The slopes at lower altitudes are guaranteed to be skiable by an impressive quantity of snow-making equipment. There are several restaurants on the slopes that have terraces where you can relax and enjoy the sun in comfortable deck chairs. LES BATACLANS is by far the most popular. It serves good pizza grilled *feu au bois* and barbecues.

Apart from downhill skiing Auron also has a wide range of other winter activities to offer. It's a center for hang-gliding and para-skiing. Several miles of carefully prepared cross-country ski trails wind through the forest and down to the picturesque village of St-Dalmas-le-Selvage. Village life is centered around the ice skating rink at Place de la Téléphérique. On this main square, the hotels LE CHAS-TELLARES and LAS DONNAS are less than a minute's walk from the *téléphérique* and face south with views of the mountains. Unfortunately, however, hotel accommodations are not up to what one would expect from a first-class ski resort. The *après-ski* spots also hover around the ice ring: LE SERAC, a little créperie, or next door LE SLALOM SNACK. For dinner, again on the main square, the restaurant LA

The restaurant Bataclans on the ski slopes of Auron offers great opportunities to catch some high altitude Mediterranean sun

When entering the Alpes d'Azur along Route des Neiges there are plenty of reminders that you are approaching a ski area

GRANGE D'AUR has a rustic decor and serves *les special-ites de Savoie*, i.e. raclette and fondue. LE PUB is a special and interesting place with only 5 tables and a small bar. Madame, originating from Bourgogne, prepares home cooked food for the lucky few and offers a great selection of very good *vins de Bourgogne*. This is also the place to have a real *vin chaud*, a spicy, hot red wine, delicious after skiing!

PART II - BACK TO THE VAR VALLEY

If you continue on the RN 202 along the Var River instead of turning north towards Isola and Auron as described

Just a few miles inland the architecture and the character of the countryside changes dramatically as you enter Little Switzerland

in part I, you will soon reach Touët-sur-Var, another small village with a lot of Swiss influence and chalet-styled wooden houses. In Touët-sur-Var you will find AUBERGE DE CHASSEUR with its small terrace "on" the main road, a true country inn, furnished with an open fire to add a couple of degrees to the warm atmosphere. You will be served specialities from the mountains of the region, like thin slices of dried ham.

GORGES DU CIANS - A ROAD THAT HAS TO BE SEEN TO BE BELIEVED

Shortly after Touët-sur-Var there will be a sign for the ski resort of Valberg. Turn north on the D28 and the road starts climbing the impressive Gorges Inferieures du Cians. Giant white vertical rocks hem in the narrow and winding road. This road is, in fact, worth an excursion on its own, being one of the most spectacular roads in the Alpes d'Azur, if not all of France. Immediately after you leave the first gorge, you enter a second rocky landscape, with the massive red rocks of the Gorges Superieures du Cians. Quickly the already narrow road gets even thinner, with upturned rocks on one side, a steep cliff face on the other, and a creek splashing some 500 feet below! Sometimes the passage is so narrow that you must wonder how this "one-lane" road can handle "two-way" traffic, until you meet a mammoth tourist bus coming from the opposite direction. At points, you drive under huge boulders, enormous icicles, and sometimes even through minor waterfalls.

Once through the gorges, the landscape turns flatter as you reach the village of Beuil, which once upon a time during the Middle Ages was the seat of the Grimaldi family - a fact that might explain why someone would build an access road like the one you have just arrived on. Today Beuil is far from what it was at that time, and serves only as an intersection where you can choose to head off to Roubillon, a relaxed family ski resort with some good cross-country skiing and a view of the perched village of Roubillon - or to Valberg.

VALBERG - A DAY OF FAMILY SKIING

Valberg, the third biggest ski resort in the Alpes d'Azur, is located at 1400 m (4700 ft) and has skiing up to 2000 m (6900 ft). Due to the fairly low altitude, it is best to confirm snow conditions before setting off for Valberg. But when there is snow, the skiing is outrageous. The ambience of the village is once again very Swiss. For non-skiers, Valberg is an excellent starting point for numerous mountain hikes on the long trails and for mountain bike excursions. Valberg is, however, a place to choose for a day visit, not for overnighting. There is a shortage of comfortable hotels and good restaurants, so it's definitely advisable, and a much safer drive, to return before dark and find something nicer closer to the coast.

The narrow "two-way" road leading up to Valberg

A happy "wooden" chef announces the existence of a nearby country inn, although he points in the wrong direction!

CONTINUING ALONG THE VAR VALLEY

Continuing along the Var River towards Entrevaux, not far after the intersection leading to Valberg and the Gorges du Cians, you'll see the auberge LES ACACIAS in the middle of an open field by the road. A large "wooden" chef with a mustache stands happily next to the road, guiding you with his thumb to the entrance. It seems that the further away from the coast you get, the more casual, "simple" and less expensive these countryside places tend to become, while the quality of food and the ambience remain good. LES ACACIAS is a popular place for family lunch on Sundays, and

during the summertime tables are set in the pleasant lurch garden.

ENTREVAUX - INSPIRED BY THE GREAT WALL OF CHINA

The last stop along the *Route des Neiges* is the old fairytale village of Entrevaux, 70 km (50 miles) from Nice. It is located on "the other side" of the Var River with only a vaulted stone bridge leading into the old town. Entrevaux dates back to the 11th century and is built at the foot of a huge rock with a fortress at the top to guard it. The fortress can be reached by a 30 minute walk on a man made walkway that resembles a mini-version of the Great Wall of China. From the top there are beautiful panoramas of the eastern fringes of the higher Var Valley. Next to the entrance of the village by the railroad station, HOTEL-RESTAURANT VAUBAN has kept all the charm of an ancient *refuge* for long distance road travelers. The food is prepared with local products and the speciality of the house is *socca*, a dish from *niçoise* kitchens. In addition to its charm and its impressive fortress, the village also offers a range of local specialities and products like a singular fruit juice, LES VERGERS D'ENTRE-VAUX, whose distinctive taste is derived from an old Entrevaux family recipe. The juice is very sought after since only about 100,000 bottles are produced each year. The local butcher BOUCHERIE PAYSANNE is the gourmet meat temple and the Mecca of all top restaurant chefs from the coast, who take pilgrimages here in search of the finest products.

PART III - SKI ITALY

On the eastern side of the Alpes d'Azur just across the border from France to Italy, you will find Limone. The village is only a two hour's drive from the coast, but very different and very Italian. Instead of taking the *Route des Neiges* from Nice, you have to head for the Tende Pass north of Monaco and Menton. This is the old road that connected the Mediterranean coast with Central Europe.

LIMONE - LA RISERVA BIANCA

A touch of Italy! How amazing that you are only 5 minutes from the French border, but you are plunged into a completely different culture! You are in Italy and here they speak only Italian. Located at only 1000 meter (3300 ft) with skiing up to 2100 meter (6900 ft), Limone is a little bit low to guarantee good snow conditions and it's advisable to call and check before heading for the slopes.

Skiing Italy you will immediately be confronted with the "Italian style." From the village, only one chairlift brings you up to the top. The chairlift looks like it was built for two people, but it carries three! And there is no security bar. You have to hold your poles and skis in your hands and jump onto the rapidly moving chair and at the same time try to avoid your fellow passengers equipment. It's quite a show to watch, but less fun to do yourself. Then at the top, you have to jump off the still moving chair onto a wet and slippery pavement.

Limone itself is a charming medieval village with lots of twisting streets where clothes billow from each window trying to dry in the cold mountain air. The main street Via Roma allows no cars and stretches along a river to the main square and the railway station. Most of the action in town takes place here. The HOSTERIA DE CARTUNE is a popular restaurant among the younger generation, located in a cavernous vaulted stone basement. During high season a line begins at dinner time and the place stays full until well after midnight. MAC MICHE RISTORANTE, a *caracteristica taverna*, is just around the corner and is more sophisticated, where the Italian upper class prefer to dine, dressed in elegant furs and jewelry. Next to the central square and the church, on a narrow little street called Via Cap Centino, you will find a modest sign for TRATTORIA DEL SALVATORE, a very "just-as-you-believed-it-should-look" restaurant. The owner and chef prepares delicious Italian pastas and pizzas while you are comfortably seated in a small dining room basking by its large fireplace. Across the square, behind the church on another tiny street, the Via XX Settembre, the entrance of IL BAGATTO RISTORANTE OSTERIA is well hidden under a vaulted stone passage. Il Bagatto is a traditional Italian osteria with home made food *à la Mama*. Reservations are a must, as it is popular and very small - only about 10 tables.

For *après-ski*, the favorite hang-out is the CREMERIA CAIRI GELATI ET SORBETI, just across from Mac Miche on Via Roma. A crowded place that you would only find in Italy, it serves coffee, tea, liqueurs, and a wide range of cookies, bakery goods, and sandwiches. Further down the street, the BIRRERIA DE LA PUNCHA is a rustic bar where the action begins later and goes on until the nightlife takes over.

The only first-class 4-star hotel in Limone is the PRINCIPE GRAND HOTEL, conveniently located just across from the spectacular chairlift, so you can sit comfortably on your balcony and watch the ongoing show which begins early in the morning. The Grand is a typically high-class Italian family hotel where you have at least one meal plus breakfast included in the price. On Via Roma, in the heart of the village, the ALBERGA TOURING HOTEL is less luxurious than the Principe Grand, and also only with half board.

The old fairytale village of Entrevaux dates back to the 11th century and is built at the foot of a huge rock with a fortress at the top to guard it

Ben - *There is too much art....*

Mur du Feu - Yves Klein

PROMENADE DES ARTS

"I dream of the south" - Renoir

I *don't understand why this countryside isn't used as an art studio…"* Renoir pondered. Of course, he was an early resident of the Côte d'Azur. If only he could have seen the explosion that would soon take place! No where else in the world, outside of the great urban centers, has a small local region had such an influence on several generations of artistic life.

The first artists came because the south of France was fashionable. Stories of its beauty and mild climate had circulated in Paris. Everyone seemed to want to come to the south of France in the second half of the 19th century - the royals, the aristocrats, the nouveau riches - even the bourgeoisie - and the artists. The artists stayed and took root, not because all those wealthy potential clients bought their work, which they didn't, but because they found a beauty and inspiration that could not be duplicated by the gray streets of Paris. Did the burst of color and energy that became the artistic force in the late 19th century come from the

Riviera? Or was the discovery of the Riviera due to the search for a new artistic life force?

Renoir and Monet came first, in 1881. The two friends were the first artists to travel across the Riviera - not yet named the Côte d'Azur until 1887 - from Marseille to Genoa on a six month expedition. They marveled at the light and at the beautiful variety of landscapes - sea and mountains. And they were thrilled that they could paint outside. Both men returned. In 1888, Monet painted scenes of the Alps as seen from Antibes (still probably one of the most fascinating views for modern-day photographers) and Renoir returned for good in 1909 to live out his life in his beautiful olive orchard in Cagnes-sur-Mer.

It's probably not a coincidence that artists began to arrive after the building of the railroad. The spectacular tales of paradise and the good life stirred the imaginations of the impoverished young impressionist artists fed up with their rejection in Paris. Trains now made the passage possible.

Van Gogh arrived in Provence by train in 1888. Somewhat miserably, he arrived at the Arles station in a snowstorm. But by the spring, his creativity was in full swing and he found vivid colors exaggerated by a benevolent sun. He invited his friend Gauguin, who withstood his quarrelsome companion for a couple of months, escaping Arles the morning after Van Gogh cut off his own ear, heading for even more exotic lands, namely Tahiti.

Paul Signac stopped by Arles in 1889 to check up on Van Gogh's health, found his recent paintings quite good, and moved on to visit the home of his ancestors, who had been sailors in St Tropez. Signac was a pointillist painter and President of the *Salon des Independents*, where young artists not accepted by the Academy could show their works. He was instrumental in bringing young Fauvist painters to the south. Their wild colors blossomed in the bright sun, and their uncomplicated figures and perspectives breathed fresh inspiration from the open simplicity and gaiety of life in the southern countryside. They found a freedom which the structure of the city had denied them.

In 1902, Signac sailed his boat Olympia into the port of St Tropez and installed himself in the village. His house Villa La Hune, which still stands on the same street as the jet-setter Byblos Hotel, soon hosted many young avant-garde artists, the most famous and enduring in the story of Art on the Riviera was Matisse, who spent the summer of 1904 in St Tropez, where he painted his celebrated "Luxe, Calme et Volupte."

MATISSE RANKS AS ONE OF THE GRAND MASTERS OF THE CÔTE D'AZUR

His was a love story with the area - with the exuberance of its colors and its luminous light, of its bountiful flowers and fruits, and of the sea. A great portion of his work was realized in Nice, where he first moved into the Beau Rivage Hotel in 1916. By 1921, he purchased the top-floor apartment of the bright yellow building at one end of the Cours Saleya in Old Nice, and until 1938 he could step out onto his large terrace and survey the lively kaleidoscope of the Cours Saleya market and the sparkle of the blue Mediterranean.

His gift to the region, he left in Vence - the Rosary Chapel for the Dominican nuns. The cool, clear colors of the sea, the sun, and nature are illuminated in stained glass windows by rays of the Riviera light, which Matisse so revered. "The richness and silvery quality of the light in Nice seem to be quite unique and absolutely indispensable."

Artists who moved south brought other artists. Most painters didn't relinquish their contacts with Paris and, in fact, often lived there for some of the year, so they had every opportunity to tell friends back home stories of the south - and to invite them down. An artistic community developed on the Côte d'Azur, which acted as a support group for comradery and inspiration. Circles formed, like at the Colombe d'Or in St Paul de Vence (see chapter on Loup Valley, Route d'Aventure - page 101). "Art" was happening in the south - and it was a powerful draw.

In Cagnes-sur-Mer, Renoir was a veritable force in bringing both young artists and famous individuals to the village, giving it a kind of status which it never even earned years later with its own wayward child, Yves Klein. Modigliani and Soutine settled in to what is now the very fine local restaurant of JOSY-JO and painted scenes of the old Cagnes-sur-Mer (Modigliani's with a sweet calm and Soutine's with eerie torment) in the 1920s.

PICASSO HAS COME TO OVERSHADOW MOST OTHER ARTISTS WHO HAVE WORKED ON THE CÔTE D'AZUR

Renoir died in 1919 and by the 1920s new artistic energy was penetrating the Côte d'Azur. Picasso became a summer resident, falling in with the very contemporary American crowd at the Hotel du Cap on Cap d'Antibes, where Scott and Zelda Fitzgerald drank champagne and had legendary "scenes." Picasso, like the poet and painter Jean Cocteau and other southern artists to this day, appreciated that the Riviera gave access to close contact with rich and famous internationals, many who were eccentric characters or lead creative lifestyles, which no doubt thrilled and awed the curious artistic spirit. Picasso became a regular at the home of Sarah and Gerald Murphy on the beach of La Garoupe, along with Ernest Hemingway, Archibald MacLeish, and Rudolph Valentino. He painted Cubist renditions of the popular new resort Juan les Pins as early as the summer of 1920.

Picasso has come to overshadow most other artists who have worked on the Côte d'Azur. His genius was totally contemporary, forcing the art world to stagger into the future. Yet his themes were often of antiquity, with new interpretations. His most vital time on this Mediterranean coast was in 1946, when he was invited to use the Grimaldi fortress on the ramparts of Antibes. He painted with the paints of the fishermen, because the war had left the area impoverished. In Antibes, he could smell antiquity and the sea. He felt a euphoria and optimism because of the end of the war, and a great love for his companion Francoise Gilot. He painted "Suite d'Antipolis" - a fantasy to mythology and the sea.

"MY STRUGGLE WITH CLAY IS MORE JOYFUL THAN MY CONFRONTATION WITH CANVAS" - PICASSO

For those artists who worked with ceramics, the south of France was essential. Picasso turned to it with a passion, followed by Léger in Biot. For centuries, ceramics was linked to an agricultural necessity. Terra cotta jars were a by-product of olive oil production, used for trade exportation from the region. At a time when its center of production, Vallauris, was slowing down, Picasso revived this artisan craft with innovative enthusiasm. His loyalty was complete.

César - Wrecked Car

Picasso - La Joie de vivre ou Antipolis, 1946

He found the red *provençal* clay sensual to the touch and proclaimed, "My struggle with clay is more joyful than my confrontation with canvas."

WORLD WAR II INCREASED THE FLOW OF ARTISTS TO THE SOUTH

Many, like Chagall and Max Ernst, were forced to flee the Nazi onslaught, others left occupied Paris on principle, preferring to live and work in the free zone of southern France. In 1945, an interesting reversal in the flow of the artistic community took place: the Maeghts moved to Paris. Aime and Marguerite Maeght, who were to open the Maeght Foundation in St Paul de Vence in 1964, originally owned a small bookshop in Cannes where they exhibited local artwork. They met the painter Bonnard who was in Le Cannet and Aime Maeght was soon printing his lithographs. Through this connection they were introduced to the art community during the war years, and they became the neighbors of Matisse, who moved to Vence when Nice was bombed. The Maeghts owned a cow and their son Adrien would lug pails of milk to Matisse. The kindness was not forgotten. When the Maeghts opened their successful art dealership in Paris, Matisse was their first show.

The Maeghts' success in Paris stemmed from their contacts in the south, but when they moved back to St Paul, they brought a new group of contemporary artists who have become associated with the Côte d'Azur: Miro, Giacometti, Calder - who form the core of the Maeght collection, along with Chagall, who moved to Vence in 1949.

Sometime in 1950s, a local crowd of Nice artists started to take stock of the art scene on their own terrain. And frankly, they said, "Enough is enough." No more of these pretty landscapes and sunsets, no more easels and paint. Art must be able to express itself in other ways. In fact, art must begin to reflect the contemporary world. They wanted reality to replace pretty pictures. In 1961 Yves Klein, Arman, and Martial Raysse were recognized as the School of Nice. They were soon joined by Ben, César (from Marseille, but close enough), Serges III, Sosno - all from the Nice area. As "new realists" they gained international acclaim. César sculpted discarded metal; Arman collected garbage; Raysse worked with plastic; while Klein explored emptiness and infinite blues. Basically they said, "Look at our wasteful, mass produced society. We can create art from it." Their ideas were accepted by the avant garde art community in New York, but in Nice they were considered cultural hooligans.

The ruckus created by the School of Nice has long since died down. Many of its artists are now respected members of the community, and in 1990 the Museum of Contemporary Art was opened to exhibit their art.

Are there signs of new life? The tail end of the School of Nice is still wagging, but the art historians are also looking to the future for signs of new development, and new artists. Plenty of museums and galleries exhibit the region's rich heritage, and many international artists live in the area or come here to work in the peaceful surroundings in between dashing off to Los Angeles and Tokyo. The tradition of artistic communities and foundations lives on with American artist Nall in Vence, who invites young artists, writers, and musicians to work. Nall's surrealistic pieces are the most powerful and original works on the Côte d'Azur today. And in true Riviera style, his N.A.L.L. Association Board of Directors includes Monaco art collector Michel Pastor, the Duchess of Bedford, and Ringo Starr.

Written by Inger Lise Eisenhour

Picasso - Le Naivre et le Centaure, 1946

The Loup Valley, the village of Caille, and Cime du
Cheiron on the eastern side of the valley

VALLÉE DU LOUP

Art and Adventureland

 eaving Nice and the Var River delta by way of the busy coastal highway, you will be traveling towards Antibes along the *Baie des Anges*, the Bay of Angels. An easily missed signpost indicates where the Loup River flows out into the Mediterranean Sea in Villeneuve-Loubet. The Loup originates upstream in a wonderland of mountains and open fields, the Loup Valley. It's only an hour's drive inland from the coast, and its passage to the sea is etched by magnificent gorges.

The coast stretches almost north-south between Nice and Antibes and is one of the low-points of the French Riviera. Its shores are wide open to the strong Sirocco winds that blow from Africa, bringing rough seas and sand-filled rain. The beach is a hard cobblestone of pebbles. The railway runs almost on the beach, the traffic chokes the highway, and the sidewalks are a scramble of cheap hotels, unappealing restaurants, and Citroën vans selling pretend-to-be pizza *au feu du bois*. Behind the railway and this seafront "strip," huge camping grounds spread across the scenery. Unfortunately, this is the French Riviera many people recognize, but those who know better only pass by in a rush to reach the golden sand of Cap d'Antibes or Cannes.

Heat haze along the cobblestone shore between Nice and Antibes

HIDEAWAYS AND MEDIEVAL VILLAGES HIDDEN BEHIND THE BEACH

But what's behind the beach scene and the wafting aroma of suntan oil? Only a few miles inland you'll find medieval villages, vast protected forests with endless trails along small creeks, romantic château hotels, and star-spangled restaurants. And what's more, you can also explore some of the richest art treasures in the world.

HOW IT USED TO BE

Further inland, half an hour from the coast, the scenery begins to reflect a more natural world, one of fresh air with slopes of olive and chestnut trees and softer colors, sometimes slashed by wild gorges, waterfalls, and caves or tamed by immense open green fields where local farmers harvest their land - all of this is the Loup Valley.

HOW TO GET THERE

Only a few roads run to this back country and they closely follow the course of the Loup River. Personal transport - be it car, bike or feet - would make this trip a memorable experience. The river itself will guide anyone who wants to hike it from the coast, a distance that probably could be covered in two or three days with comfortable overnight stops in auberges built next to the river. Driving straight up to the Loup Valley along the river will not take more than an hour, and maybe half a day on a bike.

FRESH, PURE, AND CLEAN AIR

The landscape that greets you once you arrive in the Loup Valley contrasts sharply with its closest neighbors. To the north, the pre-Alps with snow covered peaks and skiing. To the east, the more rugged hinterland of Nice. Westward, Provence lies cultivated in vineyards and to the south, the Mediterranean Sea.

The Loup Valley itself is an immense flat landscape located at 1000 meters (3300 ft) above sea level, ringed by the mountains of Thorenc and Cime de Cheiron in the north and the mountains above Grasse to the south. Peaks reach close to 2000 meters (6600 ft). Pollution is almost non-existant; the air is said to be the cleanest and purest in all of Europe - one reason why one of Europe's biggest observatories is located in this valley. Not long ago it was also a popular health resort.

The valley could almost be looked upon as a mini-western America or it could be anywhere in the wilderness of northern Scandinavia or Canada. Therefore its nickname Adventureland! Life is easy-going and focused on the outdoors.

Next page: Clear skies and the pure fresh air of the Loup Valley

Hideaways and medieval villages hidden behind the beach - above, the village of Valbonne

But what's behind the beach scene and the wafting aroma of suntan oil? Only a few miles inland you'll find the peace of nature

ROUTE D'AVENTURE

From art treasures to treasures of nature

Biot, located only 3 km (2 miles) from the coast and the beach where the Loup River flows into the sea, is - like its neighbors St Paul-de-Vence and Vence - one of the more famous hill top villages on the Côte d'Azur. The Romans developed Biot, like many other villages in the region, and left behind some remarkable remnants: the Mausoleum of the Chèvre d'Or, aqueducts, and the large wall of Vaugrenier. Today, visitors to Biot can still see some of these well preserved remains, and also study the crafts of ceramics and glass blowing for which Biot has become so famous.

As you wander the narrow streets of this quaint town, the past is evident everywhere, and openings between the old houses let you catch glimpses of the surrounding hills and the sea. It's easy to close your eyes and imagine that you are in the 17th century. You would see thousands of orange trees, olives and vineyards - where today you see the golf course, hundreds of *provençal* style private villas that have sprouted up across the hills, and Sophia Antipolis, a high-tech industrial zone with ultra-modern buildings, created to secure the future of the region.

POTTERY - A LONG STANDING TRADITION

After stone and wood the oldest craft is said to be pottery, which in Biot was practiced long before our epoch and you'll find numerous pieces of antique pottery as proof of this early activity. Pottery, traditionally in the form of *terra cotta* jars to hold olive oil, is still big business in Biot today, but not as important as artistic glass blowing. This art form took off in Biot during the 1950s when the ceramist, Eloi Monod, had the idea of recreating, in glass, rustic and traditional figurines, dishes, and vases that used to exist in Provence. Some 40 years later few visitors leave the village without stopping by LA VERRERIE DE BIOT to buy at least one piece of their world famous, hand blown Biot glass - thick heavy glass swirled in light colors with hundreds of tiny air bubbles. You

The village of Biot reflected in a handblown Biot glass

can also watch the glass being blown at the workshop just southeast of the village.

WINE GLASSES WITH A TWIST OF THE 1960s CONTEMPORARY NEW YORK

Along the main street overpriced tourist shops selling colorful and spicy "pretend-to-be " *provençal* products are mingled with the studios of true artists: potters, sculptors, and glass designers who create pieces of international worth.

Jan Paul van Lith is a glass sculptor, ceramist, designer, metal worker, and painter whose surrealistic wine glasses and sculptures are exhibited around the globe. He is an exuberant and prolific artist with tremendous versatility and provocative works that break down traditional barriers. In the late 1960s he moved to New York and lived through the craziness of Warhol, Lichtenstein, and Rauschenberg. He befriended many of the great contemporary artists of the time, many who were turning the garbage of the consumer society into colorful works of art. All these new and revolutionary ideas exerted a strong influence on van Lith and he brought them back to France and Biot, where his studio is just off the main street close to the entrance of the village. In his showroom wine glasses splashed with gold and circus colors share shelf-space with glass sculptures of make believe figurines.

The internationally acclaimed Swedish ceramist Hans Hedberg, also carries on working from his Biot workshop. His reputation is of the same dimension as his works: monumental. He creates huge realistic fruit sculptures, along with other delicious products that the region has to offer. Both artists are pleased to receive visitors, but by appointment only.

THE FERNAND LÉGER MUSEUM

The LÉGER MUSEUM, "a must" for art-lovers, stands to the southeast at the bottom of the village on the very spot where the artist, only a few month before his death, made plans to erect huge polychrome sculptures in ceramic.

Fernand Léger, famous for his cylindrical works during the cubist period and his Communist inspired working class scenes, had this museum built to honor his memory. The stark features of the building are the artistic creation of a local architect, and meant to represent a cubist temple. The facade is decorated with vast mosaics, originally designed for the Hanover Stadium. Inside you'll find a complete vision of the artist's work from 1905 until his death in 1955: oil-paintings, gouaches, drawings, ceramics, mosaics, stained-glass and tapestries.

RESTAURANTS IN BIOT

AUBERGE DU JARRIER, where olive jars were once produced, is the best known restaurant in the village. The Auberge is located on a quiet side street and has a terrace covered in bright bougainvillea facing the countryside. The proposed menu is reasonably priced compared to *à la carte* and the fact that Bellet wines are served is a sign that this restaurant is a good choice. The few wine producers of Bellet carefully select which restaurants to supply, thus setting up a sort of local quality control! Just outside the town *au pied de village* is the restaurant LES TERRAILLERS, a charming old 17th century pottery workshop with vaulted stone arches creating an intimate atmosphere inside. A small garden overgrown with greenery and flowers decorates the outside most of the year.

BIOT TO ST PAUL-DE-VENCE THROUGH THE VALBONNE FOREST - *LA VALÉE VERTE*

North of Biot lies a large protected forest that offers one of the nicest hikes close to the coast. The trail begins immediately as you exit Biot, then runs along the Brague River through the thick forest of the *Vallée Verte*, the Green Valley, and arrives three hours later at Valbonne.

If you prefer the comfort of a car to the tranquillity of a hike, then the main road towards Valbonne leads through the same forest and provides panoramic views of the coast. Shortly before Valbonne, turn right and follow signs for Roquefort-les-Pins. Continue on the narrow D7 and soon you'll be passing the Loup River before you arrive at La Colle-sur-Loup and St Paul-de-Vence.

This trip takes approximately 30 minutes by car and passes the Valbonne Golf Course before it swings through the unspoiled nature of the Valbonne forest and the lower part of the Loup Valley. It's hard to believe that in this quiet woodland, you are only minutes away from the hectic coast.

Along the road you'll come to a small auberge well

worth a visit, a lunch, or a night rest. The history of the AUBERGE DU COLOMBIER in Roquefort-les-Pins dates back hundreds of years. This old stone house is believed to be one of the oldest auberges in the region, because it was the only station on the road between Nice and Grasse where a rider could change horses and get some food and rest in earlier days. The auberge is located on a "balcony" overlooking the forests and the coast. In the beautiful flower garden, white pigeons fly free around their huge cage. The rooms are small, simple, and comfortable, some offering a private terrace. Lunch and dinner are served on the patio by the pool, which makes lunch especially nice. Mr Wolf, the owner, is always there to look after you and give you ideas about spectacular hikes and riding excursions to explore the surrounding countryside.

Shortly after the AUBERGE COLOMBIER you'll leave the forest behind and enter a more open landscape where rolling hills are covered with olive and orange trees. Looking out towards the Mediterranean you'll see an old medieval village, Le-Haut-de-Cagnes, topped by its castle tower.

LE HAUT-DE-CAGNES

The village history starts with the castle, as is the case in so many of the medieval villages along the coast, and the history of this castle is tied to the history of the Grimaldi family of Monaco. It was built by Rainier Grimaldi, Lord of Monaco in the early 14th century. In the early 17th century, at the peak of the Grimaldi's powerful hold on the coast, it was converted into a nicely decorated château by Henry Grimaldi. The Grimaldis led a life of luxury in this château, so idyllically mounted above olive orchards and the Medi-

terranean, safely protected by the French king and Cardinal Richelieu, until French Revolution broke out and the Grimaldis were driven out.

The castle and old village remain, with steep narrow cobblestone streets, vaulted passageways, and houses dating back to the 15th and 16th century, many of which have been carefully restored. But the surrounding olive fields have had to give way to Cagnes-Ville - a busy residential and commercial quarter that stretches all the way down to the coastline.

LE CAGNARD - A REPUTABLE OLD INN

LE CAGNARD is one of the oldest buildings in the village, with a history that dates it as an "inn" already in the 15th century. It has been beautifully restored into a "modern" auberge that is positively medieval in charm and decor. A small car could muster a passage up the slim street that runs to the auberge, but it is preferable to leave your car at the large parking at the entrance of the village and follow the signs that will guide you to LE CAGNARD.

Red stucco walls greet you as you enter. The low ceiling is supported by huge timber beams interspersed with painted murals creating an imposing sence of history. A small wooden stairs lead down to a balcony overlooking the medieval dining hall. The restaurant is dominated by a large stone fireplace, while the terrace has a delicately painted roof that smoothly slides open in warm weather to let the sun reach your table. The view is superb of hills and sea. In addition to its lovely decoration and warm inviting atmosphere, the auberge has won several awards for its delicious gourmet cuisine.

The artist van Lith's atelier in Biot

The medieval village of Le Haut-de-Cagnes

LE CAGNARD offers 17 rooms in the old auberge where you can enjoy all the charm and peace of living in a medieval village, yet pampered by the comforts and facilities that the modern world has added to life. If you prefer something bigger, owners Felix and Mauricette Barel have extended the auberge in recent years to include 11 spacious apartments nearby the auberge, most with big private terraces and all with the same fabulous view as from the restaurant.

ST PAUL-DE-VENCE - THE SECOND MOST VISITED VILLAGE OF FRANCE

St-Paul-de-Vence is one of the most beautiful of the French Riviera's perched medieval villages - it's also the second most visited after Mont St. Michel in Bretagne. St-Paul-de-Vence has come to be known as a mecca for art lovers and both the MAEGHT FOUNDATION and the COLOMBE D'OR have added to the reputation. Art has undoubtedly lived in St Paul for hundreds of years, but it was not until the 20th century that the village became celebrated as a favorite with artists, when the COLOMBE D'OR played host to a bevy of promising artists.

The COLOMBE D'OR is situated near the entrance of St Paul-de-Vence, an unpretentious and weathered old *mas* with a sign on the door stating: guests only! A tiny square cut out of the door allows a teasing glimpse of the heavenly terrace, all decked out with wooden tables and fig trees, set before a panorama of the Alps. Inside it houses an extraordinary private collection of 20th century art. For many years, the COLOMBE D'OR was a favorite "hang-out" for struggling young artists invited by owner Paul Roux, himself a painter. The story has it that he accepted artwork from artists in exchange for food, drink, and accommodation. Today, the works fill the dining room, guest rooms, and even the small lobby of the hotel. You can dine next to a Chagall or a Miro, walk on the terrace and pass the large Léger mural; or stroll into the hotel courtyard and be greeted by a giant marble thumb by César, while a large marble dove sculpture stares at you from the greenery. In the pool, you are sometimes shaded from the sun by a 6 meter (20 foot) Calder mobile slowly sweeping above! or you may wake up under the watchful gaze of a Foujita, a Picasso, or a Matisse above your bed. Many celebrities love the simple and elegant atmosphere of this secret museum, where even the most seasoned critic will be impressed. The collection of Golden Visitors Books are an art treasure themselves and only seen by a lucky few. They detail the secrets of two generations of COLOMBE D'OR guests and are filled with improvised masterpieces from the great and talented people who have passed through, a true art lovers dream!

A book and a place - where Chaplin shares a page of history with Miro!

A HOLLYWOOD STAGE WHERE THE CROWD SNAPS "TYPICAL" PICTURES

The CAFÉ DE LA PLACE is situated across from the COLOMBE D'OR, its dusty red playing field is the *grande place de boules*. It's a sophisticated café in the typical French style. Its regulars are boules-slinging locals, picture-postcard Frenchmen, joined by heroes of the French culture and entertainment world. The whole scene resembles a Hollywood stage with crowds of tourists snapping their pictures.

The village itself stretches along the Rue Grande, the main street that runs the full length of the village. Closed to traffic, the *"rue"* is a good place to explore the picturesque housefronts and to browse in the art galleries, artist studios and homes, and souvenir shops filled with *provençal* "arts" and crafts.

The GALERIE GAULT has come up with its own style of selling ceramic, mini-scale *provençal* houses: you simply buy each building separately - hand made and signed by the artist himself - and build your own miniature village.
Outside the village walls and just behind CAFÉ DE LA PLACE, GALERIE ISSERT is the "most contemporary" of the contemporary art galleries and one of the select along the Côte d'Azur visited by prime collectors.

GALERIE DE LA SALLE across from the MAEGHT FOUNDATION was a major force behind the *Ecole de Nice*; it was the only gallery in the region to actively promote and exhibit their experimental works in the 1960s.

THE MAEGHT FOUNDATION - THE MOST IMPORTANT CONTEMPORARY ART MUSEUM ON THE CÔTE D'AZUR

THE MAEGHT FOUNDATION is beautifully situated, at peace in the pinewoods just outside St-Paul-de-Vence. It's certainly one of the most spectacular and important museums on the Côte d'Azur. Relying heavily on Mediterranean influences, the Spanish architect created an artistic complex entirely of white concrete and rose colored bricks. The long stretches of green lawn within the natural

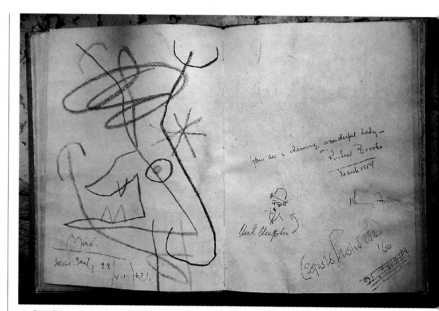

A book and a place where Chaplin shares a page of history with Miro

parkland are made enchanting by Miro sculptures and a huge Calder stabile. Devoted to 20th century art, it counts some of this century's most innovative artists: Miro, Chagall, Giacometti, and Calder in its permanent collection which rotates throughout the year.

THE MAS D'ARTIGNY - SPACIOUS ROOMS WITH PRIVATE POOLS

Hidden in a beautiful pine forest in the hills above St-Paul-de-Vence and surrounded by 16 acres of natural parkland, LE MAS D'ARTIGNY is neighbor to an exclusive international elite who make *Les-Hauts-de-St-Paul* their home away from home. The hotel is certainly not a *mas*, having been built in the early 1970s, but it's still a wonderful place for those seeking privacy, tranquility, and comfort in a countryside easily accessible, yet away from the frenzied coastline. LE

One pool for each room - Le Mas d'Artigny

Photo courtesy Mas d'Artigny

MAS D'ARTIGNY does not pretend to sell a sea view, but offers the outdoors and spacious rooms with private balconies and a great view of St-Paul-de-Vence and the surrounding hills.

The unique feature of this *mas* are the 25 apartments, each with a private pool, living room, and a spacious dressing room, plus the three astonishing "private" villas with five to eight rooms linked to all the services of the hotel. Unfortunately the private pools are too small and sometimes too hot in the summer, therefore serving more as an added attraction that you can tell friends about at home. The best choice is one of the private villas with its full-size pool.

The private garden has a huge pool, tennis courts, a

Vegetable market in the old town of Vence

putting green, and a "driving range." There is also ping pong, a billiard table, a courtyard to practice boules before conquering the "locals" in front of CAFÉ DE LA PLACE, and for high-fliers arriving in helicopter - a heliport.

VENCE - THE OLD TOWN - AN OASIS SURROUNDED BY THE 1950s

From St-Paul-de-Vence the road winds its way through a beautiful forest and valley up to Vence. Behind the *vieux moulin* outside St-Paul-de-Vence a trail in the woods leads to Vence and can be hiked in one and a half hours.

Vence itself gives a very stark, out of place impression with its huge, modern, squarish white buildings mostly constructed in the 1950s. It's big and hectic with one exception - the old village hidden in the heart of town. If you manage to reach this oasis where no cars are allowed, you'll find a charming old town with lots of cafés and restaurants. Try a pizza at the casual little pizzeria, LE PECHEUR DU SOLEIL on the square behind the church and make sure to order one of their 500 pizzas they offer on the menu. If you prefer something more *provençal* there is the AUBERGE DES SEIGNEURS, an old auberge built into the ramparts of the ancient village with 8 charming rooms to service this medieval hideaway in modern Vence. The original kitchen has been turned into a dining room with a large open fireplace where Monsieur Pierre Rodi, owner and chef, prepares the main meat dishes when he's not walking around telling guests fantastic fairy-tales about the place's history. Just looking at the rustic surroundings, where tables and chairs are made out of heavy wood with a very old touch and the walls are covered with traditional copper utensils, will make you believe most of what you are being told.

THE MATISSE CHAPEL

Opposite the ramparts of the old town on the slopes facing south you'll see the MATISSE CHAPEL embedded in greenery and olive trees. After Matisse completed the chapel in 1951, he said, "*Despite its imperfections I think it's my masterpiece... the result of a lifetime devoted to the search for truth*"

Many delightful things have been said about this beautiful little chapel, but it can hardly be described better than by American poetess Sylvia Plath in a letter to her mother in January 1956:

How can I describe the beauty of the country? Everything is so small, close, exquisite, and fertile. Terraced gardens on steep slopes of rich, red earth, orange and lemon trees, olive orchards, tiny pink and peach houses. To Vence - small, on a sun-warmed hill, uncommercial, slow, peaceful. Walked to Matisse Cathedral - small, pure, clean-cut. White, with blue-tile roof sparkling in the sun. But shut! only open to public two days a week. A kindly talkative peasant told me stories of how rich people came

Relaxing midday "nap" on the Balcons de la Côte d'Azur

daily in large cars from Italy, Germany, Sweden, etc., and were not admitted, even for large sums of money. I was desolate and wandered to the back of the old nunnery, where I could see a corner of the chapel and sketched it, feeling like Alice outside the garden, watching the white doves and orange trees. Then I went back to the front and stared with my face through the barred gate. I began to cry. I knew it was so lovely inside, pure white with the sun through blue, yellow and green stained windows. Then I heard a voice. "Ne pleurez plus, entrez," and the Mother Superior let me in , after denying all the wealthy people in cars. I just knelt in the heart of the sun and the colors of sky, sea and sun, in the pure white heart of the chapel. "Vous êtes si gentille," I stammered. The nun smiled. "C'est la misericorde de Dieu." It was!

Sylvia Plath, Letter Home: Correspondence, 1950-63, ed Aurelia Schober Plath, Faber & Faber, 1976

CHÂTEAU DU DOMAINE SAINT-MARTIN
A STAR ABOVE VENCE

High above the Matisse Chapel and Vence on a southern balcony of the pre-Alps 500 meters (1,600 ft) above sea-level and the Riviera, CHÂTEAU DU DOMAINE SAINT MARTIN is a tempting alternative to the not-too-distant COLOMBE D'OR, though much different. Since Roman times, the spectacular position held by the Domaine St-Martin - protected from the north wind by mountain tops and with a panoramic look-out of Vence and all the countryside to the sea - gave reason for the construction of a fortified stronghold on the site. Its history dates back to 350 AD when Saint Martin, Bishop of Tours and evangelist of the Gauls, gave name to the estate.

The Knights Templar set up a commandery on the Roman stronghold - their impressive drawbridge still stands to this day. History says that the Saint Martin Templars worshipped a golden goat which they hid with their enormous treasures before leaving their confraternity. This legend has persisted to such an extent that the bill of sale drawn up in 1936, when the present owners, the Geneve family bought the domaine, stipulates that "in the event of the treasure being found, it shall be shared amongst the assignees and the last owner!"

Today the treasure can be shared by everyone since the family opened the domaine as a hotel and restau-rant in 1958. The castle, as it is today, in the midst of six acres of a serene parkland planted with olive trees, was completed in 1936. Throughout the castle, all bedrooms, lounges, and reception areas are tastefully decorated with Persian and Flemish carpets as well as beautiful pieces of antique furniture. In addition to the main house, small private *bastides* and villas are scattered among the wooded estate with full hotel facilities. The swimming pool is romantically shaped as a heart. There is tennis and an excellent restaurant awarded for its gastronomic food.

TOURETTE-SUR-LOUP - WHERE NATURE BEGINS

Vence flows into the next village, Tourette-sur-Loup, which is less famous, more picturesque, and somewhat less explored. One reason for Tourettes' relative anonymity compared to its famous neighbors Vence and St Paul-de-Vence may be that it allows only through traffic and parking is very limited. Only two gates access the village and its dramatic setting on a rocky spur has always acted as a natural barrier to keep people out-or in.

This village seems to be the northern border where the stream of tourists coming from the coast believe everything ends. Minutes above the village, the small AUBERGE DES CHEVALIERS sits in a secluded garden overlooking Tourette with a magnificent view down to the coast and sea. On the hillside above the auberge, there are plenty of nice walks along huge grassy fields with small streams of ice cold water pouring down from the mountain.

Back in town, the streets of Tourette village loop around from the main parking lot, and a few minutes walk down the cobblestone lane will bring you to a string of boutiques selling local products, handicrafts, and art works.

A small restaurant, LE PETIT MANOIR, tempts strollers and is quickly filled up with local connoisseurs during lunch and dinner, since both the cuisine and the ambience are very inviting.

TRAVELING ALONG THE LOUP RIVER
INTO CÔTE D'AVENTURES

Shortly after leaving Tourette heading west, there is a fantastic view of the village atop its rock, which plunges to the ravine below. For the next 13 km (8 miles), the road runs through the wooded southern slopes of Pic de Courmettes above the lower reaches of the Loup River valley. Descending into the river valley, you'll enter the village of Pont du Loup, the gateway entrance to the impressive Gorges du Loup. This village is cut in half by the Loup River and is home to the auberge LA RESERVE with its large terrace high above the river rapids where you can enjoy an excellent *cuisine regionale*. There is also trout fishing, walks along the river in the countryside up to Bar-sur-Loup, and a spectacular pool in the park by the river.

GORGES DU LOUP - SPECTACULAR
AND IMPRESSIVE

The Loup River has cut a deep and narrow path in the mountain. Steep white rocks, sometimes with patches of lush vegetation, rise vertically from the riverbed and the road, reaching heights of several hundred meters (almost 1,500 feet). Along this impressive scenery of white water and rocks, there are two famous waterfalls. The Cascade de Courmes drops down into a natural pool next to the road. Several pathways have been cut into the mountain at this

Château de Cipières towering above its village with a majestic Mount Cheiron in the background

point, allowing visitors to climb up and under the waterfall. But walk carefully! Time, erosion, and lack of maintenance have made the excursion somewhat hazardous. Further on, the landscape opens up and a smaller, less dramatic waterfall, Cascade des Demoiselles, tumbles down the slope.

CHÂTEAU DE CIPIÈRES - YOUR OWN CASTLE

The landscape opens up dramatically as you reach the upper Loup Valley; the mountains become less colorful and much smoother. Gréolières is a hill village at the southern base of Mount Cheiron. The village is quiet and empty, but offers a good view across the valley to the village of Cipières, which will strike you with its rather unusual profile. A huge squarish castle, like a big lump of sugar, dominates the little village. LE CHÂTEAU DE CIPIÈRES, located at an altitude of 750 m (2500 feet) is a

17th century home built on top of a medieval fortress dating back to the 14th century. The early fortress was built by the *Grand Batard* son of the Duke of Savoy, a notable warrior and the uncle of Francois I, King of France. From the end of the 19th century up until 1951, the château was used for keeping sheep and storing fodder. This architectural and historical gem was then rescued from oblivion by a private family who purchased the property and had it restored and furnished as their personal summerhouse. In 1989 it was opened to the public, or rather, to the lucky few, as a luxury accommodation with six separate apartments, all facing south. The most original of them is under the roof beams, where thousands of pigeons were kept in the old days, as a sign of wealth. In the study area, several pigeon cages are still intact - and clean!

Guests have full access to the impressive living room and old dining room, where lunch and dinner are served to guests only. Outsiders are not allowed into the château to

The road climbs steeply above the village of Gréolières with magnificent views of the Gorges du Loup and the upper Loup Valley

ensure the feeling of living in a "private" château. The beautiful garden which surrounds the hotel contains the ruins and ramparts of the old fortress which was built directly on the rock. The swimming pool sits on a separate plateau and has terrific views of the mountains. Rumors persist that a ghost lives in the house, protecting a treasure hidden in the ruins, which must by law be split among the inhabitants of Cipières if ever found.

CHÂTEAU DE CIPIÈRES provides the calm beauty of an exceptional setting along with a gracious and warm ambience - a first choice for an unforgettable honeymoon right on the threshold of the great Côte d'Aventure outdoors.

GRÉOLIÈRES-LES-NEIGES - THE CLOSEST SKI RESORT TO THE COAST

The landscape north of the CHÂTEAU DE CIPIÈRES is dominated by a steep mountain covered in snow several months of the year. On top, at an altitude of 1,450 m (4,800 ft) Gréolières-les-Neiges, only an hour's drive from the coast, is probably the closest ski resort to the Côte d'Azur. Its altitude being low for a ski resort, snow conditions are rarely exeptional and there aren't many ski-lifts, but skiing is fairly easy. The village does not provide any culinary

surprises nor any hidden medieval château where you can spend the night. This is an excellent choice for a day excursion as a change from the coast when you know that there is lots of snow - and the view from the top of the blue Mediterranean Sea and the coast truly amazing.

CÔTE D'AVENTURE

Continuing from Gréolières towards Thorenc, the road climbs steeply above the village and offers magnificent views of the Gorges du Loup and the upper Loup Valley. Further west, the landscape opens up into a beautiful stretch of flat countryside as the road snakes along the side of the gorge, beneath huge rock spurs of fantastic shapes and sizes with the Loup River 400 m (1,300 ft) below.

The Côte d'Aventure in the upper Loup Valley abounds in "adventure" - most of it centered around the village of Thorenc. Large green fields and meadows stretch across the land, meshing with the smooth green hills and forests. The outdoor enthusiast can breathe deeply of the fresh country air - this landscape offers him everything. During the summer season, several shops rent mountain bikes (VTT in French, *Vélo Tout Terrain*) and any other equipment necessary to enjoy outdoor sporting which can be exercised in the valley: mountaineering, stage rock climb-

Next page: Across the wide plateau de Caussols, thousands of white stones lie scrambled in the extremely barren landscape, where only a few dry bushes and trees survive

ing, trout fishing, horseback riding, hang- and para-gliding, archery, ultra-light planes.

The valley offers more than 250 km (156 miles) of trails and marked hikes - all in an unspoiled reserve of nature with hundreds of colorful wild flowers, sheep, goats, and other wildlife. The winter season offers the added attraction of skiing, with over 100 km (62.5 miles) of cross country trails and five ski resorts for downhill skiing, including Gréolières-les-Neige.

Thorenc itself is a fairly modern village, spread over a large area on the southern slope of the Bleine and Thorenc mountains. Wooden houses are nestled into the green countryside. LES VOYAGEURS, a small auberge and restaurant on the main square, serves excellent food on a terrace overlooking the village and the valley. From here many hikes begin and end. A 45-minute hike leads up to Col de Bleine, which looks out over the entire "adventure" valley from 1,450 m (2,300 ft). This peak also provides a ramp that serves hang- and para-gliders when they take off for long sweeping flights across the valley.

To better explore all possibilities in the region, it's advisable to use a guide. EVASION ADVENTURES has a long experience in many different excursions and they offer a vast program of activities - from beginners to the most experienced mountaineers.

A LIMESTONE MOONLAND
THE CAUSSOLS PLATEAU

When leaving the Loup Valley, it is best to climb the D5 towards St-Vallier-de-Thiey for approximately 16 km (10 miles) until you come to a side road on the left - D112 - with signs pointing to Caussols and Gourdon. It is important to stay on the southernmost road while crossing Caussols, the high plateau above Grasse. A new landscape unrolls before you, one that may be different from any you have ever seen before. Across the whole wide *plateau*, thousands of white stones lie scrambled in the extremely barren landscape, where only a few dry bushes and trees survive. Every so often you spot stone huts and stone fortresses dating back to prehistoric years. The *plateau* offers peaceful walks or tough exercise on a mountain bike. There are plenty of opportunities to search out your own cave, possibly one with a patch of wild grass in the huge white rocks - unbeatable for a private picnic.

GOURDON - THE EPITOME OF A
HILL TOP VILLAGE

Descending from Caussols, you quickly approach the coast. The scenery is rugged with little vegetation until you reach

the village of Gourdon, which teeters at the edge of an 800 m (2600 ft) cliff, with a view that sweeps across the entire Côte d'Azur. Unfortunately, Gourdon's sensational site is too close to the coast, so one finds the typical array of cheap souvenirs being peddled in the streets. If you can disregard the bric-à-brac or look beyond it, you'll find products like honey, olive oil, and spices, as well as a few shops offering high quality, handmade glasses and fine antiques.

At the entrance to Gourdon next to the parking, the AUBERGE DE GOURDON dishes up good meals in warm, very French, and casual surroundings. More striking, at the very edge of the village where the rock drops vertically down into the valley below, the LE NID D'AIGLE has a fabulous view and rustic interiors. You do pay a bit for the view, but the food is good.

Leaving Gourdon on the D3 to return to the lower altitudes, the road first makes a sharp turn skirting huge vertical rocks. A waterfall can be seen in the background as the road swings around to the rocks overlooking Gourdon. From here, the village appears majestic, perched on the edge of its cliff, with vertical rocks plummeting several thousand feet into the lower Loup Valley. Gourdon is the epitome of a hilltop village. It is hard to leave this sight without wondering to yourself, "Who came up with the idea of building a village at this site, when the rock was not even accessible by road?" During the week-ends, this town becomes home to brave men and women with hang-gliders or para-gliders, who throw themselves out into the wind, often staying airborne for several hours on the upward winds from the vertical rocks before they land in the valley.

From this point, the road continues down and passes the outskirts of Grasse and the little village of Pré du Lac. At the main road junction in this village you'll find the café, BAR PERGOLA, a meeting point for mountain bikers, mountaineers and hang-gliders where they can make plans for the day or discuss past experiences over a glass of pastis.

MOULIN DE LA BRAGUE - THE OLDEST OLIVE MILL IN THE REGION STILL IN OPERATION

Le Pré du Lac is where civilization begins anew and you can literally feel it when driving through. Beautiful private homes begin to appear on the terraced slopes, tranquil amongst the ancient olive trees. A shepherd nearby watches his herd as they graze along the new golf course of Opio. Driving past the hillside village of Châteauneuf de Grasse down towards Opio you'll pass the olive mill, MOULIN DE LA BRAGUE, dating back to the 15th century and still in full operation, producing one of the finest olive oil in the region. It has been operated by the same family for six generations, and locals still bring their bushel baskets full of homegrown olives as they have for hundreds of years. The olives are then weighed and the "landlord" leaves the mill with an equivalent amount of pressed oil. Visitors can buy directly from the shop, choosing from a large variety of oils. Soaps, scents, bowls of olive wood, and foodstuffs are a few examples of the fine provençal products available.

VALBONNE

Continuing through the woods towards the coast, you reach Valbonne, which was built by the Romans following the grid pattern of ancient Roman cities, with straight streets and right angle crossings. The superb Place aux Arcades with its arched arcade occupies the center of town. One of the oldest houses on this square hosts a hotel, LES ARMOIRES, restored in 1990 by a former Parisian hairdresser, Mr Pelletier, who had had enough of Paris and found himself this auberge dating back to the 15th century.

LA TABLE AU GOURMAND is located at the entrance of Valbonne as you arrive from Opio. It has a gorgeous little patio outdoors and stone walls inside filled with local artwork and paintings. A huge fireplace fills the second floor. When it is lit in the wintertime it heats up both the room and the "home cooked" meals sizzling on the open fire. The restaurant is one of those family run establishments that you dream of finding while touring the provençal countryside. Make sure you have a reservation, the restaurant is small. On the outskirts of Valbonne next to the church there is another old moulin à huile, but it is no longer used as a press. It is in the former monastery of Valbonne, which has now been converted into the beautifully decorated LE MOULIN DES MOINES.

The neighborhood surrounding Valbonne has become one of the most popular areas for summer homes in the region and many magnificent estates can be found here. The club house of GOLF DE VALBONNE is a restored country mansion which dates back to the 18th century and hosts a lovely hotel, modern conveniences, and modest prices. The club facilities are excellent: an 18-hole golf course, tennis courts, swimming pool, and a great restaurant to lunch in, even if you are not a golfer.

As you continue along the road towards Antibes, shortly after Valbonne you will see the auberge LE MAS DE VALBONNE to the right. During the summer, lunch and dinner are served in a relaxed garden shaded by a lofty tree. During the winter, the big open fire provides a warm and romantic atmosphere throughout the several small private rooms. The food is excellent and the ambience unforgettable.

Heading back towards the coast, the road edges Mougins known worldwide as a gastronomic mecca (described in the Cannes chapter on page 143). In addition to the many fine reststaurants, hotels and auberges you will find the MOUGINS - CANNES GOLF AND COUNTRY CLUB, one of the regions most prestigious and oldest golf clubs. The road then leads through the Valmasque Forest and the high-tech center of Sophia Antipolis, before reaching the coast and Antibes.

Next page: Gourdon, majestically perched on the edge of a cliff

The old town of Antibes, the Picasso Museum, and snow covered Maritime Alps

ANTIBES

Yacht center of the world

ntibes, "the opposite city" in Latin, is located in the southern corner of the Bay of Angels, facing Nice (its former enemy) to the north and the Alpes d'Azur. Its history stretches back to 400 BC when the Greeks set up the trading post of *Antipolis*, which was later taken over and destroyed by the Romans. During the 14th century, the king of France recognized its important military potential, standing as it did at the border of France and Savoy. For more than three centuries the fortifications of Antibes were improved and expanded and finally completed by Vauban in the 17th century.

Today only the seafront portion of the fortification remains, creating a natural protection for its famed yacht harbor, Port Vauban, one of the world's largest marinas. Thousands of shiny white yachts sway along its quays, making Antibes the yacht center of the world. It also boasts a new pier and the IYCA (International Yacht Club of Antibes), home to the world's largest yachts. Circling the harbor, smaller yachts and local fishing boats are docked along the inner part of the old ramparts.

STROLLING AROUND THOSE MULTI-MILLION DOLLAR FLOATING HOMES

It's amazing to stroll along the antique ramparts and look at these modern multi-million dollar floating homes, with uniformed crews polishing every detail, keeping the yachts in mint condition in case the owner or a guest should eventually turn up, which rarely seems to happen. If you're lucky, an aft deck door might be open and you could catch a glimpse of a nautical world where interior designers have been directed to let their fantasy loose and to lay it on thick - very thick since money is not the restriction - if faucets can be gold, let them be gold. And sometimes the decor ends up looking like Liberace meeting Louis the 14th.

Through the ancient gate, you face Antibes charming old town, a truly authentic, cobblestoned village far removed from the technical bustle in the port or the plush new carpets behind the mahogany doors of mega-yachts! This unique village has survived the modernization and tourist development of the last 50 years and retains its dignity and atmosphere from a seafaring past. As you pass in through the main gateway, there is a TABAC where locals congregate and where you might take a coffee or a French draft beer *"un demi pression"*. Later in the evening, it's a good choice for a late night drink after a good dinner, but you would do better dining elsewhere.

THE PICASSO MUSEUM

Behind the TABAC, a narrow square leads to steps which bring you up onto the old ramparts, offering a beautiful view of the entire Port Vauban harbor, with the 16th century Fort Carré, the coastline stretching towards Nice, and the Alpes d'Azur in the distance, their peaks glistening with snow on a crisp winter or spring day. From here, there is easy access to Avenue Amiral de Grasse, the seafront promenade that runs along the 17th century ramparts, directly beneath the cathedral and Grimaldi castle - today the home of the PICASSO MUSEUM, a must for every visitor to the French Riviera!

Picasso spent the year of 1946 painting at the castle, invited by the town of Antibes. The outcome is prodigious. It allows the visitor's fantasy and imagination to wander, with an eye on how an artist can transform the soft colors, light, nature, and richness of the region into exceptional works of art. The majority of what he painted and sculpted during this period is permanently displayed at this wonderful museum. The Antibes paintings on the first floor include a

series of canvases known as the *Suite d'Antipolis* - all are inspired by marine and mythological life in the Mediterranean and express delight and fantasy. In the ceramics collection, Picasso's unique imagination and creativity are highlighted in accents and adornments of great beauty and originality. This museum is a major attraction along the coast, not only for its collection of Picassos, but also for its genuine beauty and perfect location.

COURS MASSENA - A MARKETPLACE AND A DRIVEWAY

From the PICASSO MUSEUM you can follow any of the old cobblestone streets which lead down to the Cours Massena, the local marketplace each morning. In the afternoon, the Cours Massena is transformed into a driveway, where throughout the evening cars must give way to tables spilling out from the restaurants along the sides. Around the market, a network of narrow cobbled streets are filled with small shops offering a wide range of local products: everything from the butcher, antiques and artistic, handicrafts. Although centrally located on the Côte d'Azur, Antibes has avoided as much as possible becoming too "touristy."

Walking along these tiny streets, you will ultimately arrive at Rue de la Republique, which stretches all the way through the old town of Antibes to the central square, Place Nationale. La Place - an obligatory *locale* in every good French village - and the streets surrounding it are full of small, cozy-looking restaurants, which unfortunately do not always serve the quality of food you would expect. One exception, AUBERGE PROVENÇALE, is located in a quiet corner of La Place, with no tables on the sidewalk in front.

Antibes and Port Vauban, one of the biggest yacht marinas in the world

*Juan-les-Pins at sunset with the
new yacht harbor of Golfe-Juan*

The entrance greets you with the usual French seafood and oyster bar. Once inside, you will find a warm atmosphere, antiques, wood, and a collection of porcelain hung from the ceiling. Taking his place in front of the large open fireplace, Helder, an elderly chef, prepares appetizing grilled dishes of local fish and the unforgettable Beef Helder, served with delicious "Belgian" French-fried potatoes and a tasty *sauce bearnaise*. During summer, the little backyard overgrown with greenery opens, and on top of the restaurant a few nicely set hotel rooms are available for very reasonable prices.

Two blocks away towards the harbor, CHEZ PAUL LE PECHEUR, is an authentic fishermen's hang-out. The entrance is a mix between an oyster bar and a fish market and inside local fishermen sit at the few casually arranged tables discussing the day's catch. Upstairs on the second floor, the decor is straight off a comfortable old cruise liner, a marine blue salon with faded pictures of ships entering the port of Antibes. Fisherman Paul, appropriately dressed in a captain's hat and a big smile, will tell you all about today's catch and happily go on about everything to do with the marine life in the Mediterranean, the history of Antibes as if it were his own, and harrowing stories of hardship endured by *Antibois* fishermen in heavy seas and gale winds. For an informal dinner, the restaurant is a good choice for Mediterranean fish, preferably with their specialty, the *palengre*, a rare local fish. But do watch out! Due to his success, Paul has opened a second restaurant in Antibes away from the harbor that also bears his name followed by LE BASTIDE. This place is a total contrast to the first, with no maritime ambience and where the fish dinners strangely don't taste as good, even if the kitchen is said to be the same. Make sure you join Paul in the harbor and that you have a proper reservation.

Also in the old town along Rue de la République, you'll find the oyster and seafood bistro L'OURSIN, a very small, informal eatery. Much fancier, LES VIEUX MURS, is a rustic *cave* with a view of the sea and Cap d'Antibes, located on the ramparts close to the Picasso Museum. The owner and chef, Mr Georges Ramono, worked the restaurant several years ago when it had one star in the Michelin Guide. Recently returned to Antibes from a successful restaurant venture in Paris, his ambition now is to regain the lost star in Antibes.

JUAN-LES-PINS - A THREE MONTH EXTENSION OF SPRING BREAK

West of Antibes, only minutes by car across the Cap, Juan-les-Pins was "discovered" in the 1920s by the "Lost Genera-

Many consider the Juan-les-Pins scene to be a three month extension of Spring Break

tion" of Americans who flocked to the recently fashionable resort. Juan-les-Pins has none of the old world charm typical of nearby Antibes and is purely a modern summer resort, virtually closed during the winter. In summer, the sandy beaches are filled with fun-seeking teenagers and sun worshippers from all over the world. After beach hours until early morning, the two main streets attract a pulsating crowd. The carnival atmosphere is heightened by two pseudo Brazilian bars with steel bands that try to outplay each other with samba rhythms.

Many people would consider the Juan-les-Pins scene to be a three month extension of Spring Break. The ideal place to sit and watch this kinetic show of holiday makers and street entertainers - including fire-eaters, sword swallowers and magicians - is at LE CRYSTAL on the main square. There is no food, just snacks and an enormous selection of different beers, including what they claim to be the strongest beer in the world, "*Trapista*." If you care to dine while watching the show, the VESUVIO opposite LE CRYSTAL has a terrace with tables placed on the narrow and crowded pavement, plus more relaxed seating inside. The food is Italian with some delicious "catch of the day" selections. Juan-les-Pins also offers many nightclubs with such names as WHOOM WHOOM and WHISKEY A GO GO. Every night a new theme is presented: "Miss Teenage Topless" is among the most popular. The many boutiques of Juan-les-Pins sell the latest hot summer fashions and the smallest bikinis in existence - and they seldom open until the afternoon, since most of their customers are on the beach, or in bed, but instead they stay open long after midnight.

During the month of August, the annual Jazz Festival adds a touch of culture and glamour to the summer craziness. It takes place in a small park shadowed by lofty pine trees next to the sea that ordinarily serves as the *boules* court for the locals. This is the highlight of the season and traditionally attracts such well known artists as Ray Charles, Eric Clapton, Joe Cocker, and Phil Collins.

RUE DE DAUTHEVILLE - WHERE THE RESTAURANTS ARE

A typical street of Juan-les-Pins, the narrow Rue de Dautheville, is located a block behind the main square. Restaurants with appealing names such as LA BAMBA, LA BODEGA or PAM PAM are lined up side by side, featuring all the symptoms of tourist traps, including gaudy signs which read "pizza *feu du bois* - for home delivery." They are crowded, pumped with loud music, fun, very young, and have some good value for money as well. LA BAMBA serves excellent food at very reasonable prices in an artificial Provence "mish mash" décor. The owner, always attired in a wide pair of suspenders and an unbuttoned shirt, shows a chest which matches his big, black Fidel Castro beard. He smiles patiently as he does his utmost to find empty seating at tables overcrowded year-round, while waiters joke and smile. Next door, POUSSE POUSSE serves Oriental-Vietnamese food and some vegetarian meals and is frequented by Americans and English hungry for something other than the traditional French cuisine.

THE CRAZINESS AT THE BEACH

Soft sandy beaches run the entire shoreline of Juan-les-Pins. Long sections are kept public, and during the summer the main problem is how to reach the water without tip-toeing over oily, topless youngsters crushed shoulder to shoulder or how to avoid being hit by beach balls flying like uncontrolled bees through the air. The safest and most convenient solution is to stay away from the public sections and choose one of the private beach establishments, each offering a different taste. Instead of eating in the sand with children dashing to and fro, you'll feel quite civilized with a proper restaurant, your own *matelas*, table and parasol. Your favorite drink will be brought by the tanned young beach boys.

LE MOOREA is the hotspot for young, beautiful people. The beach is "furnished" in a Tahitian decor, plays Pacific music, and has several shady "beds" and hammocks to sprawl in. The wooden deck has been replaced by a cabana covered in palm branches. Ping pong, beach balls and other activities will allow anyone the opportunity to show off, but it is amusing to sit quietly, eat a tropical salad or a grilled brochette out of bamboo plates, while studying the ritual of new arrivals to the beach: the right look, who to say hello to, which mattress to choose, how to change into a bathing suit to obtain optimum attention, and which body position allows maximum body exposure to the sun. On Sundays, a band adds to the ambience and dancing in the sun goes on until late afternoon. To say the least, Juan-les-Pins is unlike its charming neighbor Antibes and a contrast to the peaceful Cap d'Antibes, but it is a lot of fun.

Parc Pinède, shaded under parasol pine trees is the local boules court

Young and trendy, enjoying every minute in the sun at the Moorea beach.

The beach in Juan-les-Pins on a busy summer day

CAP D'ANTIBES - EXCLUSIVE AND CALM

Due to the hectic nightlife which takes place in the streets, it is not advisable to choose a hotel in Juan-les-Pins, especially when the Cap is so close. If you have to - there is a small hotel with a private garden where breakfast is served under palms by the pool: HOTEL DU PARC. Surrounded by huge apartment blocks, it faces the sea and the beach. But because of its hidden location, you might find some rest there.

Exclusive and calm, Cap d'Antibes is a spit of land that juts into the Mediterranean where its hectic neighbor Juan-les-Pins ends. Though the name originally only referred to the southernmost tip of the land, it now encompasses the entire peninsula. Cap d'Antibes is one of the most popular Hideaways around for luxurious private villas and sumptuous hotels. The sea is all around and enchanting gardens add soft colors and scents. Avenue de Marchal Juin begins in Juan-les-Pins and runs along the western shore of the Cap, offering beautiful views out to the Lérin Islands, La Californie, and fashionable Super Cannes where magnificent summer homes include the 2000 square foot seaside summer residence of King Fahd of Saudi Arabia.

The seaside walks of the Cap are breathtaking experiences along rocky shores and take between 2 and 3 hours, or an inner trail leads to the lighthouse on the Plateau de la Garoupe. It ushers you along a narrow road shadowed by huge umbrella pines to the highest point of Cap d'Antibes, where a spectacular panoramic view awaits you of the entire Côte d'Azur, Alpes d'Azur, and the surrounding Mediterranean Sea. By the lighthouse, there is a small church built in the 17th century which hosts a small café on a calm gravel square.

BELLES RIVES - A DREAM COMES TRUE

The hotel BELLES RIVES and its famous restaurant are situated on the seaside road that leads out to the Cap, less than a five minute walk from the center of Juan-les-Pins. The hotel is perched majestically above the water with its own pier, dock, and private beach. The building reflects the Golden Era of the late 1920s when F. Scott Fitzgerald and Florence Gould made the Cap their favorite playground. Just as the Colombe d'Or in St Paul de Vence is a mecca for art lovers, the BELLES RIVES is truly a mecca for lovers of the art of fine furniture signed "art déco."

The hotel is still run by the family of its creator, Boma Esténe, an exiled Russian who came as a poor refugee to the Côte d'Azur in the early 1920s. While working as a servant, he met Scott Fitzgerald, who lived in a nice little house by the sea. Boma dreamed of building a great hotel in the increasingly popular Juan-les-Pins and with the help of Fitzgerald, he managed to buy the little house by the sea. Together they transformed it into a hotel. Shortly before the hotel opened, they got the idea that the hotel should be decorated by first class furniture of the day. They went to a much admired craftsman, who made an entire line of unique handmade pieces, all beautifully styled "art déco" furniture, aimed at pleasing the important guests. Somewhat later, an article was published in a magazine extolling the beauty of this seaside haunt. The article was a tribute to the hotel, the rooms, its restaurant, and the beautiful location, with only one criticism - the furniture - so hideous it could only be compared to soap cups! Mr Esténe was furious, but the expensive furniture had to give way to a more traditional style. Years later, even in France, the beauty of "art déco" was appreciated and the family brought the furniture out of the dark, almost as new, to be admired by today's visitors.

The rooms are comfortable, beautifully decorated, and some offer guests a private balcony. To enjoy the hotel to its utmost, be sure to reserve a room facing the sea. Its nostalgic atmosphere is best captured on the jetty where lunch is served by the sea, *pieds dans l'eau*, just next to the private beach. Dinner is served in a romantic setting on an upper terrace wrapped in bougainvillea, with a splendid vista of the sunset behind the craggy Esterels. In most hotels guests seek the spots where locals go instead of vice versa. The BELLE RIVES is an exception. It is one of the few hotels where locals from all over the coast come to enjoy lunch by the water, to be spoiled on the private beach, or to go water-skiing behind one of the hotel's shiny wooden Rivas.

HOTEL DU CAP EDEN ROC
A QUEEN WHERE CASH IS KING

Just south of the Belles Rives in the small fishing harbor of Port du Crouton, fresh catch from the Mediterranean is sold each morning directly off the fishing boats. The little harbor is also home to a small private beach, PLAGE LE PECHEUR.

Located at the southernmost point of the coastal road, the HOTEL DU CAP EDEN ROC, a favorite of jet-setters, is rumored to be the most pre-eminent resort hotel in the

*Panoramic view from the Hotel du Cap at Cap d'Antibes:
a peaceful bay and snow covered Alps*

world. It stands like a gracious chateau in a park of pine trees, while its first class restaurant and luxury pool are set in the cliffs by the sea.

The hotel security guards rigorously enforce the privacy of guests, even the French prime minister - a prime terrorist target - feels secure here. Liza Minelli, Barbara Streisand, Robert de Niro, Madonna, Bill Cosby, Henry Kissinger.... the list is endless. Why then has the HOTEL DU CAP EDEN ROC become a hideaway of celebrities? Perhaps because it has a *hauteur de prestige* accompanied with a comforting elegance that makes even its most luminous guests feel privileged to be here. Plus its incomparable ambience, here again the present is redolent of the past.

Originally named Villa Soleil, the HOTEL DU CAP was inaugurated in 1870, at one time planned as a house for tired intellectuals! The inauguration was attended by "the most beautiful women and the most distinguished gentlemen," a great event for the region that got enormous publicity. After having been ushered in under such favorable auspices, Villa Soleil might have been expected to go from strength to strength in a glow of mounting prosperity. But, alas, hardly had the hotel opened than the Franco-Prussian War burst on Europe and the hotel soon went bankrupt and for years it underwent dire financial misfortunes.

Its redemption came through a successful Italian hotel owner who was inspired by the writing of Stephen Liegeard, a poet of the times who resided in Cannes and coined the phrase "Côte d'Azur" as the title of his book published in 1887. In the book, awarded a prize by the French Academy, he described Antibes:

Towards the entrance to the rustic dune which is the Cap d'Antibes, villas begin to mount. They have a genuine magnificence, with pavillions, balconies, colonnades, and Greek statues.

With prodigious labor and lots of patience the hotel was turned into one of the noblest dwellings on the Côte d'Azur.

Today the hotel is a vision of pale white, with green shutters and yellow awnings. From the third floor a magnificent view looks across the pine trees to the sea and the Esterel Mountains. There are nine garden rooms below the reception floor, each has a loggia or private garden. The grounds slope gently downwards from the hotel to the sea, occupying 22 priceless acres. A nearby rose garden provides the fresh roses that are placed in the rooms of arriving guests. There is even a small cemetery for love-pets.

The broad esplanade below the steps of the hotel leads to the PAVILLION EDEN ROC, where the British at the turn of the century sipped afternoon tea, to the seawater pool, and the private cabanas.

The HOTEL DU CAP is open only in the summer season and upon arrival you'll be greeted by a small golden sign reminding guests that whether their credit cards are gold or platinum, they have no value here. Cash is king and nothing else counts!

THE AUBERGE DU CAP - THE ANTITHESIS OF THE HOTEL DU CAP

Only a few minutes walk from the HOTEL DU CAP, you'll find an auberge, or a little manoir as they prefer to call it, CASTEL GAROUPE AXA, on a green open field in the middle of the countryside - truly a fabulous manoir! Here in the very heart of fashionable Cap d'Antibes, encircled by the greenhouses of florists, the pretty manoir offers a pool and tennis courts, along with a few sweet rooms at very reasonable prices.

The owner, a wonderful character with her family of dogs and cats, gives everyone a warm welcome. If you plan to stay out late, you will be entrusted the front door key. When Madame goes to bed, the door will be locked carefully with a handwritten message pinned to it stating that no rooms are available, to prevent latecomers from waking Madame during the night.

THE GAROUPE BAY - A BEACH FACING NORTH

On the other side of the Cap, you'll find La Garoupe, a bay well protected from the Mistral wind, with a nicely tended sand beach facing north to the Bay of Nice and the snow covered peaks of the Alpes d'Azur. This is the same beach that Gerald and Sara Murphy raked every morning for their summer guests: Ernest Hemingway, Rudolph Valentino, Scott and Zelda Fitzgerald, Dorothy Parker, Archibald MacLeish - in the 1920s when the beach belonged to the Villa America. Today, the public beach hosts several private restaurants, each with its own character and colored umbrellas, some with outdoor wooden decks. PLAGE KELLER and its restaurant CEASAR, named for the owner, offers either *al fresco* dining on the deck or an air-conditioned restaurant with a gastronomic menu including specialities of local fish and moules, truly one of the best beach restaurants on the entire coast.

BOUILLABAISSE AT LE BACON

Not far away when heading back to Antibes, there's another oasis for the rich and famous and lovers of expensive seafood. LE BACON has for years attracted travelers of the Côte d'Azur with its excellent bouillabaisse. This poor man's dish was created at a time when food other than that of the sea was rare in the region, but today bouillabaisse has become a culinary extravaganza that diners are willing to pay exorbitant sums for, especially when it is served along the coast in restaurants with open views of the sea.

A summer dream - alone with the sea, the sun, and the blue sky

If the beach gets to crowded - use your imagination

Leave crowded beaches and identical hotels behind....

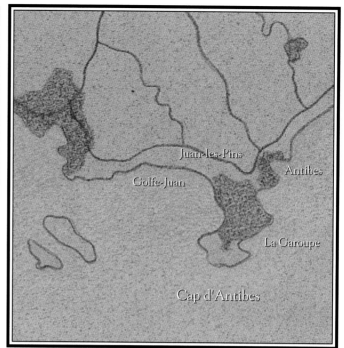

DREAM VACATION

Your own "private" yacht

We all know about power lunches and power business - now get ready for the ultimate one-up-manship - power vacations! Your own private yacht cruising the French Riviera for pleasure is the ultimate in holiday luxury and comparably priced to other vacation alternatives. No longer just for celebrities and royalty, a private yacht is a symbol of wealth, luxury and style.

Leave behind the crowded beaches and the seaside hotel rooms from where you can see your "dream" sailing out the window. Get out there and live that dream first hand... in the company of other glamorous *bon vivants* and their immaculate crews.

ALL THE AMENITIES OF A FIVE STAR HOTEL

In a world dominated by hurried travel and pre-packaged tours, chartering a private yacht is the only mode of luxury travel left that puts you at the helm - in charge ! And it comes equipped with an experienced crew who know the ropes, ready to take on the daily business of logistics and let you get on with "easy living." Yachts have all the amenities of a five star hotel, but add the freedom and privacy of a customized world - your custom made world - your itinerary, your

Baie des Milliardaires - a quiet bay on Cap d'Antibes just around the corner from Hotel du Cap

favorite cuisine, your schedule! The cabin crew will pamper you, while the chef prepares the gourmet meals you've requested. You can roam indoors or out, from the airy salon and dining room to the largesse of the outdoors, where a sundeck and aft deck are perfect for lounging about.

Naturally, the crew has separate living quarters, so you and your guests enjoy total privacy. Businessmen need never be out of touch - yachts of high caliber are equipped with state of the art communication systems (fax, phone, telex). Far away from crowded beaches and identical hotels, you can create your own world. Your yacht can bring you to the dramatic tranquillity of the high seas or to the isolated beauty of coastal coves reachable only by sea. Clean water, empty anchorages, and deserted beaches, yet always close to comfort and safety, delicious food, fresh sheets, and soft towels.

HOW TO CHOOSE YOUR BROKER

To make it perfect - spend some time pre-planning your adventure, getting to know your broker and your options. It's not only the yacht that you must consider, the captain and the crew are equally important, so get in touch with a good charter consultant who specializes in customizing vacations. All aspects are arranged - from menu and itinerary planning to arranging a car to pick you up at the airport. A good broker knows the yachts and crews at hand and what they offer, as well as the cruising territory.

We suggest : ASSOCIATED YACHT BROKER of Monte-Carlo, FIGURE HEAD of Cannes, and CAMPER & NICHOLSONS of Antibes.

All of these agencies have expert knowledge of cruising the Riviera and know the ships that operate out of the region. Professional yacht charter agents assist the client in putting together the ultimate private cruise by learning about their client's special requests and linking that information to the captain and crew. The agencies have a catalogue of their boating selections, along with full color brochures describ-

ing details on each yacht for hire, and your yachting consult-ant will assist in matching your objectives with the perfect holiday.

HOW MUCH DOES IT COST?

The price of chartering a yacht is "fixed" ; it depends on the season and, of course, the size of the yacht. To ensure a good selection, bookings should be made at least 4 to 6 months in advance. Cost is only negotiable if the charter period will last longer than 2 weeks or if you book with very short notice, but then the selection will be very limited and there will be less time to prepare for your personal requests.

The charter fee includes the yacht with its equipment in working order, the crew's wages, and the insurance of the yacht. Fuel for up to 5 hours cruising per day and food for the crew are also in the fee. All other expenses will be charged to the charterer : food and beverages, berthing and harbor expenses, telephone and other communication costs.

All added together at the end of the charter, the cost per person (if all beds are occupied) will be approximately equal to a first class cabin on a premiere cruise ship or the presidential suite in a 4-star hotel.

WHATEVER YOUR WISHES, WITHIN REASON AND LEGALITY, THEY CAN BE FULFILLED

Private yachts for charter range from 60 ft (18 m) up to 250 ft (75 m) and can accommodate 4 up to a maximum of 14 guests. You have a choice between sailboats, traditional motor-yachts, or jet-powered superfast mega-yachts depend-ing on your preference and budget. A smaller yacht 60 to 100 ft equipped with 4 crew members is ideal for leisure cruising along the coast, anchoring in secluded bays, and visiting small harbors. It will comfortably accommodate 8 guests in 4 separated cabins, all with their own facilities ensuite.

For more extensive cruising in the Mediterranean, to Corsica, Sardinia, or Mallorca, for example, it is advisable to chose a yacht sized between 100 to 135 ft. Such a vessel has up to 8 crew members and the number of cabins is 5 or 6, providing accommodations for up to 12 guests.

Then there are the priceless "super" mega-yachts, which don't actually involve more guest cabins, only more space, more luxury, more gold, and much more money ! The charter price could easily exceed $170,000 a week, which makes $24,000 a day or $1000 an hour...

If you prefer to travel fast, St Tropez is just an hour from Monaco, cruising at 50 knots on the jet-powered 132 ft Octopussy ! The price for chartering this high-tech float-ing spaceship is comparable to other yachts of the same size, but then you also have to pay the fuel bill: she burns over 2000 liters (550 gallons) an hour !

Sit back, relax, be pampered - it's your choice.

Next page: Cruise into the sun - the ultimate mode of luxury vacation that puts you at the helm…

First class privileged entry at sun set in the harbor of St Tropez

Bigger boys - bigger toys

ROUTE MÉDITERRANÉE

Cruising the Côte d'Azur

Ah, the romance of the sea... the irresistible combination of water and sun that make the Côte d'Azur one of the world's top yachting centers. The short 40 km (25 mile) coastline contains beautiful bays, enchanting harbors, villages, islands, restaurants, and glamorous nightlife. How's this for a typical week at sea in this sun-splashed sailor's paradise?

Most of the charter yachts are based out of San Remo, just across the border in Italy. The crew will pick you up anywhere along the coast and bring you to the yacht in San Remo. Everything is taken care of, and as charterer on a first class yacht, you will soon appreciate a crew trained to anticipate your every whim.

Departing at noon, you'll enjoy lunch at sea while cruising close to the coastline and the Italian towns of Bordighera and Ventimiglia. Four hours later you will arrive at the first of the three main *Caps* of the French Riviera - Cap Martin, offering beautiful anchorages on both sides of the peninsula. On the eastern side, there is the town of Menton, on the western side the shores of Roquebrune and Monte-Carlo. The view is spectacular. The ancient village of Roquebrune sits high in the mountains which rise sharply here out of the sea to become the Alpes d'Azur.

Along most of the shoreline, there are huge estates and mansions with manicured gardens built close to the water and protected from the land by large gates and walls, but from the sea, you'll see it all. While you take in this splendid scenery, the crew will set the aft deck table in an elegant fashion for an afternoon tea. No restaurant can compete with such a combination of privacy, service, scenery, and food!

MONACO - A BEDAZZLING ENTRÉE

After a cup of tea and a refreshing afternoon dip in the clean, azure blue water, the cruise continues into the sunset, moving closer to Monaco just a 30 minute cruise away. Any sailor will tell you - a Monaco welcome is bedazzling. The Casino

Some of the finest private yachts in the world docked side by side in Monaco

and the HÔTEL DE PARIS tower to the right, and to the left the old town with Prince Rainier's Palace.

Your yacht will be docked "stern to" right in the middle of Monaco, just a short walk from all the best shopping, restaurants, nightlife, or the famous Casino. Your very own first class gourmet chef aboard will present the week's menu, based on information received from the charter agent. Every meal can be served on board, but of course you always have the option of eating ashore.

You'll find that your neighbors are a selection of the finest and most luxurious yachts existing in the world and that you are a yachting person yourself - at least for a week. You have entered a new world, with new dimensions. You don't have to stand on the quay curious about what and who are behind those doors at the other end of the gangway - you are one of them and your captain can arrange visits or why not host a welcome party yourself! Let's pretend one of your neighbors is M/Y MARIDOME ex. STEFAREN, the 16th biggest private yacht in 1992 and often based out of Monaco. This is what you would find while visiting her: In the main salon, the most formal compartment on board, light floods through gigantic round windows and is then reflected by floor-to-ceiling columns of mirror. The sofas are of white leather, a gambling table stretched with snake skin, and there's a boudoir grand piano. Don't worry if you can't play it, just slip in a cassette of your favorite oldies and it plays itself.

The master bedroom, or call it a duplex apartment, is stunning with 180 degrees of window that give an unobstructed view of the horizon. And on the ceiling above the bed, star-sign constellations twinkle electronically by touch-button controls.

On the "entertainment deck," the second floor, you'll find a mind boggling treasure house of the most advanced electronic equipment available, providing hi fi sound, TV from all over the world shown from a drop-down ceiling unit, pulsating disco lights with a laser show, plus disco smoke effects. Even the carpet, interwoven with fiber optics, pulses and changes color to the rhythm of the music. But best of all, aboard M/Y Maridome, you can also practice "Hollywood" scuba diving, great for salty sailors who prefer to stay in bed. The yacht is equipped with a remotely controlled mini-submarine carrying underwater color TV cameras which relay back to all TV monitors on board. From your bed you can "drive" the sub and view the watery world beneath the keel.

Or maybe the eccentric billionaire Prince Leo is in town, hosting a party on his floating castle, the NEW HORIZON, where all that glitters is gold. The crew consists of 13 uniformed British gentlemen officers and some dozen Asian stewards with white gloves and silver platters. The running cost of this home is rumored to be $40,000 a day.

The "King" of this aquatic castle, who believes he is the happiest man on earth, has the largest stateroom aboard, with a one of a kind chinchilla bedspread which required 138 chinchilla pelts to create. His bathroom is solid lapis lazuli from tub to sink to Kleenex dispenser; the faucets and tooth brushes glitter of solid gold... The Prince entertains lavishly, with formal dinners in New Horizon's brilliant dining salon, where a solid gold dinner service and gold plated porcelain are set beneath a ceiling of white goatskin, supported by black marble pillars, and accompanied by a live orchestra.

In the new world of yachting you've entered, money seems to flow and anything is possible.

CAP FERRAT

After a hectic night with your new friends and some morning shopping and sightseeing in Monaco, the yacht will leave after lunch as you have instructed. The second day's cruise of about 2 hours will head for the next of the *Caps - Cap Ferrat -* and the Bay of Villefranche. Along this coastline where cliffs drop sharply into the water, there is a beautiful view of the hilltop village of Eze. A little further

An 8 hour cruise from Monaco will take you to the picturesque village of Portefino in Italy

A helicopter on the sun deck means easier access for friends if you have a party at sea

up the coast, you will pass the small pleasure craft harbor of Beaulieu-sur-Mer. On the eastern coast of Cap Ferrat, you glide past the former fishing village of St-Jean-Cap-Ferrat. Elegant private seafront mansions dominate the shoreline. At the original Cap Ferrat, only the southernmost tip of the peninsula, you will see HOTEL BEL AIR and the CLUB DAUPHIN, with its swimming pool and private cabanas by the sea. After slipping by this beautiful landmark, the Bay of Villefranche opens up and provides another favorite anchorage for yachts and cruise ships. It offers protection against all Mediterranean winds and is "a must" to visit for every yachtsman.

THE PRIVILEGE OF YACHTING. TO DO AS MUCH OR AS LITTLE AS YOU LIKE

The Bay of Villefranche is one of the superb spots along the coast for a morning dip, peaceful yet animated by a busy shorelife. It would be very easy to spend hours relaxing in the sun on the sun-deck, taking in the sights around you while being spoiled by the crew. But can you resist such "toys" as waverunners, windsurfing boards or waterskis? For joggers and walkers, the path around the cliffs of Cap Ferrat will take up to two hours and access to shore is easy; the crew will *chauffeur* you at any time in one of the speedboats called "tenders." One beauty of yachting is that you can do as much or as little as you like.

And everyone has his/her own way of enjoying life. Once while visiting this bay on a warm summer day, a large white yacht anchored shortly before lunch. The only people to be seen on deck were the crisply uniformed crew, setting a table with white linen, crystal glasses, and silver candelabras in the shade of the aft-deck. Suddenly - as if the captain had signaled over the satellite telephone that lunch would be served -the sound of a helicopter broke the silence of the bay. The satcom dome, the masts and radar antenna of the ship vanished hydraulically and the sun-deck was magically transformed into a heliport ! The helicopter landed and a party of 6 elegantly dressed people disembarked and sat down for a formal lunch served by the crew. After a two hour meal, the guests disappeared inside the yacht, maybe for a short nap. They later re-appeared on deck, now dressed in swim wear. The crew members slipped a life vest on each guest and attached a line to each one, almost like a dog's leash. The guests then eased into the water. The crew walked them, one by one, on their leashes a few laps around the vessel. When the swim session was over, the guests were blown dry by warm air, they dressed in more casual afternoon clothes, and were lifted back ashore by the helicopter, as the yacht slowly sailed back to its port.

HEADING FOR CAP D'ANTIBES IN THE FAST LANE

Leave Villefranche early in the morning and cruise down the coast in a wide circle to avoid the smog from Nice. This is a heavily trafficked area in the summer, so you'll have plenty of boats to look at while cruising. If you hear the sound of a jet-engine, it might very well be a plane taking off from Nice airport, but it might also be super-yacht OCTOPUSSY or one of her fast sister ships speeding between harbors.

Speed is a passion and has made its mark on every facet of our society. When it comes to possessions, fast means desirable. John Staluppi, a New York born garage mechanic who over the years built himself a strong empire of car dealerships, adheres to the idea that toys should be faster and bigger as one gets older. His target was to build a luxury yacht 42 meters in length, guaranteed to reach a speed in excess of 50 knots ! i.e. faster and bigger than FORTUNA, the Royal Yacht of King Juan Carlos of Spain. A penalty clause in the contract obliged the yard to buy the boat back at full cost plus interest if it failed to achieve this speed with 2000 gallons of fuel, 500 gallons of water, a full crew, and 16 passengers! On the other hand, if the speed was achieved, Staluppi agreed that the price would increase by $200,000 for each knot over 54.

The goal was achieved - she was officially named the fastest super-yacht in the world, as she reached a top speed of 53.7 knots powered by her 11,000 HP water-jet engines. As OCTOPUSSY hurries by, flying over the water, you might catch a glimpse of Staluppi eating his favorite fast food. There is no kitchen, only two microwave ovens, as per the owner's instructions! Life in the fast lane doesn't give room for any time consuming luncheons.

Cap d'Antibes offers wonderful anchorages on both coastlines. On the Antibes side facing east, you'll find the little cove Plage de la Garoupe. This sandy beach has small waterfront houses under pine trees on one side and a magnificent private estate on the other.

On the western side, the spot to anchor is directly in

The romance of the sea.... the irresistible combination of water and sun that make the Côte d'Azur one of the world's top yachting centers

Sunrise over Cap d'Antibes

front of the majestic pine tree alley leading up to the world renowned HOTEL DU CAP, where your tender will dock you at the hotel jetty for a visit.

ANTIBES - CAPITAL OF THE YACHTING WORLD WITH AQUATIC PALACES FROM A THOUSAND AND ONE NIGHTS

Late in the afternoon, a 30 minute cruise will bring you to Antibe's Port Vauban, the world's largest and most impressive yacht harbor. The entrance is filled with the exclusive multi-million dollar, floating mega-palaces, mostly owned by Arab citizens, poised side by side - like KINGDOM, ex. TRUMP PRINCESS and ex. ex. Adnan Kashoggi's NABILA - 282 ft (86 meters) of pure luxury. Chances of being invited on board are minimal and she is not for charter, but let's take a quick look anyway :

She could easily be described as the ultimate toy. A 52 man crew is needed to run this "private" yacht rumored to have cost more than $90 million to build in 1980, more than half of that spent on the interior. This is where Kashoggi lavished money with utter abandon. And the shipyard went bankrupt! Insisting that she should be totally self-contained, Kashoggi had included in the specifications

everything from a *patisserie* and a three-chair hair salon to a screening room with an 800 film library and a hospital with an operating theater. Many of Kashoggi's most opulent parties took place aboard Nabila, at a secure distance from long papparazzi camera lenses.

On one occasion five heads of state - including three kings - were entertained simultaneously. Often, NABILA'S guests were Arab princes, Third World officials, shadowy European and American businessmen and diplomats, plus lots of beautiful young women, all ensconced in various suites and free to use the 180 telephones and other facilities that make life more enjoyable. A tour of the yacht, which has five decks and some 100 cabins, would take a separate book, so a look at the owner's apartment (his wife had her own somewhat smaller apartment) should suffice to get an idea of how to spend some $40 million. The bedroom has a tortoise shell ceiling, a 3 meter (10 ft) wide bed, and bedside remote controls for the entertainment center, for room service, even for the curtains - and a secret exit for discretion. In the bathroom the onyx floor tiles are carved in a sunburst pattern. The owner's barber chair stands to one side next to the sauna and the shower - with 13 nozzles - which is carved in the shape of a scallop shell from one single piece of the finest onyx - a task that took one year to

The monastery on Ile St Honorat outside Cannes as seen from the sea

complete. Across from the bathroom is the televesion room and a study from where a private elevator leads to the owner's private sundeck. An enclosed section houses the bar, pantry, video games, poolside sauna, and shower. Outside, behind bullet-proof glass, the circular swimming pool is situated next to a hydraulic lift which raises the sunbed high above anyone else on the boat, enabling the sunbather to bask in total privacy. Anything else you need?

THE LÉRINS ISLANDS - WHERE CHAOS IS PART OF THE GAME

The cruise from Antibes to the islands takes about one hours and it is suggested that you arrive there before lunch, to be able to choose a good anchorage. During the summer, there can be a mob of up to a thousand yachts, boats, and virtually anything else that floats anchored between these islands. The larger of the two islands, Ste Marguerite, is separated from Cannes (Palm Beach Point) by a shallow channel. The smaller island, St Honorat, is separated from Ste Marguerite by a narrow strait with shallow, crystal clear, azure blue water. The view from here stretches from the Esterel Mountains to Cannes and all the way to the Cap d'Antibes. Getting to the beaches and rocks on both islands is quite easy, either by tender for those who prefer to stay dry, or by a relaxing swim. St Honorat has a well known restaurant on

its eastern side, CHEZ FREDERIC, shaded by tall umbrella trees. There is also a 2-hour excursion across the island to visit the ancient monastery where St Patrick of Ireland lived for one year in the 5th century AD. The local monks who lead quiet lives of prayer here year round, produce their own liqueur "Lérina 2" along with lavender honey from their fields, all available at a small shop.

On the northern point of Ste Marguerite, the tiny village of Bazaine offers a small harbor for pleasure and fishing boats. The restaurant L'ESCALE has a wonderful terrace overlooking Cannes and serves fresh lobster, the catch of the day, and fantastic plates full of fresh vegetables, the *corbeille de crudités*. Shady, pleasant walks are laid out all around the island, providing up to three hour walks among the beautiful pine and eucalyptus woods or along the shore. Guided excursions are also offered to historical monuments on the island. Fort Royal was built by Richelieu and contains the cell where "the man with the iron mask" was held prisoner from 1687.

If you prefer the sundeck, music, and a cold drink on board your yacht, this anchorage offers a comedy game show: watching a flotilla of luxury crafts desperately seeking anchorage! The game has no rules, which makes it chaotic and we suggest keeping the captain's binoculars handy! What you're most likely to witness are scenes occurring from a total lack of seamanship. Yachts show up late in the morning,

*Along the main quay in St Tropez, yachts are docked
"stern to" with their aft decks facing the cafés*

overcrowded with people desperate for some sun and swim. They find a mooring in the crowded water, turn off their engine and they then all happily jump into the salty sea and start to play. What they were never told was that a boat, any size, needs an anchor. Suddenly they realize in the middle of a watergame that their boat has left them and drifted far away... the rest is up to the reader's imagination.

Small inflatables zig-zag through the middle of this chaos of people and boats, announcing their appearance with loud horns. From these boats you can buy almost anything : a full lunch, ice cream, hot chocolate or pretty male or female companionship.

In the late afternoon, plan to leave for Cannes and dock in the *vieux port*, the old harbor, close to the center of Cannes and the Croisette, next to the Palais des Festivals. From this harbor, it's a short walk to all the best restaurants, the Carlton Hotel, the Majestic, or shopping at the Gray d'Albion and along Rue d'Antibes.

SAILING TOWARDS ST TROPEZ ALONG THE ESTEREL MASSIF

Allow most of day five to explore Cannes, but be back after lunch to set off for St Tropez. The cruise takes approximately six hours - you'll arrive just in time for the late afternoon rush into the St Tropez harbor, after a cruise along the red Esterel Mountains.

Arriving in St Tropez is a memorable experience. Even for experienced yachtsmen, this is a show not to be missed! It's very important that the harbor is notified well in advance either by the captain or charter agent, especially during high season. Most captains have a long term relationship with the harbor master, who is rumored to be one of the richest locals in St Tropez !

Coming closer to St Tropez, Ste Maxime is situated on the right hand coast and the Cap of St Tropez with the beach Les Salins will be seen on the left. As you glide around the Cap, St Tropez emerges, shimmering in soft pastel colors, its unique setting facing the warm late afternoon sun. The harbor itself is small and crowded, as though everyone wants to be there. Along the main quay, yachts are docked "stern to" with their aft decks facing the cafés. That's the place to be! The captain slowly maneuvers the yacht backwards into the narrow space between two other yachts. For entertainment, the charismatic harbor master screams directions in broken English and blows his whistle, supported by a shouting crowd waiting for that tiny mistake to happen. The yacht, which seems small on the sea, suddenly feels gigantic as she maneuvers into her berth. The lines are thrown ashore and the harbor master, with a cigarette dangling from his lips, twists them quickly around a pole, not forgetting for a moment to scream and whistle at the next yacht, faithfully followed by the applauding crowd.

Early evening is the time to "people watch" - and to be watched. The aft deck which originally was a work area for crew members has now become the most popular area among the guests, especially in St Tropez. A crush of curious onlookers stroll the quay, admiring and comparing the yachts, straining for a peek of the passengers on the visible aft deck. Meanwhile, yacht guests make self-conscious appearances, and look out at the crowds, deciding perhaps when would be a good moment to dart past them for dinner.

HE WHO DIES WITH THE MOST TOY'S - WINS: AN UNWRITTEN RULE OF THE GAME IN ST TROPEZ

You'll find a different type of yachting person in St Tropez than you did in Monaco or Antibes. He is the ultimate funseeking, daredevil show-off. If most super-yachts are designed to impress - to dazzle the onlooker with their rakish appearance, their flashy speed, their opulent interiors - then St Tropez is the greatest showroom. Nothing should surprise you. On the yacht next to you, the crew is constantly on full alert, setting up magnificent luncheons and dinners, but you see no guests, no people at the tables, no one enjoying the caviar and champagne. Finally you ask the captain what they are up to and his in-the-yachting-world, self-evident explanation is, that the boat is on a stand-by charter ! He continues... the charterers are on another yacht chartered somewhere else in the world and in case they should decide to change their minds, to come back to St Tropez... Well, they could show up at any time without notice, so the crew has to be prepared every minute. On another fast-looking monster of a super-yacht, the captain will tell you that he's been on the yacht for a few years with the same crew and that he is frequently ordered from one port to another, but only once has he seen the owner or a guest.

There are other multi-million dollar jet-powered crafts kept in St Tropez year after year, their only function to serve as a "bathing boat," transporting the owner and guests plus their daily "catch of the day" to the beach everyday.

Nightlife in St Tropez begins very late and is often still swinging in the early morning. Being a night town, it is also a very slow starter. It stays quiet until noon, when the rush for the beach begins and by lunch St Tropez is quiet again. The cruise to Pampelonne Beach takes an hour (it takes 5 minutes to drive and about 30 minutes to walk!) Each beach restaurant has its own anchorage facilities and the crew will know the best spot. Small dinghies pick up those guests who do not prefer to swim ashore or stay on board, watching from a distance. The hazy view of the landscape with vineyards rising up the slopes behind the beach is breathtaking. The cool afternoon breeze makes life on deck much more pleasant and as it picks up in the late afternoon, windsurfers with colorful sails and fast ultra-light boards will zoom by. This is a time when you wish time could stand still.

Late afternoon brings the same race back to the harbor, time to win the best spot in front of the SENEQUIER café. Only a few yachts fit in that much desired berth and it's a matter of negotiating with the harbor master or being first! But as your yacht must be back in San Remo tomorrow, it's a wise idea to cruise leisurely back towards Italy, anchoring in one of the bays along the Esterel Mountains. There you can enjoy one more fabulous dinner on board, while watching the sunset explode over these red mountains.

The short 40 km (25 mile) coastline along the Côte d'Azur contains beautiful bays, enchanting harbors, villages, islands, restaurants, and glamorous nightlife. Discover the secrets of the yachting world and your next holiday could be the ultimate vacation - limited only by your own imagination

"The Big Wedding-Cake" - the Carlton Hotel
a sweet sight on the Croisette

Cannes and Le Golfe de la Napoule below the Esterel Mountains

CANNES

Heart of the Côte d'Azur - City of Festival

Prior to 1834, Cannes was a peaceful village, sheltered under the rock known as le Suquet and flanked by its Saracen tower. Then destiny took a turn! Lord Brougham, a young English baron and a prominent British political figure, decided to escape the cold, foggy climate of London for sun-drenched Italy. When he could not cross the Sardinian frontier at the Var River, closed due to a raging cholera epidemic, he stayed in the small fishing village of Cannes.

As days passed, he became enamored with this town and decided to settle. He bought land and built a luxurious Italian-style villa, Chateau Eleanor-Louise, a tribute to the memory of his daughter who died on their trip.

After settling in Cannes, he wrote to one of his closest friends in London, *"In this enchanted atmosphere, it is pure delight for me, with my fondness for dreams, to forget life's ugliness and misery for a few moments in this fairyland."*

These words spread quickly through high society and soon "the English quarter" sprang up, surrounding Lord Brougham and Chateau Eleanor-Louise. From that time on Cannes continued to draw people, and the quiet fishing village became a favorite winter resort for the cream of English society - soon followed by Russian nobles, Americans, Italians, Germans, Scandinavians and people from all over the world!

A WINTER RESORT JUST LIKE NICE AND MONACO

Originally, Cannes was a winter resort just like Nice and Monaco, an escape for the wealthy from the bitter cold winters further north. By the beginning of the 1920s, the first casino was built and the population of Cannes grew rapidly. The idea of hosting a Film Festival in Cannes was born to counter-balance the Mostra Festival in Venice, which was closely linked to Mussolini and Hitler. The opening gala was scheduled for September 1, 1939 and

Le Suquet and Mount Chevalier Tower, a 12th century watch tower which rises above the old harbor of Cannes

movie stars such as Gary Cooper, George Raft, Tyrone Power, and Mae West flocked to Cannes via a trans-Atlantic cruise liner. The day of the opening, war was declared and Hitler invaded Poland. Within hours, the palatial hotels were emptied and the trans-Atlantic cruise liner, with its celebrity guests back on board, had pulled anchor and was steaming back to the safety of America. It took until 1946 before the festival started up again and today, of course, it has become world famous.

LE SUQUET - THE OLD TOWN OF CANNES

A pleasant walk about town begins with an early morning stroll along the old harbor to watch the fishermen sorting out the night's catch in time for the market to open! Continue up to the Suquet by following Rue St Antoine through the old town, keeping close to the cliff with its many charming restaurants. This picturesque area is in strong contrast with the rest of the aristocratic city. When you've walked up these winding streets, you'll reach Place du Suquet at the top of the hill, nestled around the old castle. Once called Castrum de Canoïs, it was built in the 10th century by the Phoenicians to protect the town. A magnificent view sweeps across the entire Cannes area: the famous

seaside walk la Croisette, the beach, the two yacht harbors, the islands *Iles de Lérins,* and even the mountains.

LE MARCHÉE FORVILLE - THE MARKET PLACE

After a peaceful "early morning tour," it's time for the *Marchée Forville,* the Forville food market, a covered marketplace at the bottom of the rock. This very authentic, hectic, and bustling event takes place each morning, with farmers from the region and local fishermen doing their best to persuade "the locals" - restaurant owners, chefs, and housewives - to purchase their products. During market hours, the surging crowds with baskets on their arms float from stand to stand. The noise and crush of people is fascinating and makes a happy atmosphere. Only in such a marketplace can you understand the rich variation of available produce and why fresh food is so important to the French. The aroma of herbs, vegetables, and fruits permeates the air and the sight of fishermen with their colorful fresh catch-of-the-day provides a truly unforgettable scene. Forget about electronic cash registers! An old woman behind her stand scribbles numbers on a piece of paper and the food is placed in your basket in exchange for francs. And if you think it's less expensive here than in a supermarket, you're wrong.

LA CROISETTE - AN ELEGANT PROMENADE BORDERED BY PALM TREES, FLOWERS AND GARDENS

From the marketplace, it's only a minute's walk down to the Croisette and the old harbor by way of the Allée de la Liberté and its colorful flower market, where locals meet for a morning game of *boules*. What an ideal place to sit down at an outdoor café and enjoy a coffee and a freshly baked croissant while watching the activity!

As you walk away from the old harbor to the Palais des Festivals et Congrès, home of the Casino and the main scene of the Film Festival, you'll pass by the Gare Maritime, where ferry boats depart for the Lérins Islands. The relatively new Palais building is surrounded by gardens and fountains, a children's playground, and a walkway between the beach and gardens where roller skating, jogging, and skateboarding take place, while musicians and street artists entertain.

Past the Palais, the beautifully manicured Croisette, with its palatial grand hotels centered around the splendid white "wedding cake" facade of the Carlton, is decorated with palm trees and floral gardens as it brushes against the sea and the sandy beaches. Colorful beach umbrellas and matching sun mattresses belong to the various private seaside establishments, each with its own restaurant, charm, and character. During the summer - especially in July and August - it is recommended to arrive early at the beach, or to have a space reserved several days in advance. By midmorning, until late afternoon the beach and sea will be spilling over with sun worshippers.

La Croisette ends at the new yacht harbor, Port Canto, but the promenade continues along a magnificent rose garden and leads to Pointe de la Croisette, a point of land that juts into the Mediterranean and an area with some of the most fashionable residences with a breathtaking sunset view of Canne's miracle mile and the Croisette as it stretches the length of the bay.

LUNCH IN CANNES - STAY ON THE CROISETTE

After an energizing morning stroll, selecting the right spot for lunch is important, and actually very easy, despite Canne's many different restaurants. You simply stay on the Croisette or at the beach, which is where you'll be seen and see others! Along the Croisette, the ultimate casual choice is LA GALLERIE DU ROYAL, better known as the ROYAL BAR, with its authentic mixture of locals and tourists. There is an indoor restaurant on the second floor above the bar, but it's the terrace where you want to be, shaded by large blue and white parasols.

On the beach, the LIDO PLAGE and the PLAGE VOILIER provide a graceful contrast to their more sophisticated neighbor, the CARLTON BEACH. It's hard to tell if it's the

La Croisette, the palm-trees and the beach

Catching some afternoon sun at the Croisette

good looking guys and girls, the mannequins showing the latest in Cannes fashion, or the quality of the food that draws the hottest people of Cannes to these two places, but this is where they are.

OR THE LÉRINS ISLANDS....

Even more relaxing, take the ferry boat from the *Gare Maritime* out to either of the two islands in the bay for a leisurely lunch. The trip will take only 15 minutes and the ferries leave about every hour (except during lunch). On Ile St Honorat there is only one restaurant - CHEZ FREDERIC, nicely shaded by pine forest and somewhat overpriced and snobbish due to a lack of competition. This place has become very *à la mode*. The restaurant has its own dock so that guests arriving aboard private boats can hand over their keys to the dock master while lunching. On Ile Ste Marguerite, there are a few restaurants, but L'ESCALE has it all. Food is served on a terrace facing Cannes with a beautiful vista of the coastline from the Esterel Mountains to Cap d'Antibes with the Alps as a backdrop. The

ambience is casual, the clientel is "chic - in the know" and the food is excellent. Try the lobster or if you're looking for something light, *la corbeille de crudites -* only vegetables.

AFTERNOON SHOPPING IN CANNES

If you have had enough of the sun and the beach and long, lazy, rosé-drenched lunches, a small American-oriented bistro called WARNER CAFÉ is located only two blocks from the beach. At lunchtime, it's full of locals who actually work! Such people do exist - even in Cannes - even if most people think they don't. Try their *Hamburgers à la Française*, that's the best. And when you exit the restaurant, you're right where the shopping starts.

Shopping anywhere in France, but especially on the Côte d'Azur, is strictly for the afternoon and shops stay open quite late. In the morning, they are only open for a few hours, if at all. At noon, everyone closes for lunch until 3:00 pm, when they re-open until 7:00 or 8:00 at night. For the good life, only a few places in the world can compete with Cannes at offering such a range of prestige and luxury shopping *à la Mediterranean*.

Most of the boutiques are concentrated in a very limited area, making it ideal for shopping after a day in the sun. Along the entire Rue d'Antibes, hopefully soon to become a pedestrian zone, you will find all the world-famous brand names: Gucci, Hermès, Boucheron or Yves St Laurent. Rue Cdt Andre hosts more modern designer names like Alaïa and Sonia Rykel.

The Gray d'Albion, a big gray bunker between Rue d'Antibes and the Croisette, houses a hotel, apartments, and an exclusive indoor shopping arcade. Those looking for the glitter of jewels, for Cartier and Boucheron, for watches or couture clothing, can stay on the Croisette where it's all to be found.

A SUN-SET COCKTAIL

In the late afternoon, as the fresh sea breeze cools off the air and the sun lowers itself behind the Esterel *massif*, people get "on the move." If you just like to watch people or be watched, then it's the terrace of LA FESTIVAL on the Croisette where you want to be seated with a rosé colored Kir Royal - a traditional French aperitif invented when someone realized that even bad champagne could taste good if you just added some *Crème de Cassis*. The chairs pretend to be from a film set all decorated with the names of movie stars, and the people who sit in them try their best to look like one. A trendy, chic atmosphere with dark sunglasses, relaxed poses, and all that glitter - that's not necessarily gold.

A much quieter choice, more elegant, less crowded, and where the glitter is gold - have a cup of tea on the CARLTON TERRACE.

WINING AND DINING

If you want gourmet food in a stuffy, quiet atmosphere with little charm, white linen table cloths, and a tuxedo-clad head waiter fawning over your every need, then life is very convenient, because you still don't have to move from the Croisette or your favorite "palace" hotel. This is where they are, the elegant 4-star restaurants with look-alikes in every major big city. Prices are obviously not cheap, dogs are not allowed and young people look suspicious! In less than a 3-minute walk, you'll find 7 Michelin stars and 82 gourmet points out of the 100 possible in the Gault Millau: PALME D'OR on the terrace of the MARTINEZ, LA BELLE OTÉRO under the roof of the CARLTON, LA CÔTE also at the CARLTON on the ground floor, the ROYAL GRAY at the GRAY D'ALBION, and finally LE SUNSET at the MAJESTIC. All are names with a certain familiarity for Arab princesses and the very rich, proving that gourmet nominations and Michelin stars move from the super chefs' own establishments to the grand hotels that can afford to pay for them.

IF YOU HAVE HAD ENOUGH OF THE CROISETTE LET'S SEE WHAT'S BEHIND

If you have spent most of the day on the Croisette, then use the evening to explore behind the "main stage" and you'll be positively surprised. There is a vast selection of nice and affordable restaurants - even in Cannes. Starting in the old town and the Suquet: Rue St Antoine is narrow and charming as it climbs the rock from the old harbor, lined by restaurants where from early evening to late at night you'll have to zig-zag between tables and street musicians to find your choice. LE MACHOU has been there for a long time and remains as popular as ever, mainly because of the excellent cuisine and the fact that you don't have to bother with a menu. Just decide whether you want fish or meat and you get what they are serving that evening. The dining room is small but in the summertime it spills into the street to make room for more guests. A reservation is an absolute must. Across the street you'll find L'EMBUSCADE, much more traditional with no lack of ambience. It has long been a favorite of stars and celebrities who have expressed their appreciation with enthusiastically autographed comments on the walls. A few years ago the owner decided to give the restaurant a face-lift during the off season and left on vacation. Local workers efficiently wiped out all the scribbles, white-washing the walls as a surprise for the dismayed owner upon his return. Only a small portion of his unique guest book "on-the-wall" was saved.

Moving back towards the center: Rue Félix Faure, the prolongation of Rue d'Antibes, provides another selection of restaurants with terraces extended onto the side-

Restaurants are lined up side by side along Rue Félix Faure

A relaxed artist tries to capture the beauty of Cannes

walk in an effort to minimize room for pedestrians. But why walk when you can sit down and eat! Some of these places have obviously concentrated their efforts on making colorful signs in English and German, to show that they have a reasonably priced tourist menu, rather than on the food itself. In the summer, it also seems as if they are trying to be nominated to the Guiness Book of Records for serving the greatest number of people, in the least amount of time with only a minimum of waiters.

You guessed it! There is a watering hole for lovers of seafood, shellfish, and oysters. The best oyster bar in Cannes is ASTOUX ET BRUN , simple and casual, with lots of locals in the know. Forget about the decor and you'll enjoy the fresh sea food delights offered without any fuss with a carafe of local wine.

*Desperate photographers trying to capture the
beauty of starlets at the Cannes Film Festival*

Only a few blocks behind the CARLTON, just off the Rue d'Antibes, there's another hidden treasure of Cannes, LA CAVE, a small modern bistro run by a young couple. The menu changes from time to time depending on what is seasonally fresh and is chalked up on large blackboards hung on the walls. The food is cooked up front. It's affordable for what you get and you're right, it's full all year - make sure you have your reservation.

THE CARLTON

Even if relatively few visitors know the history of the Côte d'Azur or Cannes, most have heard of the CARLTON, so closely linked to the myth of the Côte d'Azur. As a monument it represents everything the Côte d'Azur stands for: luxury, easy elegance, celebrity, and extravagance, all in a playground of sea and sun and palms. This seaside palace with the white wedding cake curlicues of its facade dominates the coastline of Cannes. After Cannes was "discovered" by Lord Brougham a palace was needed to welcome Russian aristocrats and British nobles, so the CARLTON was created. The Grand Duke Vladimir of Russia lent his financial support and architect Damas began to work, the fabled twin cupolas on the roof said to be inspired by the ample bosom of the lovely Belle Otéro, an illustrious courtesan whose company was sought by most of the crowned heads of Europe. The opening of the hotel in 1911 was heralded as a great event, but times changed rapidly and the early years were difficult ones. The first world war broke out, the fashionable clientèle stayed home and soon the CARLTON was converted to a hospital. After the war, it lost its clientèle of Russian aristocrats, who were ruined in the Russian Revolution. In 1919, the hotel was put up for sale at less than one million francs ($150,000). Not until the post-war period did things start to improve. In the 1920s, Cannes was still looked upon as a winter resort, but by 1930 Cannes and the Carlton were experiencing the new wave of summer season holiday makers - and the hotel has been open year round ever since.

Renovated in 1990 for F170 million, the 7th floor was redesigned to start a new era for the hotel. The CARLTON CASINO CLUB opened its doors at a convenient distance from the BELLE OTÉRO restaurant, located under the eastern cupola of the lady's legendary breasts. An elegant dining room and a small terrace offer stellar views of the beach and the Bay of Cannes. Under the western cupola, a gigantic 12 room suite! was installed, unequalled anywhere else on the coast or in the world for its size and its genuine luxury. It has 4 bedrooms, each with its own bathroom, there is a library, a study, a huge private terrace, plush living and dining rooms, hammam, jacuzzi and a private butler, fresh flowers, and as a generosity of the CARLTON, they offer free transport to and from the airport!

Indicative of the management's determination to keep up with modern life-styles, a new health club has been

The private beach and wooden deck
of the Majestic on the Croisette

opened. A glass roof provides natural light for this deluxe center which offers a fitness room, gym, swimming pool, jet-stream pool, etc. - all supervised by specialists for various treatments. All in all, the CARLTON of the 1990s offers its guests just about everything in the way of entertainment and leisure, plus a fascinating world just outside its doors!

WHERE ELSE TO STAY IF NOT AT THE CARLTON

The Carlton is flanked by two neighbors who are good, but not quite as elegant, palaces of the early 1920s: the MAJES-TIC and the MARTINEZ both with their own small gardens and swimming pools on the Croisette. For something less chic but still high-class, the newly restored Hotel L'HORSET SAVOY is located in "the second row" behind the Croisette. Upgraded in a distinctly modern design, it has a sumptuous foyer and beautifully painted pillars and a bar. The best rooms are above the third floor where you have a bit of a view or even better, on the fifth floor, where all rooms have a private terrace. A major feature of this hotel is its rooftop terrace, bar, and aquarium pool with a panoramic view of the rooftops of Cannes, the sea, and the mountains.

Only two blocks away, the Hotel PROVENCE is a quiet and relaxing little hotel with "a family touch." It has its own garden where breakfast is served, but there is no sea view, which explains the more reasonable price. It is recommended to reserve a room above the 4th floor, where you will have a private balcony.

The Hotel SPLENDID, a miniature copy of the Carlton, is ideally situated across from the Film Festival Palais, right in the middle of everything. The rooms are comfortable, but decorated in an old French style, a bit dark and drab. Above the 3rd floor, there's a nice view from the balcony of the old harbor and the Suquet.

CITY OF FESTIVALS

Cannes is an international center of festivals, Congresses, exhibitions, and the like, and each week, year round, new marquees headline what sort of people will be in town: the television festival, the duty-free festival, the popular music festival MIPCOM when rock music is the talk of the town, or the advertising film festival when trendy, young individuals with two-day beards transform the bar of the Martinez into their playground for a week.

But in May of every year, Cannes hosts the Film Festival, two weeks that must be seen to be believed. Approximately 50,000 people gather for an orgy of movie-going and deal-making, with Hollywood and Beverly Hills moving to Cannes. Someone has described it as Disneyland for adults. During the day, it's trade screenings, while distributors, journalists, and "God-only-knows-who-else" run in and out of the sunlight looking for a good movie. At night, a more elegant crowd dominates the "screenery" with official black-tie screenings and parties attended by stars! Naked starlets romp on the beach, while movie moguls sign multi-million dollar deals on paper napkins. The palace hotels are guarded by Tyson look-alikes, forcing photographers to climb the palm trees of the Croisette for that sneak photo. Then suddenly it's all over and things get back to normal, and chances are that not one American movie will be shown in English in Cannes until it's time again a year later.

TOWARDS MOUGINS

While the Lérins Islands outside Cannes are an excellent daytime outing, Mougins - Roger Vergé territory - is a good choice for the evening, if you prefer to get out of town. Ideally located in the countryside behind Cannes, Mougins is a peaceful hill top village where gardens merge into olive groves hundreds of years old. In the first century B.C., the tiny village was the regional center of a Ligurian tribe, and later during Roman times, the village gained a certain importance as a stage post on the Via Aurelia. The village became prosperous in the 18th and 19th centuries as a result of hard work by the inhabitants in their olive groves. In the middle of the 19th century, the fame of Mougins charm and the pleasant countryside had spread, attracting Parisian holiday seekers and a vast number of foreigners.

It wasn't until the late 1960s that Chef Roger Vergé bought a centuries-old *moulin* olive mill, where he opened his restaurant MOULIN DE MOUGINS and received 3 stars in the Michelin guide within 3 years, the highest award a restaurant can get. As a kind of "temple of gastronomy" the *Moulin* has attract other chefs and restaurants of high repute to settle in Mougins over the years. Today Mougins is a mecca for international food lovers and has more Michelin stars and other important awards for its gourmet kitchens than any other small village in the world! Unfortunately, this reputation has from time to time also attracted a few "luck seekers," those who have profit instead of culinary expertise on their minds, creating an expensive "tourist trap" that will leave the fastidious connoisseur with a bitter taste.

A visit to the MOULIN DE MOUGINS quickly convinces anyone skeptical that *la gourmandise* can become a way of life. But where does it begin? With the eyes, the nose, or simply the decoration and ambience? It's a combination of everything. A winning combination that you rarely find. While your eyes are feasting on antique furniture and out-standing works in Vergé's contemporary art collection, you'll find yourself comfortably captivated by the sweet fragrance of beeswax and logs burning in the fireplace. This isn't the place for pretentiousness or stuffiness, the atmosphere extols a 16th century olive mill, still crushing olives shortly before Roger Vergé took over.

THE VILLAGE

Arriving at the village, a large parking lot twists around the hill behind the post office. Best to stop here, no cars are allowed within the town. Despite the popularity of the village, life here has managed to retain a human dimension. Walk up into town past the Place de Patriotes where locals play *boules* and a panorama opens up north to Grasse with the Alps as a backdrop. Opposite the Place, Roger Vergé has installed himself in three of the old houses. The old storage cellar for the community's olive oil has now become LA CAVE DU MOULIN stocked with 5000 fine wines. Just up the road in LA BOUTIQUE, Denise Vergé has made a selection of attractive gifts for the table, plus a range of products bearing the Vergé label primarily based on the "Cuisine of the Sun:" herbs of Provence, peach and ginger mustards, black fig jams, and other delights. The same building is home of Roger Vergé's cookery school which offers week-end courses, a food week, or single *à la carte* lessons. Next door in yet another old *moulin*, Roger Vergé opened his second restaurant L'AMANDIER in the late 1970s. An almond tree planted on the inaugural day marks the entrance, and its 14th century oil-press of polished wood stands as a centerpiece in the stone vaulted dining room. Stairs mount to multiple levels and two hanging terraces draped in climbing roses are open to the starry skies. For long this restaurant was equal to LE MOULIN, but today the formula has changed: it's more bistro-oriented, casual and affordable, ideal for lunch.

Higher in the village, the old Town Hall carries the

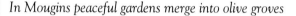

In Mougins peaceful gardens merge into olive groves

Mougins coat of arms on its facade. A fountain in the corner fills the square with mysterious gurgling and all around are quite a few restaurants. Opposite the Town Hall, FEU FOLLET is a restaurant that has been a favorite for residents since it opened.

Only steps away but in a completely different setting, LE BISTRO is another favorite, established since the early 1970s in a vaulted stone chapel. Alain Ballatore and Jean-Pierre Giordano, who worked for many years in popular restaurants in the States, decided to move back home to try their luck in Mougins serving *provençal* dishes at affordable prices. With some of their neighbors terribly overpriced LE BISTRO and FEU FOLLET continue to attract clients all year around - a reservation is a must.

AND IN THE COUNTRYSIDE OF MOUGINS...

Mougins is not only the village, but also the countryside. Before turning up to the village at the bottom of the hill, you will find a very special, romantic haven of high gastronomy, LA FERME DE MOUGINS, nestled in a garden oasis of greenery and flowering shrubs, with its own tiny brook. This stone *provençal* farm house was made into a restaurant in the mid-1970s. In this idyllic setting, you can choose to sit on either of two sunny terraces to enjoy an *al fresco* luncheon or linger over a sumptuous five course dinner in the warm *provençal* evening. Next door, in a completely different setting, the same owner has opened the ST PETERSBURG, a Russian cabaret restaurant which is crazy and wild with live Russian music. The night spot is inspired by the owner's previous success, La Bergerie in Courchevel, that has for

years been one of the most popular spots in that fashionable winter resort.

LE MANOIR DE L'ETANG

After World War II, Mr Gridaine, a successful cinema architect, received this astonishing manoir on the olive slopes facing the village as a gift in return for his efforts to build a film studio on the grounds for the village, which unfortunately ran out of funds for the project. Until his death in the late 1980s, it served as a summer home for the lucky family. Recently, the family decided to transform the property into a small country hotel and restaurant - a lucky decision for all of us. Le Manoir is just about the best the Côte d'Azur has to offer! A place where you want to get to lunch early, so you can hang out by the pool or take in the rose garden before your *provençal* lunch on the terrace above the lotus ponds. Some products like the olive oil and honey come from the Manoir gardens and are made from old family recipes. Dinner is more formal, served by the fireplace, yet the mood here is one of family. Fifteen romantic rooms face south to the cypress lanes and ponds. Whether it is for exploring the many restaurants around Mougins, business, pleasure, a honeymoon or simply enjoying a peaceful week-end, this is our choice. The following words are picked out of one of France's most important guides, Gault Millau: "*Le cadre, un luxueux manoir prolongé d'une terrace dans le parc, est exceptionelle....*" You'll dine and sleep like the star of a Pagnol script in this cinema setting of a bygone era - and if "Gone with the Wind" had been filmed in France, it would have been here.

Below: Manoir de l'Etang beautifully located in an olive grove outside Mougins

Next page: Mougins village peacefully nestled into the countryside on a small hill

DÉBARQUEMENT DE N

Le 26 février 1815, à une heure après-midi, la garde impériale et les officiers de la suite de NAPOLÉON reçurent l'ordre de se tenir prêts à partir. Les dispositions nécessaires à cet... l'Empereur! À huit... un coup de canon donne le signal du départ. À neuf... l'Empereur et sa suite ont quitté l'île d'Elbe. *Le sort en est jeté!* s'était écrié Napoléon, en mettant le pied en... Bertrand, et ses cent grenadiers. Jusque-là Napoléon avait gardé son secret: *Grenadiers*, dit-il alors, *nous allons en France, nous allons à Paris!* Les grenadiers l'auraient suivi partout... au cri de *Vive la France* domma celui de *Vive l'Empereur*. — Le 1er mars, à trois heures de l'après-midi, la flottille de l'île d'Elbe entre dans le golfe de Juan, quitte le pavillon blanc... À cinq heures, Napoléon met pied à terre, et son bivouac est établi dans un champ d'oliviers *Voici un heureux présage*, dit-il, *puisse-t-il se réaliser!* Aussitôt le débarquement effectué... comme des déserteurs de l'île d'Elbe, reconnaître les dispositions de la garnison, et chercher à se la rendre favorable; mais un zèle imprudent fit échouer cette tentative. Enfin, après p... Napoléon reparaît à Paris. Il est accueilli avec enthousiasme par la foule qui se rassemble, se grossit sur son passage, et lui forme un cortège jusqu'au Carrousel; là citoyens et soldats... ...leurs font répéter que ce moment fut un des plus beaux de sa vie

Propriété de l'Éditeur. (Déposé.

POLÉON.

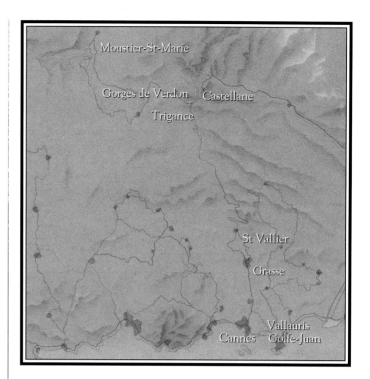

NAPOLÉON'S RETURN

An important part of French history

Route Napoléon commemorates an incredible event in the history of France and Europe: Emperor Napoléon's return from exile and the resumption of his reign over France for one hundred days. The story is so strange that it is certainly of interest to everyone.

Emperor Napoléon, defeated by his adversaries, had abdicated in 1814. The monarchy under the Bourbons was restored in France and the Allied powers met in Vienna to re-establish peace in Europe. The French people were exhausted after twenty long years of war. Napoléon had to be protected from the wrath of the populace as he was brought down the Rhone Valley towards his place of exile, chosen by the victors of war: the small island of Elba, off the coast of Italy.

NAPOLÉON LEARNS THAT THE FRENCH ARE NOT SATISFIED WITH THEIR ROYAL REGIME

Napoléon was left on this island with a small army and navy of his own and an English colonel to supervise him. Colonel Campbell, however, left Elba time and again to court an Italian duchess who lived on the mainland. Napoléon had a network of informants on the continent and learned of plans among the assembled delegates in Vienna to have him deported to Australia or even to have him murdered. He longed for his wife and son, who were not allowed to join him. He learned that there was a growing dissatisfaction on the part of the French people towards the incompetence of their royal regime. The King also failed to provide Napoléon with an agreed upon allowance.

NAPOLÉON DECIDES TO RISK A COUP

In the spring of 1815, a frustrated Napoléon decided to risk a coup rather than stay on Elba; he made detailed plans. He counted on the loyalty the French army and on the charismatic sway he exercised over their rank and file. He relied on the enthusiasm of the French people, which he could generally arouse with his dramatic gestures and stirring appeals. He prepared his proclamations:

"The Imperial eagle will fly from steeple to steeple until he reaches the towers of Notre Dame."

On March 1st, Napoléon's flotilla, filled with over a thousand grenadiers, landed at Golfe-Juan. The troops assembled in an olive grove between the beach and the road to Antibes. To the few inhabitants, the arrival was a complete surprise and the local authorities were thoroughly confused. At that time, it took five days for news to reach Paris. This gave Napoléon his opportunity. *"We shall fly,"* he said. *"We shall be in Paris without having to fire a single shot."*

They marched through Cannes towards Grasse. He had chosen the road over the Alps rather than the ill-remembered one along the Rhone. At Grasse, the main road ended and guns and carriages were left behind, the money bags were loaded on mules. The party marched in single file along the narrow trails across the mountains. It began to snow heavily and a mule slipped on the ice and fell, and thousands of gold coins showered the precipice.

" SOLDIERS, IF THERE IS ANYONE WHO WISHES TO KILL HIS EMPEROR, HERE I AM."

So far, in the remote countryside, they had met no resistance. People in the villages were friendly and helpful, the magistrates hid or looked the other way. The crucial hour struck, after five days of marching, as the party approached the city of Grenoble. Troops from their garrison, a battalion of the 5th Royal Infantry had been dispatched to confront and resist Napoléon at Laffrey. The two contingents met near a bridge and faced each other, eye to eye. There were some palavers, indecisions. Then Napoléon, alone, walked toward the line of soldiers barring the route, their officer cried *"Fire,"* but not a shot was heard. Napoléon, unbuttoning his riding coat, called out: *"Soldiers of the 5th regiment! If there is anyone among you who wishes to kill his Emperor, here I am."*

There was an outburst among the troops of *"Vive L'Emperor."* Fascinated by the legendary figure in his grey coat, soldiers rushed forward, clasped his hands, and touched his sword hilt.

That was the turning point. The next day the whole garrison of Grenoble, 8000 men, rallied for the Emperor. A few days later the situation repeated itself in Lyon. On March 20th, Napoléon entered Paris, the king had fled the day before. Not a shot had been fired.

We know what followed. Napoléon and the army he had assembled were beaten at Waterloo by the Allied forces under the command of Wellington and Blucher. He abdicated, and was exiled again, this time to the distant island of St. Helena. The adventure, which began on the Route Napoléon, was over. When he left his beloved France forever, he was 46 years of age.

At Café Escale in Golfe Juan, Napoléon started his march towards Paris

All along the Route Napoléon there are reminders of Napoléon

ROUTE NAPOLEON

They did it on foot - Let's do it by car

ust between Cap d'Antibes and Cannes on the western shoreline of the Bay of Golfe Juan, there is the ancient fishing village of Golfe Juan, sheltered by the heights of Vallauris. Its place in history was secured on March 1, 1815, when Napoléon Bonaparte and his 1200 men landed here en route from Elba to Paris through the Alps and Grenoble - on the road now known as the Route Napoléon.

On the sandy little beach next to the old fishing harbor of Golfe Juan, a monument embedded in flowers marks the historic site where Napoléon disembarked his men on his return from exile to re-capture the French empire. He chose this bay because it was well protected and little known, no one would pay much attention or be able to warn the King of France. Nearly 200 years later, Golfe Juan still lacks the luster and fame of other villages along the Cote d'Azur. Its "discovery" is attributed to a French sailor named Ernest in 1918. After sailing five times around the globe, Ernest decided to settle down in what he thought was the most beautiful place on earth - and surely he must have known. Ernest, nicknamed Ernestou, gained his fame as an "on-board" chef and was regularly sought after by the big ships of that time for his delicious bouillabaisse. Shortly after he chose this tiny fishing village to be his home, he decided to open his own restaurant. He built a little shack on the beach, called it TETOU, and cooked his bouillabaisse over a wooden fire. An institution of French Gastronomy was born, TETOU is known today worldwide from Tokyo to Los Angeles.

As the years went by, the late 1920s international jet-set started to flock to Cannes and Juan-les-Pins in the summertime, Golfe Juan, which already provided its rich and famous neighbors with one of life's necessities - food - soon developed a second necessity - sex. Golfe Juan became the center of prostitution on the Riviera with over 40 bordellos. History doesn't tell whether it was the divine girls named Loulou and Foufou or the delicious fish soup at TETOU that was the main attraction for the royals, the rich,

and the famous artists at nighttime, but everyone needs food and TETOU was there and still is - more popular than ever, even if the girls left a long time ago. TETOU hasn't changed much, it's still the same house though rebuilt 4 times, the same family going on its fourth generation, and the same traditions, i.e. cash is the only mode of payment, credit cards are unheard of.

The biggest asset apart from the old recipes and a private parking lot twice as big as the restaurant, is the booking situation. Make sure you have your reservation a fortnight in advance and, if it is film festival time, remember that Hollywood won't miss the opportunity to eat the world's most expensive fish soup. Reservations are accepted a year in advance. Next door is NOUNOU, another appropriate name and a similar looking restaurant serving almost an identical menu at half the price of its neighbor. Rumor had it that the reason for the lower prices was that NOUNOU served leftovers from TETOU, but that is not the case. It's the Michelin star and the fact that the bouillabaisse is much tastier that accounts for TETOU'S substantially higher prices. NOUNOU has a nice terrace and both restaurants offer their private beaches during the summer, where you can lay down and rest after consuming a generous garlic-filled meal. Close your eyes and imagine the scene two hundred years ago, when galleons anchored up in the harbor of the tiny village and the Emperor returned to France.

Across the street, facing the old fishing harbor, there

Ceramics and pottery have been the lifeblood of Vallauris for the last four centuries

Mimosa flowers and orange trees make the hillsides of Vallauris shimmer yellow and gold

is a quiet and comparatively inexpensive fish restaurant, CHEZ CHRISTIANE, which doesn't look like much from the outside, but when you open the door and the kitchen scents billow out, you know that it is a special place. On chilly evenings, you are comfortably protected by a glass wall while surveying the activity in the harbor and well attended to by the gracious and smiling Christiane, who serves the food prepared by her husband Marc.

GOLFE-JUAN - A DIVING CENTER

Further out in the Gulf of Juan Bay, there are over 30 different sites and wrecks ready to be explored in the clear blue water. C.I.P. *Ecole de Plonge* (Diving School) offers full diving courses and guided excursions in the bay and elsewhere on request. IMAGE MARINE, at the old port, will also arrange such adventures and they have a special course in underwater photography.

When entering Golfe-Juan on the coast road that edges the seaside from Juan-les-Pins, there is a small and casual *pizzeria* for those looking for a quick bite with a very Italian touch - look up for the sign CHEZ GIGI. The waiters run across the busy highway to reach the tables set up on the harbor walk. Antoine and his wife, originally from the south of Italy, prepare crispy thin pizzas in their wood burning stove - *pizza au feu du bois* at its best. If it's the season for *moules marinières*, the moules here are among the best you'll find anywhere.

At the "main" intersection, CAFÉ DE L'ESCALE provides an active corner for breakfast while catching the first glimmer of sunlight or for a beer in the late afternoon. A road sign next to the café indicates that the Route Napoléon begins here and points you to Vallauris 10 minutes inland.

VALLAURIS - THE POTTERY CENTER OF THE CÔTE D'AZUR

The village of Vallauris is located at the foot of the Vallauris heights, where the hills and slopes form a lovely residential area which includes fashionable Super Cannes. The overwhelming mass of mimosa and orange trees makes the slopes shimmer yellow and gold, in a beautiful contrast to the blue sky, between January and March when the mimosa is in full blossom.

Ceramics and pottery have been the lifeblood of Vallauris for the last four centuries. The traditional art of pottery was in severe decline after the war, but when Picasso decided to settle into a studio in the village for a period during the 1940s, he infused life and confidence into the town, which soon attracted a new and young generation of artists.

During the last few years, however, there has been an influx of mass produced pottery, sold along the roadside and geared to tourists, instead of the traditional handmade ceramics. Recently the village has been going through a major facelift, and slowly tradition and quality are coming back to Vallauris. If you stroll the main streets, you will find shops selling fine porcelain and pottery at good value. The MADOURA GALLERY is located in an old stone house, one block from the main street. It hosts many high quality pottery exhibitions during the year and - it has the exclusive right to sell duplications of Picasso ceramics !

Restaurants in Vallauris are still a rare asset, but there is one that is excellent, hidden on a residential back street, LE MANUSCRIT, in a rustic stone-walled distillery. The restaurant has handmade lace tablecloths and a warm atmosphere with two reasonably priced menus. The terrace is glassed in for the winter, and the garden is a burst of brightly colored flowers and mimosas.

The *old chemin* from Vallauris to Cannes takes you right across the heights of Super Cannes, where a detour to the Super Cannes observatory located at 325 m (1065 ft) is "a must." The panoramic view above the Mediterranean shoreline is breathtaking - overlooking the snow capped Alps and the entire coastline from Italy to the red Esterel Mountains, and below, Cannes. It's not hard to understand why the "richest of the rich" have chosen this slope as the Mount Olympus of their multi-million dollar estates.

Among the invisible residents, perhaps the most famous is the Emir of Qatar, the Arabian businessman Al Middam, who is closely linked to King Fahd of Saudi Arabia. His property, which consists of 8 mansions on 8 acres of land, is said to be worth over $ 100 million, if such a buyer were to exist. There is also the property of Saddam Hussein, purchased for $ 40 million in 1981, although rumor has it that the owner has been busy at home and still hasn't had a chance to visit his beautiful Super Cannes summer house.

When Napoléon made his way over these heights almost 200 years ago, none of this existed. The view consisted of vast olive groves and vineyards as far as the eye could see. At that time, this was still a largely impoverished and undiscovered area of France, 20 years before Lord Brougham and the English noblesse began their invasion of Cannes and the surrounding hills.

When Napoléon's small army reached the fishing village of Cannes, they set up a bivouac on the beach for a short rest and later, the same morning, set off from the church *Notre Dame de Bon Voyage*, located behind the old harbor and the Palais des Festivals, commemorated today by a plaque on the wall. Continuing inland, the straightest road to Grasse leads through Le Cannet, a beautiful village which is easily overshadowed by the glitter of Cannes. Passing Le Cannet the road leads on through the commune of Mougins and Mouans Sartoux, a very industrialized area, until it reaches the outskirts of Grasse. Napoléon tried to avoid Grasse for fear of potential aggression by the inhabitants, such as he had encountered from locals along the coast. He took a short break on Plateau de Roquevignon, better known as Napoléon's Plateau, not far from the quaint village of Cabris. It occupies a magnificent site on the edge of *Le Plateau de Provence*, overlooking hills and valleys all the way to the coast. The village has long been a favorite among young artists and writers searching for peace, beauty, and fresh air - attributes abundant in this area. A 17th century church and the ruins of an old castle perched on the edge of a cliff dominate the village. In ancient times Cabris was occupied by the Moors and when they were driven out, a golden goat *cabris* was thrown into a nearby lake by their leader - a lost treasure searched for ever since. If you don't plan to hunt down the goat, there is another treasure that's easier to find: the restaurant LE PETIT PRINCE, a rare gastronomic gem that can only be found in a small French village. The food is excellent, the ambience friendly, and prices modest.

THIS IS WHERE THE ROAD ONCE ENDED AND WHERE THE CÔTE D'AZUR ENDS TODAY

For Napoléon, the road ended here, so he and his men had to trudge on, tackling the steep slopes of the pre-Alps on local mule trails. Nowadays the road is excellent as it leaves the perfumed air of Grasse and enters the limestone *provençal* mountains. Between the mountains and their passes, immense green fields open up where lambs graze in the pastures - what a contrast to the tightly developed coast! Life's pleasures almost instantly seem simpler - the natural scents of thyme, rosemary, and pine mix with lavender to fill the air. Dazzling light bathes this land of black cypress and crooked olive trees; the sunny clear skies are washed deep blue by the Mistral winds. It's a landscape that will make even the most volatile Latin temperament cool down considerably.

The Route Napoléon cuts across these mountains and fields, then crosses three passes in succession. The first, the Pilon Pass at 782 m (2570 ft) catches a last view back to the coastline from its southern slope. Then the Faye Pass at 980 m (3234 ft) comes shortly after the small village of St-Vallier-de-Thiey, where a bust of Napoléon on the main square commemorates his quick rest under a great elm tree on March 2, 1815. In the late afternoon he achieved the third pass, the Valfèrriere at 1169 m (3810 ft), and continued down to the village of Séranon, located in a pine forest, where the Emperor halted at dusk to spend the night at Le Château de Brondet, the country home of the Marquesse of Gourdon, mayor of Grasse. Today only the ruins remain. Considering the fact that walking distance from the coast was nearly 50 km (30 miles) and included climbing 3 mountain passes averaging just under 1000m (3300ft) each with 1200 men and equipment - across wilderness trails in snow and rain - then Napoléon's first day must certainly be seen as an exploit of bravery and determination.

The countryside is splendid with green valleys, alpine pastures, animals, and lots of fresh air

THE MARCH CONTINUES TOWARDS CASTELLANE

Along this road up from the coast, there are many sites that will remind today's traveler of Napoléon's brave march. Halfway between Grasse and Séranon there is the little AUBERGE NAPOLÉON where a sign notes that the army stopped here for a rest. It is still an ideal stop for refreshments, a stretch and a look at the beautiful scenery around. Later, arriving in Séranon, there is another country inn along the road, CHEZ MARIUS, a favorite with locals and a very popular place for Sunday lunch, as you'll understand once you've sampled the good food and authentic country atmosphere at such attractive prices.

At dawn the next morning, Napoléon's party set off for its second day and the Luens Pass at 1054 m (3480 ft) where one is able to catch the first glimpse of Castellane. Going downhill to the north, you will pass the village of La Garde about 6 km before reaching Castellane where AUBERGE DU TEILLON is a splendid place to eat and it also offers nine charming small rooms.

Napoléon and his small army lunched at the Sous-Préfecture of Castellane before continuing to Digne, Chateau-Arnoux, Sisteron and Gap to Grenoble, where they arrived only five days after their departure from the coast, with 340 km (155 miles) of marching behind them. The alpine village of Castellane is dominated by a single monolithic crag of 184 m (605 feet) on top of which is built the chapel of *Notre Dame du Roc*, creating Castellane's "sky-line," perhaps one of the most striking sights in the Haute Provence. Located in a valley at the beginning of the Gorges du Ver-don and just south of the large man-made lake, Lac de Castillon in the upper Verdon Valley, Castellane is an excellent base for excursions and long walks. The countryside is splendid with green valleys, alpine pastures, playful brooks, and lots of fresh air. It is important to choose the right season to visit this area. Avoid the end of July and August when the village is cram packed with cars and campers from all over Europe. Winter is a bit dull and grey and almost everything is closed. The best times are spring, pre-summer and autumn. Seasonal demands aside, Castellane is centered around the picturesque main square Place Marcel Sauvaire with its restaurants, bars, traditional games of *boules*, bustling street life, and the charming MA PETITE AUBERGE for dining or staying overnight. Around the corner is a lovely, very small *vieux quartier* with its old church, St Victor, which has a 12th century clock. No cars are allowed and there are quite a few shops to browse through. Behind the church, starting at the main square, a 30 minute hike is marked up to the chapel on the peak of the rock, from where you'll have a magnificent view of the village and the countryside.

Another short excursion which can be done by car or hiked (about 2 hours), begins on the winding N85 and continues north to the Leques Pass at 1146 m (3780 ft) only 5 km away. This fairly steep road circles the verdant hillside and presents another spectacular view of Castellane, the massive peaks to the south, and beautiful lakes to the east.

Previous page: Between the mountains and the passes, natural scents fill the air and dazzling light bathes the land

GORGES DU VERDON - A PROVENÇAL GRAND CANYON

The region offers a wide range of activities from slow easy fishing to the rush of kayak rafting through wild rapids

If you plan to make this area a base for a couple of days, to explore the landscape and tour the sights, and if you want to stay in style, then you should leave Castellane behind and go west towards Moustiers-Ste-Marie, driving along the Verdon River until you reach *Pont de Soleils*, the gate to the Gorges du Verdon. Turn left and continue to the village of Trigance, a charming 16th century village built on the slopes of a big rock.

Dominating the peak of the rock is an eagle's nest, a fortress named CHÂTEAU DE TRIGANCE. The chateau is an ancient fortress built by the monks of *l'Abbaye* over 10 centuries ago! Later it became the private property of the *Comtes de Provence*. The decoration remains medieval with lots of wood and stone. The beautifully vaulted dining room serves gastronomic food and regional specialties. On top of the fortress, designated seating areas offer a magnificent panoramic view of the surrounding Haute Provence landscape.

Nicknamed the Little Grand Canyon, Les Gorges du Verdon are an impressive 21 km (13 miles) long gorge, with steep cliffs dropping down several hundred meters to the flowing water of the Verdon River below. They create a breathtaking natural phenomenon. In spring and early summer there is some great river rafting to try, with exciting

Previous page: Castellane's skyline dominated by a single monolithic crag of 184 m (605 feet) on top of which is built the chapel of Notre Dame du Roc

rapids and lots of white water. The total tour of this canyon is about 155 km (70 miles) and takes two days. The width of the gorge varies from 6 m (20 feet) to over 100 m (330 ft) and the height of the surrounding rocks ranges from 200 m (660 ft) to an impressive 1500 m (5000 ft). There are a couple of different roads to choose from and several fantastic hikes, some of them very difficult! The higher road *la Corniche Sublime* on the southern side is probably the best for starters, be-cause it leads to the most spectacular points and sights. It's a very narrow road - a real "cliff-hanger" - that edges the mountainside with awesome dips into the valley and "gorgeous" views. After passing *Balcons de la Mescla*, where the river takes a 180 degree turn, you will descend 500 meters to a bridge, Pont de l'Artuby, which makes its way over a small creek that flows into the Verdon. The bridge offers a spectacular 180 m (600 ft) bungee jump for the brave with a boat that will pick you up afterwards in the small creek down below. Beyond this point the road continues to twist along the river at an impressive height until you reach the end of the gorge, where the Verdon flows into the man-made lake, Lac de Ste Croix. The landscape opens dramatically and there is a superb view of the Plateau de Provence on the other side with the blue lavender fields of Valensole.

MOUSTIERS-STE-MARIE - HOME OF FAIËNCE

Moustiers-Ste-Marie is a medieval village situated at the end of the gorge, and is a renowned center of *Faïence*. It is perched high on the edge of a ravine with an amazing backdrop of craggy cliffs. High above the town, the two sides of the ravine look as if they are held together by a massive chain, 227 m (750 ft) long, from which hangs a huge man-sized star, suspended there several centuries ago. Hiking up to the star is enjoyable and easy on the well marked path which offers wonderful views. Since the 16th century tradition has it that *la terre rouge* is the poor man's version of pottery, while *faïence* is the rich man's. It is made from the finest clays combined with various mineral elements to produce a grayish-white body that later is formed in molds.

Driving back towards Castellane, take the northern road which leads through a landscape of large open fields that stretch between the mountains, where a wide assortment of hikes and bike tours are possible. In the tiny village of La Palud sur Verdon, you can rent horses or bikes, and excursions are organized every day. River rafting trips also begin here.

RETURNING TO THE COAST

When leaving the Castellane area to get back to the coast, you can return via the same road or go east along the beautiful Lake St Julien de Verdon until you reach the main road from Digne to Nice N 202 also known as *la Route des Neiges*, described on page 81.

Above: Les Georges du Verdon nicknamed Little Grand Canyon, a 21 km (13 mile) long canyon with steep cliffs

Next page: The Gorges du Verdon and the Verdon River before it flows into the man-made lake, Lac de St Croix

*Previous page: Lavendel fields
close to Moustiers-Ste-Marie*

*Above: Côtes de Provence grapes - soaking up the
Mediterranean sun before becoming Vins de Lumière*

Newly baked bread, fresh vegetables, olive oil, and un verre de rosé - c'est la vie!

CÔTES DE PROVENCE

Vins de lumière

Wine cultivation in France began in Provence and dates back to the Greeks, who planted the first vines in 600 BC, almost 2600 years ago. At that time wines were only to be found in the Middle East and Egypt. Much later, under Roman rule, *provençal* vineyards began their real expansion. For many years the *vignerons* produced only rosé wines, but with the advent of better technology red and white wines appeared on the tables.

As grapevines do not like much variation in climate, Provence - with its hot dry summers, low humidity, and a favorable soil - proved to be an ideal spot to produce the wines that were previously produced further south. The Roman Empire expanded rapidly and from its many harbors along the coast, wine was easily shipped throughout the empire. New domains were established and new grapes introduced, some of which are still used today.

During the Middle Ages, the wines of Provence were among the most prestigious of France. Unfortunately, during this time quantity came to count more than quality. Wine was produced by mixing all the different grape varieties, whether good or bad, in the easiest and quickest way to produce a lot of cheap wine. This tradition continued into fairly recent times, while wine production in other parts of France and around the world developed into a form of art dependent on taste. This is one reason why the wines of Provence still have a slightly bad reputation in many people's minds, a reputation that Provence wines of today no longer deserve. Times have changed rapidly and today most of the better domains in the region make their wine with solicitude and respect!

Since many of the Provence wines were sold very cheaply, it was hard to make a living either as a wine producer or by simply selling one's harvested grapes to the cooperative wineries. Instead land became more and more valuable as wealthy travelers from all over the world discovered the beauty and the climate of Provence. Farmers realized that by selling their land, they would make far more money than they ever would by producing wine. The

Nowhere else in the world does a rosé wine taste as good as in Provence or on the Côte d'Azur - simple, fresh, and delicious

new landlords often made no use of their vineyards. The huge properties became prestigious estates, or sadly, were developed into condominiums, golf courses, or other commercial attractions.

STATE OF THE ART TECHNOLOGY

But there were also new owners who felt attracted to owning their own vineyard, and since they were most likely wealthy business people, they looked at their substantial investment in the vineyard as a challenging business venture. They took on their new enterprises with a full commitment, realizing that there was nothing prestigious about owning a vineyard if the wine was not of a good quality and well reputed.

In the past 50 years, enormous amounts of money have been invested in *provençal* wine production. The latest in state of the art high tech equipment is being implemented in the production. Experts on wine growing from Bordeaux and other top wine districts are being lured to Provence by the climate - and higher salaries. The AOC, *Appellation d'Origine Contrôlée* is accorded to the highest quality wines of France and imposes very strict rules as to cultivation, vinification, grape varieties and production limits. Many wines of the region are no longer cheap and the quality has increased to become very good. In certain categories, they even belong among the best wines.

A PRIVILEGED CLIMATE - LOTS OF SUN AND GOOD SOIL

Côtes de Provence wines are not produced in all of Provence. Only carefully chosen areas, limited by a government commission, have the right to AOC status. There is not only one Côtes de Provence wine, but several. Some are light and fruity, others are robust and rich in aroma, but they all come from soil capable of producing quality wines: permeable, stony and *in humus*.

Good soil however is not the only requirement for making great wines. An appropriate climate is also needed. The climate of Provence seems to have been especially conceived for grape vines. Rainfall is concentrated in two periods: the end of autumn to revitalize the earth after the harvest and mid-spring to nurture the young shoots. As for the sun, there are enough sunshine hours from one year's end to the next that the vineyards benefit from mild winters where frost is rare, warm springs that hurry the flowering, and hot summers which allow full development of the juice-filled grapes!

A vineyard outside St Tropez lit by early morning sunshine

ROSÉ WINE BELONGS TO THE REGION
A GIFT FROM THE SUN

The truth is that the Côtes de Provence is most famous for its rosé wines and that the rosés certainly belong to this region. Even so, a surprising array of great red wines and even a few white wines come out of the region. Red wines represent more than a third of the total production. They are fermented in a classical way and, depending on the soil, some are tasty and smooth with an aroma of berry fruits or flowers, while others are more robust and rich reds that with ageing will develop roundness and a more complex bouquet. White wine is still limited to 5 % of the total production, but its lovely golden color and its aromatic qualities should see it making great strides in the coming years.

RUMORS ABOUT ROSÉ WINE
WHAT'S TRUE AND WHAT ISN'T

Contrary to what is often believed, rosé wine is not a recent product. Rosé has been found to be the earliest wine in history! And another inexactitude: rosé is not a mixture of red and white or artificially made! To put an end to all this confusion it's important to note that rosé wine is without doubt the most difficult wine to make. It's a result of a special

way of vinifying (cultivation, vinification, conservation). The color of the wine depends on the length of contact between the grapejuice and the skin where the natural pigments are found. The whole art in making a great rosé wine is in the knowledge of how long this contact should be. This procedure is complicated by the particular nature of each variety of grape. In order to bring out the quality of rosé wine to its fullest extend, the wine maker must "marry" the personality of each of these varieties as harmoniously as possible and the fermentation has to be very rapid and constantly supervised.

Word also has it that rosé wine does not travel very well, but imagine these scenarios: sitting in sunny Provence with a dazzling blue sky over your head, enjoying a lovely lunch and a bottle of nicely chilled rosé amongst good friends; or, taking a few bottles of rosé home, where ever in the world, and opening them on a cold rainy day. Surely, it's not going to taste the same. The wine hasn't changed but the people traveling with it have! Rosé wine belongs to summer, to Provence, and the Côte d'Azur!

BELLET WINE - A HAPPY STORY OF
A GREAT LITTLE WINE

Tucked up in the hills above the fashionable playgrounds

*CHÂTEAU DU CREMAT just outside Nice, a
label for the local aristocracy*

of the "Big Olive" - Nice - there are a few vineyards that are
not considered to be Côtes de Provence. The micro-appel-
lation of Bellet wines is much less known and has a very
limited production. It is centered around the village of
Bellet only 15 minutes by car from Nice. High quality wines
have been produced here for centuries and, just like the
invisible border between the *provençal* and the *Niçoise*
kitchen, these wines are a lot different from its nearby
neighbors on the other side of the Var River. The high
altitude, the purer and cooler air, and the southern slopes of
these vineyards, make their wines taste much lighter. Contrary to the modern methods and more aggressive business-
like production of Côtes de Provence wines, Bellet wines are
made with a unique sense of traditional French taste, noble
and superior. The two best known wines from these hills are
CHÂTEAU DE CREMAT and CHÂTEAU DE BELLET both with
ancestry dating back to the 14th century and royal families.
In the Côtes de Provence vineyards, doors stay open to
visitors and vintners are pleased to see you, whether you
come as a client or just drop by to explore. In Bellet, be
happy if they even sell you one or two bottles! The production of CHÂTEAU DE CREMAT is 80,000 bottles a year of
which you might find a few in one of the better wine or
delicatessen shops in Cannes or Nice. CHÂTEAU DE BELLET
owned by Baron Ghislain de Charnacé, has a production of
only 25,000 bottles sold primarily to restaurants that the
Baron favors. A label of local aristocratic quality for the
restaurant! and history will explain why:

*Since the Middle Ages, a little hamlet called the Hameau de Bellet
has been clustered around the manor house of the Dettalia-*
*Doria family. Its people have for centuries worked the little
vineyard, unaware of the good Fairy Queen who keeps watch
over the place.*

*One day long ago, Anne-Rose, the pretty daughter of the
family, married Pierre Roissard, a Savoyard closely related to
the Duke of Savoy. The Duke, inspired by the good Fairy Queen,
ennobled them and their manor with the hereditary title of Baron
de Bellet.*

*The years went by. The Domaine de Bellet passed from
father to son for centuries, each generation caring tenderly for
their house and property. The good fairy kept watch over them.*

*In the middle of this century, Rose de Bellet married
Monsieur de Charnacé. They set about renovating their vineyard
and their son, Baron Ghislain de Charnacé, continues their
work. Cautiously he has married the finest grapevines of Champagne to the good old vines from Nice county. While the equipment is the most advanced of the day, the notes and counsels left
behind by earlier generations are not forgotten. And the Fairy
Queen, watching over Bellet, sees to it that the breeze is mild and
the sun caressing over its vineyards.*

VILLARS SUR VAR

Further north along the Var River towards the Alps, the
little village of Villars has some wine production on the
steep southern slopes of the pre-Alps. Located only an hour's
drive northeast of Nice and surrounded by mountains, this
area has a unique micro-climate with cold nights and hot
days, almost similar to conditions for wine producers in
Switzerland. CLOS SAINT-JOSEPH wines, especially the
white, could easily be mistaken for a light and fruity Swiss
wine. Keep in mind this area is also nicknamed Little
Switzerland. With a production of only 4000 bottles of white
and 7500 bottles of red, each bottle is numbered. It is not
difficult to understand that the wine can be hard to find.

WHEN VISITING THE CÔTE D'AZUR - DON'T HESITATE TO ORDER A LOCAL WINE....

When visiting the Côte d'Azur, don't forget about the local
wines, especially not the rosés. Don't order a Bordeaux at a
restaurant just because you feel insecure about the reputation of the Côtes de Provence or Bellet wines. Ask for a local
wine and you won't be disappointed.

Take a break from the coast and spend a day or two
visiting the Côtes de Provence vineyards to taste their wine
and feel the warmth of their hospitality. You'll find out that
you get good value for your money, especially when you buy
directly from the vineyard. Some essential advise: see how
clean the cellars are; dirty cellars produce dirty wine. Another rule is always to taste before you buy as you're not able
to do so in the supermarket back home. And remember, the
Côtes de Provence wines are steadily regaining their reputation as one of the great classifications.

Close your eyes, breathe, taste......

Soft light, a vineyard, a farmhouse

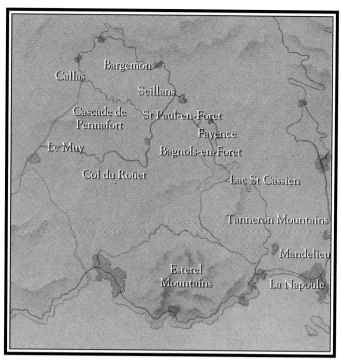

PLATEAU DE PROVENCE

A touch of the "real" Provence

When you feel you have had enough of the glamorous Côte d'Azur coastline. Enough of the crowds, beaches, and sun. Enough "authentic" *provençal* restaurants and enough *pizza au feu du bois* from either the swarming street side cafés or from the fleet of old rebuilt Citroën pizza vans, whose smoke stacks jut everywhere into the Mediterranean sky, pretending to grill pizzas on open wood fires... it might be the perfect time for a getaway to the fields of the Provence countryside only a few miles away.

This trip invites you to taste a bit of the "real" Provence, to travel the countryside which lies just north of the coastline at Cannes and is bordered to the east by the Alpes d'Azur. Flatter than its neighbors, the *Plateau de Provence* is dotted with the tradition and character of hundreds of years. You'll find the *provençal* village of your imagination here. The locals still earn their living from the land, harvesting their olives and tending to the vineyards. In contrast to the more famous and more accessible southern villages that have become suburbs of the coast, these *provençal* villages are inhabited by farmers, artists, potters, and stone and wood carvers. They are proud and authentic reminders of the history and culture that have made Provence world famous.

*An authentic pizza van making
pizza au feu du bois*

The pristine countryside which surrounds the villages is scattered with stone houses: rustic *mas* farm houses, the more noble *bastide* estate homes, and rural auberges typically built of stone, serving real *provençal cuisine* around open hearth fires at prices far more reasonable than those found along the coast.

HOW TO TRAVEL

A car or bicycle is a necessity when traveling through the Provence countryside, because no public transportation is available. Traffic is generally light most of the year, except in late July and August.

It is important to allow lots of time when driving in

*The pristine countryside of Provence
offers three long seasons*

Provence. Most of the locals aren't in any hurry. The roads can be narrow and curvy as they wind through the open landscape. Since beautiful new vistas, ideal for eager photographers, present themselves around each corner and since wine tasting *degustation de vins sur place* at the small private vineyards is a temptation not to be missed, it is easy to tire after only a few hours drive, even though you have only covered a short distance.

And then there is the long French lunch, religiously served between noon and 2:30 pm. It is best to stop and join in, or you will find your stomach grumbling from 4:00 pm to 7:00 pm when all kitchens are tightly closed. If your breakfast was a typical one of hot croissant, marmalade, and strong coffee, you'll be hungry enough to enjoy a leisurely lunch. And besides, all shops and other businesses are closed during the lunch hour, so not much else can get accomplished anyway.

MENU DU JOUR

As you settle into the restaurant of your favorite auberge, you are likely to notice that the menu does not always provide *à la carte* choices for you to compose your own meal. Most small inns of the back country offer a *menu du jour*, a daily menu chosen by the chef, *le patron*, according to the availability of fresh produce, seafood, etc. He might offer menus in three different price ranges. For each he will have made several choices of excellent dishes for a full meal of 3 to 7 courses. Diners are usually allowed a couple of options for the main meal or dessert. The easiest way to decide is probably to explain to the chef that you love *provençal* food, tell him your preference of meat or fish... and since *le patron* knows what is best for the day... let him make the choice, served with his favorite local wine, of course!

Sit back and enjoy dish after delicious *provençal* dish.

THREE LONG SEASONS

The trip through the Provence countryside described in the next chapter gives a good look at what this quieter, simpler region just a few miles up from the coast has to offer. Don't expect to find anything similar to the big fancy hotels and restaurants along the coast. In Provence you'll find only authentic family owned inns. Clean, simple and comfortable. Every season of the year sparkles with a life of its own. Summer is scented with pine, cool and refreshing in comparison to the haze and aroma of suntan oil along the hot and humid coast. The autumn vineyards are brilliant in dark green, yellow, red and saturated with the sweet smell of juices as the grapes are being harvested. Winter provides shelter from the cold Mistral winds and hearty six-course lunches in front of a roaring log fire, shared no doubt with the hospitable hosts of a local auberge. Pick a village or a good auberge and make it the goal of a full day excursion. Or wander the roads to your heart's desire.

*Next page: The market place,
a daily ritual in French living*

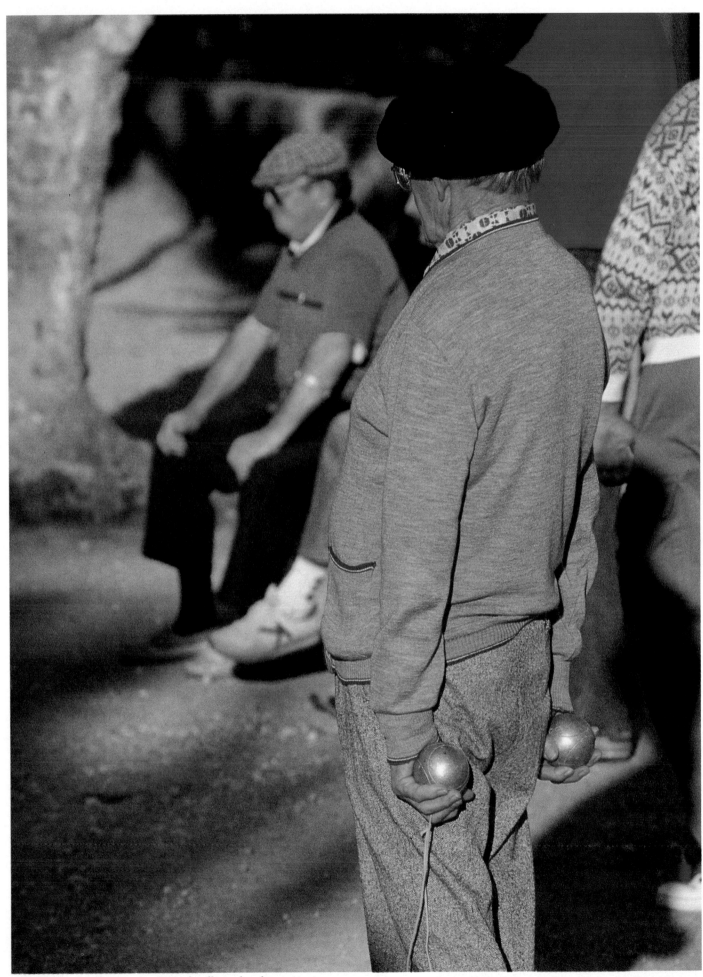

A traditional sight in every French village, locals
playing a game of Boules

A provençal vineyard dressed in the colors of autumn

ROUTE DE PROVENCE

Hidden behind the beach

The fastest way to escape the coastline on a hot summer day is to drive to the Autoroute de L'Esterel, which runs from the Italian border along the coast to Marseille, where it turns north to Paris. Once on it, take the Mandelieu-La Napoule exit, the gateway from the coast to summertime Côte de Provence. During the rest of the year, the preferable route is along the shore.

Mandelieu-La Napoule is located only 15 minutes from Cannes in the western curve of Golf de la Napoule, right at the foot of the Esterel and the Tanneron Mountains. From the main road in the center of Mandelieu, turn north onto a smaller road which winds its way up the Tanneron slopes, known locally as the Mimosa Mountain. During the winter months of February and March, these slopes are bathed in yellow and gold as the blossoms of the mimosa forests burst into color. Unfortunately, severe forest fires in the late 1980s caused intense damage to the vegeta-

tion. Tourists and campers are generally blamed for these fires, but local rumors rumble that it may be volunteer firemen, who only get paid when there is a fire to fight.

THE MIMOSA MOUNTAIN

Climbing this serpentine road you'll notice that the hillside has become a favorite summer residential area and it's fascinating to observe how every inch of this fairly steep location is being transformed by fantasy and concrete into new versions of old-fashioned *provençal* style houses. By reaching the top, only a mile from the coastline, you will be greeted with a magnificent panorama of Provence, the Alpes d'Azur, and the Côte d'Azur that you left minutes ago. Going downhill towards Tanneron, the road narrows and winds down a huge valley embedded in a lush green forest with thousands of mimosa trees. The view consists of vast fields and vineyards with Grasse and the snow covered peaks of Alpes d'Azur as a backdrop and small stone houses scattered along the way.

Calm and restful - Lac St Cassien in early autumn

Below: Local products are often sold directly by farmers along the roads

LAC ST CASSIEN

Continuing along this road, follow the signs for St Cassien du Bois located along the Siagne River in the Siagne Valley, then head to the northern point of Lac St Cassien with its wonderful view of the lake, which offers an array of sporting possibilities: gentle hikes, rentals of sailboats, canoes, paddle boats (no motor boats are allowed), fishing, and swimming. Unfortunately, several areas around the lake have become over-crowded in the summer with tourists and campers and some of the food facilities reflect this, although there is one exception, AUBERGE PUITS JAUBERT, a picturesque *bergerie*, dating from the 15th century with a majestic location close to the lake and surrounded by forest and open fields. Well hidden from the main road, this gorgeous little place is not that easy to find. On the road between Grasse and Draguignan, opposite Montauroux, you will have to look out for a weather torn sign. It points to a dusty road that leads through the vineyards and up to this isolated and tranquil place. A wonderful restaurant with a huge open fire in the middle is located in one of the old stone vaults. The food is excellent and the AUBERGE PUITS JAUBERT also offers 8 comfortable rooms and a terrace facing south. It's an ideal place to stay as a base for local excursions. Here you can find secluded and idyllic locations along the lake, and with a paddleboat and a picnic complete with a bottle of local *provençal* wine - there is always a hideaway along the shore.

THE MEDIEVAL VILLAGES OF CALLIAN AND MONTAUROUX

By crossing the main road, just minutes after the lake, you will "enter" Provence. Suddenly there is nothing but vineyards and a few scattered farmhouses, with the tiny villages of Montauroux, Callian, Tourettes, and Fayence on the slope in the distance.

Montauroux, a charming village originating back to the 12th century, is built around the ruins of an old fort which was destroyed in 1592. The main square overlooks St Cassian Lake and the Tanneron Mountains. Many craftsmen live in this village, which also offers a selection of very nice restaurants. AUBERGE LA MARJOLAINE is a tranquil small auberge with a pretty view from the terrace and reasonable prices.

The village of Callian is well worth a walk - about an hour through a beautiful valley. Its streets are lined with ancient houses that encircle a castle dating from the 13th century. The main square, which looks out to the vineyards in the southwest, has an old fountain and is shaded by huge trees. Close to the castle is a small restaurant, AU CENTENAIRE, where the owners, Monsieur and Madame Martellino, will offer you delicious local food in their delightful atmosphere.

FAYENCE

A few miles west down the same slope is the small town of Tourettes, which serves as a gateway to the more famous village of Fayence. Dating back to the 10th century, Fayence is a pleasant village on the edge of the *Plateau Provençal*, facing west with a commanding view of the vineyards that stretch across the countryside, and a breathtaking sunset. The town is centered around the main square and the *Hotel du Ville*, built over the main street forming a gateway. Some people may believe that *Hotel du Ville*, a familiar sight in every village you visit, is a chain of hotels, but it's definitely not - this is the Town Hall with the mayor's office. Opposite the town hall in Fayence are two typically *provençal* restaurants with a decor and cuisine that reflect the French art of dining: LE FRANCE, elevated from street level to a small terrace with a view over the main street and LE VIEUX BUFFET, which is very casual and nestled on a leafy terrace. Less than a minute's walk from here is the main square. From the square numerous narrow cobblestone alleys lead up and down the village with many arts and crafts exhibitions and small shops filled with the artwork of local artisans at very affordable prices. Just outside of Fayence, located in the vineyards with a *magnifique* view of the

Just a few miles inland nights can be very cold, sometimes even with frost

village is an old stone watermill built along a tiny creek, MOULIN DE CAMANDOULE, which has been converted into a quaint restaurant and also offers lodging in 11 charming rooms.

SEILLANS

Continuing northwest from Fayence the road is narrow and swings up through the deciduous forest which opens at intervals to stunning views of the wide landscape. In autumn the golden vineyards that dot the scenery are framed in the red, yellow, and green of the woodland leaves. Unfortunately, there are no marked paths, but if you are adventurous

Auberge Puits Jaubert - a restful bergerie dating from the 15th century

and independent minded, the woods are not too difficult to penetrate for a walk or a quiet picnic.

Seillans - whose name is a reminder of invading Saracens, and refers to "the boiling pot of oil" poured from the ramparts over their heads - is a favorite with artists. German painter Max Ernst made the village his home during the last years of his life. The steep cobbled streets leading up to the church and castle are tightly lined with houses in pastel pinks and ochre, the soft colors appropriate for this center of perfume making and flower cultivation. FRANCE ET REST CLARION provides travelers with excellent food and a beautiful little park with its own terrace and view. AUBERGE MESTRE CORNILLE restaurant exhibits local artwork and offers 3 delicious menus.

BARGEMON

The cool, shady square of Bargemon has a couple of bars that tumble out into terraces, functioning as lively local hangouts, and a restaurant AUBERGE PIERROT with a positively *provençal* ambience, so popular that it's best to make reservations. But don't fret, the nearby AUBERGE DES ARADES is also good for its food .

A one hour excursion leads to Col du Bel-Homme 6 km (4 miles) to the north, the perfect spot for a walk. The road writhes up to over 1000 m (3000 feet) where the expansive 360 degree view extends all the way from the coast of the Mediterranean to the peaks of the Alps.

THE WILDERNESS OF GORGES DE PENNAFORT

From Bargemon, the D25 will take you through the old village of Callas, its houses clustered around castle ruins on a hillside of olive trees. The D47, nicknamed the ROUTE DES VINS, the Road of Wines, continues into the Prignonet forest where it winds along the wooded slopes beside a tiny creek. The HOSTELLERIE GORGES DE PENNAFORT appears suddenly at the entrance of the gorge, where curious rock formations have been carved by the trickle of the tiny St Pons Creek over thousands of years. The HOSTELLERIE has transformed this old olive grove into a romantic haven, quietly surrounded by trees and water. The natural fragrance of Provence fills the air. Ducks and small boats glide across the stillness of a private lake, and dining is possible at either the barbecue area, on the shaded terrace for *al fresco* luncheons, or in an elegant dining room "decorated in the colors of the sun." Across the road, a tiny sign points into the forest with a one-word message - CASCADE - meaning waterfall, presumably to lure rugged naturalists to a unique local site, because no path exists and the trek to the advertised waterfall is tough going through 45 minutes of wilderness. As you penetrate the thick vegetation, almost jungle like, your heart skips a beat as you expect to hear the shrieks of wild animals, but in fact a stillness lies over the forest, as if life had not yet touched it. The creek guides you. Awesome vertical rocks tower on either side of it and you find yourself climbing on the rock sides and jumping across stones in the water until you finally reach the acclaimed waterfall, which in the end is not nearly as impressive as you had fantasized. Instead, it's the solitude of untouched nature that leaves an impression: the hike, the light, the echoes between the rocks become imprints in your memory... A world apart, just across the road from olive groves, vineyards, and auberges.

ROUTE DES VINS

Within minutes of leaving the gorge and this lovely HOSTELLERIE, you will be back in the Provence that you already know - the long stretches of flat fields open again, with the reddish rock formation of the Rouët Mountains towering as a backdrop. The road passes vineyard after vineyard. You have entered the valley of Esclans, once owned by the Grimaldi family, where vines have grown for centuries in the wake of powerful abbeys and monks who cultivated the fields until the French Revolution chased them away.

In the early 1930s, a well known doctor in Nice, Dr. Jean Lapouge, bought the vineyard DOMAINE JAS D'ES-CLANS because he loved the beautiful countryside where he had spent his childhood summer holidays. The grapes that grew at the domaine at that time were sold to the local wine co-operative, since the doctor was more interested in long solitary walks and hunting the wild game on the property than in wine production. But he soon became friends with Baron de Rasque de Laval, owner of the vineyard SAINTE ROSELINE, who taught him the secrets of making wine and infected him with a different love for his vineyard. New vines were planted, cellars and storerooms were constructed, and soon the domaine was labeling its own wine. An Italian named Livio whom the doctor met during the transition, was hired along with his entire family to be responsible for production. Livio turned out to be a technical magician, who constructed original vehicles, registered as prototypes, for the efficient harvesting of grapes. A few years later, an official commission inspecting the vineyards of the valley, re-instated DOMAINE JAS D' ESCLANS as an honored *Cru Classé* of the *Côtes de Provence*. The wine is still listed among the greatest. When visiting the vineyard, you might still find Livio, now a grandfather, who still repairs his original prototypes that even today continue to work the harvest.

LE MUY AND LA MOTTE - WINE CENTER OF THE REGION

Before you reach the autoroute at Le Muy, there is a large roundabout where normally you should continue on the ROUTE DES VINS towards Bagnol-en-Foret. A minor *détour*, however, following signs to La Motte in the

At the summit of Colle de Roüet a panorama opens onto the plains of Provence where spectacular sunsets flood the fields

opposite direction might be interesting; you'll continue past vineyards with wine tasting almost everywhere along the road - and a few nice auberges as well. LES PIGNATELLES is located shortly before La Motte, nestled amongst vines in a pretty field. Summer lunch is served in a shaded garden, but an open fire heats the dining room the rest of the year. Three menus range from a very affordable 3 courses to a gastronomical 6 courses. Wine is of course local, carefully handpicked from the "backyard."

CHÂTEAU SAINTE ROSELINE

Close to La Motte in the quiet countryside of Les Arcs-sur-Argens, you'll find the vineyard and chapel of Sainte Roseline, once part of the old abbey of La Celle-Roubaud. The beauty of the CHÂTEAU SAINTE ROSELINE, owned by Baron de Rasque de Laval, its rich and fascinating history and a taste of its wine, are all worth this short detour.

The legend of Sainte Roseline dates back to the 12th century when the château was owned by the Marquis de Villeneuve. The Marquis, fearing an attack by Saracens, ordered as much food as he could get from the poor farmers in the region to be brought to the castle store rooms. His daughter Roseline pitied the poor peasants, so every night she quietly snuck out of the château bringing with her food for the hungry. The Marquis noticed the thefts and put out guards. One chilly night when Roseline was on her way in the dark with armfuls of ham and bread hidden under her cloak, she was stopped and ordered by the guard to show what she was carrying. When she unfolded her robe she discovered a bouquet of flowers. A miracle of God had saved her! At 19, she entered the Monastery of Bertaud and took her vows to become a nun. She returned to the abbey of Celle - Roubaud, where she was the prioress until her death in 1329. When her brother Helion returned from the Crusades, he ordered her tomb opened and found Roseline's body intact among the other skeletons. She was made a saint and her eyes were put into a golden box. Two hundred years later, Louis XIV was traveling in the area and decided to stay at the château. When he saw the body and heard about the eyes, he ordered his private doctor to open the box and check their authenticity. The doctor plunged a dagger into Ste Roseline's left eye and blood gushed out, proving that the eyes were alive. When visiting the chapel today, you will find the shrine of Ste Roseline with her body amazingly well preserved. The eyes hang on a small golden tree created by

Giacometti, the left one shrivelled and the right one perfect. Contemporary artists inspired by her legend have decorated the chapel: a mosaic by Chagall, windows by Jean Bazaine, and a bronze frieze by Giacometti.

Early in the 20th century, Henri de Rasque de Laval married the daughter of the château's owner. He became the Baron when her father died. He started replanting vines, carefully protecting the authentic *provençal* varieties that the monks had tended hundreds of years before. He has dedicated his time to improving the wine of the château, which is today one of the most prestigious *Crus Classes* of Provence.

BAGNOLS AND ST-PAUL-EN-FORET

After this detour we re-join the initial ROUTE DES VINS heading for the forest of Bagnols and the Colle du Rouët. On this road, CHÂTEAU DU ROUËT is one of the better known vineyards with good *vins du table*, well worth a visit, if only to have a chat with the friendly owner, Monsieur Savatier. His vineyard sits at the foot of a small extension of the Esterel Mountains. Nearby very steep, imposing red rocks rise up suddenly from the floor of the *Plateau de Provence*, creating a miniature mountain and a spectacular valley, Gorges de Blavet. The Blavet River has cut a deep passage through the mountain, leaving a perfect track for hikes up to large caves. At the summit of this mini-mountain, a panorama opens onto the plains of Provence and the sea, where on clear evenings spectacular sunsets flood the fields with an extraordinary light, like an impressionist work of art.

Passing through the valley to Bagnols-en-Foret and St-Paul-en-Foret, vineyards seem to hug the edge of a shady forests. The two small villages are on the road which leads up from the coast to Fayence. In Bagnols, AUBERGE BAGNOLS-AISE has 10 cozy and simple rooms, a good menu, and a pleasing view of the forest from its terrace. L'ESTABLE, next to the church, has 3 rooms! and a restaurant which dishes up genuine "home cooked" meals. In St-Paul-en-Foret, 6 km (4 miles) north, there's no doubt about it, the place to stop is the restaurant, CHEZ ANNIE. Annie prepares delicious meals with the pure, strong flavors of Provence. Her husband takes care of the guests, serving their 5-course menu with local wines, all at a cost less than most appetizers on the Croisette in Cannes. A big stable in the village offers guided horseback riding through the forest, up to the vineyards around Fayence, or down to a secluded lake *La Soulies* where trout fishing is good.

A typical provençal lunch - soaking up the sun

The herbes de Provence add a savoury touch to regional foods

SUN-DRENCHED DISHES

The art of *provençal* and *niçoise* cooking

The name Provence is often associated with thoughts of food - the cuisine of Provence. Imagine a steaming pot of *bouillabaisse* with its colorful ingredients and unique flavor. Or picture a table with large pieces of fresh country bread surrounded by freshly picked *courgettes*, tomatoes, peppers, and eggplants waiting to be baked into a tasty *ratatouille*. Just the images of these fabulous dishes can make you hungry.

Provençal cuisine is very special and savory! It originates from a period when poverty was rampant throughout the region and food was in short supply. The region has never been self-sufficient and is located far from the richer farming areas of northern France. The land is not terribly fertile, there are not many animals, very few cows, a chronic shortage of wheat, and no grains! This is a short explanation as to the history of simplicity and moderation in *provençal* dishes. It's more economical and less lavish than one would believe, having been created originally by poor people for poor people.

A CULINARY HARMONY WITH OLIVE OIL AND GARLIC

Fresh fish are available all year round. Vegetables and fresh herbs flourish in the ideal Mediterranean climate. Some of the best herbs in the world, *les herbes de Provence*, are found here: wild thyme, marjoram, rosemary, bay leaf, fennel, basil, tarragon, and chervil. They are all used extensively, but with moderation. There are hundreds of different mushrooms to choose from, including the black truffle and the truly rare white truffle. The region's treasure is its olives - black and very dry with virtually no bitter taste. Tradition and time have developed the most delicious oil out of these olives, *l'huile d'or*, the golden oil - which when combined with garlic, creates one of the region's unique culinary gems!

"If the aroma of olive oil is the first violin in a culinary symphony, garlic is the equivalent of the trumpet. Together the two create a harmonious taste as old as the region's history"

PROVENÇAL CUISINE NEVER COMES WITH A SAUCE, NEVER USES BUTTER ONLY FRESH OLIVE OIL

Authentic *provençal* olive oil can only be purchased in the region, in markets or shops which specialize in quality products or at *moulins* like Nicholas Alziari, once the favorite oil of Nice gourmand ex-mayor Jacques Médecin. *Provençal* olive oil is much more expensive than ordinary oil, but is prepared in a time consuming process with a cold press in a stone mill which leaves only the aroma of the fruit and the oil.

SISTERON LAMB AND GOAT CHEESE

The famed Sisteron Lamb - truly incomparable! *L'agneau de Sisteron* has a spicy herb flavor, the juiciest of meat, and very little fat. The Sisteron Lamb lives its life in the fresh air of the protected hinterland of Nice, that stretches all the way up to the village of Sisteron in the cold Hautes-Alpes. Here, the grass is frozen in the wintertime and burned away in the summer. The lamb grazes the meadows and is fattened only on corn. It is raised in a much slower way than its ordinary milk fed cousins elsewhere. Shepherds drive their

sheep over the big fields in a very ancient and relaxed style, and the lambs nibble thyme, rosemary, and sage in a true *provençal* fashion. Goat cheese is derived from goats being raised and fed in a manner similar to the lambs. Their cheese is dried then dipped in water and marc, before being wrapped in a chestnut leaf. It will be placed in a cool cellar for ages - left to develop its strong characteristic flavor. Many years later, a true gourmand cheese lover can easily tell, by eating the cheese, which herb the goat preferred.

A "REAL" PROVENÇAL MEAL IS VERY SEASONAL AND ALWAYS FRESH

A "real" *provençal* meal is very seasonal. And its natural produce is very fresh - plucked from the sea or the earth the same day and sold by farmers in the local markets each morning. Buying vegetables, fish, cheese, fruit, etc. is not a simple walk down a supermarket aisle. Finding the freshest ingredients is an important ritual of daily life - and herein lies the secret of the savory taste of *provençal* food.

During the summer, menus offer lighter meals of vegetables, asparagus, fruit, monumental salads with olives, and fish. Winter menus are much richer with heavier portions and much less colorful than the light summer fare: pizzas with anchovy, cheeses and huge country *patés*, artichokes, and wild game like ducks and rabbit and local fish, all served with wild mushrooms fried in olive oil and finished off with huge portions of desserts.

Cuisine Niçoise

While almost everyone has heard about *provençal* cuisine, few are aware that Nice has a cuisine of its own. An invisible border stretches up the Var River, just west of Nice, delineating the two cultures and their taste in food. In the old town of Nice where residents still speak *niçoise*, they have created a lexicon of names for their *niçoise* food such as: *Lu Toumati or Toun, Li Sardinia Soùtat, La Sallada Nissarda* the world famous *Salade Niçoise,* and *Lou Pan Bagnat - Salade Niçoise* in a big sandwich. For more than 500 years, prior to 1860, there was little, almost nothing French about Nizza's culture. The inspiration of *la cuisine niçoise* is from the mountains behind Nice, the Alps, and Italy, including both Neapolitan and Genoese *cuisine*. Olives and the unique cold-press processing of olive oil are said to originate from Nice.

Estoficada in exchange for olive oil

In those days, Nice's large harbor made it an important trade

Ratatouille waiting to be baked

The provençal sun brings out the best in vegetables

center. In exchange for fruit, vegetables, and olive oil, various provisions from other countries were brought in such as the wind-dried cod fish, moure, not to be found in Mediterranean waters. This fish, now called "stockfish" or *Estoficada* came with sailors from northern Scandinavia, where it is a delicacy served on Christmas Eve. With a slight change in the Scandinavian stockfish recipe, the *niçoise* added the *provençal* touch of olive oil, thus creating a trademark dish for *la cuisine niçoise*. This is how it's prepared:

* After the moure has been dried for several months, it is as hard as wood and must be sawed into sections before being placed in water for 10 days to soften it for preparation.

* A good six hours before it's served, place the skin, bones, and mucous membranes from the stomach wall into water. Add onions and garlic and let it boil.

* Shred the flesh of the stockfish into a bowl. Heat some olive oil in a sauté pan and add the stock-fish. Stir continously with a wooden spoon.

* When the shredded fish turns golden brown, add some grappa and lots of pepper, plus the rest of the onions and garlic. Cook at low heat for at least 2 hours.

* Quarter potatoes and steam them. Add olives and the potatoes to the *casserole* half an hour before the stockfish is ready. Add salt before serving.

Recipes from a "Mediterranean Kitchen," J. Médecin

This unusual dish is appreciated by some adventurous tourists intelligent enough not to be put off by its powerful, to say the least, aroma.

A FISHING-PORT SURROUNDED BY VERY DEEP WATERS

The fishing industry, based in the very deep waters outside Nice, has never rivaled Marseille or any of the other large fishing ports along the coast, but fish versus meat is still the major diet of its inhabitants. There is an old local saying, *"Fish are born in water and die in oil."* Anchovies and sardines are common ingredients in *niçoise* cooking, and small delicious baby anchovies called *poutine* are not allowed to be caught anywhere else in France. *Lou Pissala*, a very *niçoise* dish, is made of these tiny and rare anchovies and sardines. Though nowadays they have become hard to find, so *Lou Pissala* is often made with fully grown anchovies. Never the less, it is much appreciated by the locals in Nice as a flavoring for a wide range of dishes or simply served on cocktail breads.

"Fish are born in water and die in oil"
goes an old local saying

THE REAL SALADE NIÇOISE - SALLADA NISSARDA

For those who want to familiarize themselves with the *cuisine* of Nice, there is unfortunately very little which has been written about it, and genuine *niçoise* food simply cannot be found except in *niçoise* homes and a handful of restaurants in Nice. Tradition and recipes, handed down from generation to generation can be found in the market of old Nice. While serving as a mayor of Nice, Jacques Médecin wrote an excellent cookbook entitled, *Cuisine Niçoise* with a large selection of secret family recipes that have been handed down to him by his dear grandmother. She had received them from an elderly peasant woman, Tanta Mietta, who lived a long time ago in the hills behind Nice. One reason the Mayor wrote a cookbook was that he had been all over the world and had had quite a few unpleasant experiences of being served leftovers masquerading as *Salade Niçoise*. As he explains, "*The real Sallada Nissarda does not have vinaigrette dressing*," and he continues, "*I beg you, never include potato or any other boiled vegetable. It is simply fresh tomatoes, hard boiled eggs, anchovy filets, cucumber, spring onions, small beans or tiny globe artichokes (depending upon the season, and never mix them), garlic, black olives, fresh basil leaves and, of course, olive oil.*" Then he adds "*On Sundays, or for special occasions, you can also use tuna fish.*" This will give you a true *niçoise* dish with a touch of Provence!

Today the ex-mayor claims from his refugee-residence in Uruguay that his sole income is from his cookbook!

A provençal kitchen filled with the sun-drenched products of the region

Mont Vinaigre, the highest peak of the Esterel Mountains

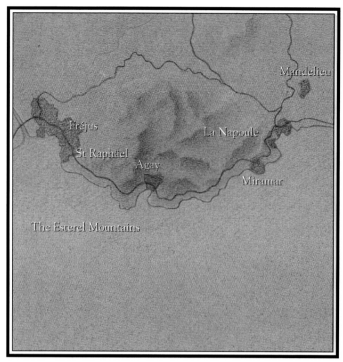

THE ESTEREL MOUNTAINS

Where rocky red mountains highlight
a cool blue sea

The porphyry rocks of the Esterel *massif* with their craggy formations - almost like great hands reaching for the sky - are a vivid color contrast to the azur blue Mediterranean. This isolated rock mass on the short coastline between Mandelieu and Fréjus is separated from the Maures Mountains by the lower Valley of the Argens River and represents the oldest geographical area in what today is known as Provence. Its highest peak is Mont Vinaigre at 620 meters (2000 ft) above sea level, less than 0.5 km (a quarter of a mile) from the sea.

Along this distinct coastline, the mountains thrust great promontories into the sea, which in turn cuts deeply into the mountains. There are few beaches, but you'll find small secluded bays and inlets between the impressive rocky outcroppings. At sea the surface is scattered with thousands of rocks, making all boating difficult, while submerged reefs can be clearly seen under the sparkling water.

The Esterels are made up of volcanic rocks which were forced up at a period of the Hercynian folding, thus differentiating them from the Maures. Once upon a time this *massif* was covered, as the Maures are today, with a verdant vegetation consisting of pines and cork oaks. Following

In a peaceful countryside an artist captures the scenery of reddish mountains, an azur blue sea, and the Mediterranean sky

severe forest fires in the 1960s and 80s, the forest exists only in a few places, mostly on the northern side.

ONE OF THE MOST BEAUTIFUL PANORAMAS IN THE WORLD

The Esterel Mountains are protected as a giant unspoiled nature reserve - with only one road open for cars - but there are numerous trails for hiking, mountain biking and horseback riding excursions. A unique flora of wild shrubs and bushes cover the ground: arbutus, cistus, gorse heaths, lavender, and wild sage. The scent of herbs in the air is like a divine perfume by the best "noses" of Grasse. And, just think, you're only half an hour away from busy Cannes, yet you are on the coast and in the mountains - nature pure and fresh - with one of the world's most beautiful panoramas: the Mediterranean Sea, the Alps, Provence and the Côte d' Azur! This is the choice for the visitor to the Riviera who prefers to leave the well-trodden tourist path for the pleasure of exploring on his own.

In contrast, La Napoule/Mandelieu offers everything you'd expect from the Côte d'Azur. The northern road connecting La Napoule with Fréjus is the historic Via Aurelia - the Roman link to Spain which runs through green cork forest. Fréjus itself was an important Roman stronghold and "a must" for lovers of the past. The southern link is the coastal road full of spectacular vistas and countless rocky bays with tiny isolated beaches.

FOUR DIFFERENT SEASONS

Touring the Esterel Mountains can be done all year around,

especially excursions in the mountains, a landscape that seems to be forgotten even during "peak" season. The reason: camping is not allowed and leaving a mobile home behind might make the adventure too risky. On the other hand, the coastal road, the public beaches, and the area around Fréjus and St Raphaël are packed in summer by campers and caravans and in these spots it's not very advisable to bring a car.

During the spring and autumn you're practically alone and the flowers in the Esterels weave a glorious tapestry of color. During the winter you are alone with the Mistral, that fierce wind that blows the air clean and leaves an amazing visibility from the heights: the coastline of Corsica to the south 160 km (100 miles) away and deep into the Alps to the north. The stormy Mediterranean shows its force by sending huge white waves crashing onto the red rocks.

HOW TO GET THERE

During summer when the roads are choked with traffic, the ideal alternative is the MétrAzur that conveniently transports you from anywhere along the Côte d'Azur to anywhere along the Esterel coast - in practically no time at all. Going by car from Cannes to St Raphaël in the summer can easily be a very hot and unpleasant experience that might last up to 2 hours. The MétrAzur takes half an hour of relaxation and beautiful vistas. In other seasons a car is no problem. There are only two entrances for cars, one just outside Mandelieu and one close to Agay on the coast. Hikers and bikers however have many access roads especially from the villages along the coast.

Next page: The Esterels weave a glorious tapestry of color with a unique flora of wild shrubs and bushes

Old town of Fréjus

The rocky coastline of the Esterel Mountains where red rocks meet the blue sea

ROUTE DE L'ESTEREL

Via Aurelia - the Roman link

La Napoule borders Mandelieu at the western corner of the Golf de la Napoule, where the two rivers Siagne and Riou emerge into the sea. This coastal neighbor is most famous for its golf course - the oldest in France, for the Henry Clews Foundation, and for being the mimosa capital of the coast. It is less well known that a wide range of sporting activities are to be found here and that long excursions up into the wilderness of the Esterel Mountains are within easy reach.

Right next to the little beach of La Napoule and a few steps from the train station, one's attention will undoubtedly be drawn to a medieval castle that looks more like the stage scene of an opera than a real feudal fortress. It is one of the Riviera's most endearing curiosities, all thanks to American born Henry Clews who purchased the property. Originally built in the 14th century, the chateau is a strange mix of Romanesque, Gothic, and Oriental styles. In 1919 Henry Clews, grandson of a wealthy American banker, and his wife Marie decided to retire to the South of France after his imaginative works of sculpture were rejected as shocking by New York art society. Safely settled into their own Saracen castle, they created a world, a cloister, a myth of their own - a world far away from everything that Henry detested in modern life. They razed and rebuilt, added crenellations, modern conveniences and... a fairy-tale sheen. Atop the main entrance you can still read the words "Once Upon A Time" carved into the stone. Throughout his life Henry insisted on looking upon himself as a modern Don Quixote, so it comes as no surprise that his private servant was called Sancho and the castle itself Mancha.

Until his death in 1937, Henry, who preferred being seen in his own setting, spent all his time in the castle. Afternoons were spent in his studio making portrait busts and grotesque sculptures out of stones that came from his own quarries in the Esterel Mountains, which he believed to be medieval material. After his failure in New York, Henry never again exhibited or tried to sell his works.

American born Henry Clews feudal fortress along the coast-line of Mandelieu/La Napoule

THE FIRST CONTINENTAL GOLF CLUB

It all started a little more than 100 years ago and it's easy to assume that it was Lord Brougham and his wealthy friends who brought this upper class English gentlemen's game with them from home, especially since it is true that the English created many of the golf courses along the Côte d'Azur at the beginning of this century. But this is not how continental golf got started. It began with a love story in 1891, which is when Russia became the creator of the GOLF CLUB OF CANNES MANDELIEU.

The Grand Duc Michel, nephew of Tsar Alexander, was exiled from Russia after he married a non-blue blooded German girl without his uncle's permission. On his extensive travels around Europe from Cannes, his temporary home, he discovered the famous golf course where golf was born, St Andrews in Scotland, while hunting with Scottish noblesse. He immediately became enthused with the game and upon his return to Cannes, he started to look for land on which to build a golf course. Next to the sea in Mandelieu he found the perfect terrain, an idyllic setting shaded from the sun by lofty parasol pines and mimosas. To keep up the true British tradition of golf, thousands of cubic meters of earth and grass had to be imported from England to give the golf course "the real touch." The 9-hole course, PARCOURS DU GRAND DUC, was inaugurated a year later and soon became a very important part of Riviera social life, particularly appreciated by the English and European aristocracy. The Prince of Wales, future King Edward VII, played with other kings and queens on this first golf course outside England.

WHERE TO STAY AND EAT

LE DOMAINE D'OLIVAL close to the golf course is a hotel built on the bank of the Siagne River, with its own dock and surrounded by a "mini park" with a pool and tennis. There are 16 apartments, all with their own kitchen and small living area. Next to HENRY CLEW'S medieval fortress on the main coastal road, you'll see LA MAISON DE BRUNO AND JUDY. Bruno works the kitchen while Australian born Judy bids you welcome with her charming accent. Being squeezed between the road and the railway and in the midst of numerous other restaurants may sound less than appealing, but once you are there you won't mind. It's a great place, where you'll be comfortable on the terrace or inside - and the food is excellent. But La Napoule does also have its own temple of gastronomy.

AN OASIS OF DELICIOUS TASTE

Back in 1954, Chef Outhier, a young man at that time, but already with an inclination towards fine cuisine, bought a house in La Napoule and opened L'OASIS, a small auberge where he served lunch and dinner in the garden. Only a few years later Chef Outhier's star started to rise as international gourmet diners came to his tables and he was one of the few French chefs awarded 3 stars in the Michelin Guide. Today after a few years of retirement, the restaurant L'OASIS is back and Chef Outhier has teamed up for this new venture with a younger chef Stephane Raimbault, who worked for years in Japan. The new concept: to interpret the subtle flavors of the Orient into the traditional French cuisine. The food is enjoyed in Outhier's oasis, a cool summer patio where streaks of bright sunlight spill in through the canopy of plane tree leaves, illuminating an almost Romanesque inner courtyard of columns and arches. In this oasis of palms and tiles a little pond bids guests to come refresh their souls.

LES ADRETS - PLAYGROUND OF THE BANDIT GESPARD LA BASSE

Continue towards Fréjus on N7, historically known as Via Aurelia, built by the Romans and once the playground of the infamous bandit Gespard de Basse. The road ran along the coast from Rome through Provence to Spain and was one of the most important routes in the Roman Empire. For many centuries, it provided the only land access to Italy from France. The Esterel Mountains that stretch to the south of the road offered escape and protection to road bandits and were fraught with danger for the ordinary citizen. A long standing local saying warns, "You have to survive the Esterel Gap." The most perilous stretch was west of Mount Vinaigre, where a cave in the high cliffs served as a refuge for the legendary Gespard and his gang after their forays onto the Aurelian Road to plunder coaches and horsemen who passed by. Even at that early date, many auberges lined the road, providing food and a night's rest for travelers and their horses. The most renown was AUBERGE LES ADRETS, the favorite of Gespard de Basse, who was after all an accomplished crook who loved style and elegance. He dressed in silky red, hand-tailored suits bedazzled with jewels and silver buttons. He met his end at 25, when he was arrested and killed. His head was nailed to a tree near the auberge, on the very road which had been the scene of his many escapades.

Today the road is safe and the AUBERGE LES ADRETS still exists. As the road continues you drive through forests of wild cork and oak trees and when gaps open the greenery you see wide vistas of Provence, with vineyards scattered between the villages and snowy mountains on the horizon - a separate world from the impressions most people have of the Côte d'Azur. Coming out of the forest you re-enter modern reality as you approach Fréjus, an important stronghold for the Romans in the past and an important stronghold for campers today.

FRÉJUS - FOR LOVERS OF THE PAST

If you are interested in history and archeology, you'll find Fréjus fascinating. It was founded in 49 B.C. by Julius Ceasar and has Roman ruins, an 11th century cathedral with a 5th century baptistry, dilapidated ramparts, and a lively old town. The Roman amphitheater is the oldest in Gaul and is still in relatively good shape despite its age. Situated in a green park, it accommodates 10,000 spectators who come for open-air music events, rock concerts (temporarily halted because they were shaking the very foundations), even Davis Cup Tennis, and for those with a taste for the

The coast is filled with restaurant that will suite anyone's taste and budget

The Fréjus Plage located west of St Raphäel is rumored to host up to 40,000 people each day during peak season

Along the Esterel coastline there are few beaches, but you'll find small secluded bays where you can bask in the sun solitude

drama and cruelty of the "corrida" bullfights, can watch the spectacle during summer, with all the trappings of its Spanish equivalent .

Two thousand years ago ramparts enclosed Fréjus, pierced by gateways corresponding to the two perpendicular main streets, thus quartering the town in the tradition of a Roman settlement. Soldiers, sailors, and citizens enjoyed the arenas, theater and bath free of charge. At this time Fréjus was a major naval base in the Roman world, even though it was not located immediately by the sea. The port was created by dredging and deepening a lagoon and was linked to the sea by means of a man-made canal. The entrance was guarded by two large towers, one of which still rises high at the end of the "south quay." At the beginning of the 10th century, the town was raided by Saracens.

Today most of the ramparts are destroyed, but a walk along the remains can get you thinking about how such a construction was feasible 2000 years back. In the middle of the old village, restaurant LE VIEUX FOUR with its rustic interior or the LOU CALEN with its typical *provençal cuisine* are two excellent places to eat and feel the history around you.

Just outside Fréjus towards the Esterel *massif*, you'll find the town's aristocratic extension, the heights of Valescure. Elegant villas are scattered in the pine forest recalling the early 1920s when an English gentleman, Lord Aschcomb, made this area his home-away-from-home and brought his wealthy friends with him. To uphold the best of English traditions and for entertainment, the clique of friends constructed the VALESCURE GOLF CLUB, claimed to be one of the oldest in Europe, after CANNES-MANDELIEU. In this "sophisticated" neighborhood, you'll also find the only "true" first class hotel in the vicinity of Fréjus - St Raphaël, the SAN PEDRO, an elegant Mexican styled villa that also hosts a gastronomic restaurant.

ST RAPHAËL - A CAMPER'S HONEY POT

St Raphaël is a gateway to the Côte d'Azur for those arriving by train. The name has a certain association with the French Riviera, its location being "right in the middle" - meaning in the Gulf of Fréjus between Cannes and St Tropez, under the Esterel Mountains, and on the beautiful seaside road Corniche de l'Esterel.

You do not read or hear much about the town and there is a reason for this. The town has been overrun by summer tourists, choked by traffic pouring through it, and turned into an urban mess by modern high-rise developments. Overcrowded in the summer and grim in the winter, it has unfortunately lost the charm and class it once had and today this "city" is filled with average hotels, restaurants, bars, and discotheques.

The nice sandy beach located west of St Raphaël, Fréjus Plage, is only about 2 km long and not very wide - it is rumored to host up to 40,000 people each day during July and August. People are packed next to each other like hot dogs on a grill in the intense heat, anesthetized by the perfumed air of suntan lotion, and fed by the horde of restaurants announcing special *menus touristiques* in German, Spanish, and English.

Obviously there must be people who enjoy this atmosphere, but others choose one of the many rocky, much less crowded bays, which can be found a few miles east or west, where the water is crystal clear, almost like an aquarium with many colorful fish and red rocks. Although you have to search out these spots, the narrow coast road is packed in a gridlock of cars, an endless stream of Dutch, Belgian, French, German, and Swedish cars and caravans from dawn until late in the evening. How to avoid it: leave your car and board the MétrAzur or escape into the wilderness of the Esterel.

The MétrAzur from Fréjus or St Raphaël swings eastward along the seafront of the Gulf of Fréjus, passing a huge modern marina for pleasure boats, until it reaches the first station, Boulouris. This small resort is dotted with private villas and beautiful gardens in the shade of tall pine trees and with stunning views of the sea and the Cape of St Tropez. Along this coastline before the next station - Le Dramont, only 10 minutes from St Raphaël - there are four or five small beaches and several rocky little bays, all much quieter than the Fréjus Plage. Right across the street from the station, La Plage du Dramont is a pleasant beach where the US army landed on August 15, 1944. Not far, on the very edge of the sea *pieds dans l'eau*, the HOTEL SOL ET MAR is a modern complex offering sunny views of the sea, of Cap du Dramont, and of Ile d'Or, the Golden Island, from the balconies of most of its rooms.

Walking up to the top of Cap du Dramont is an attractive excursion, which follows a well marked trail along the purple-red cliffs. Once you reach the top and the lighthouse, you'll have a wonderful panorama of the Esterel Mountains, the coastline, and the sea. From the "top of the rocky point," the path continues all the way down to the sea and the rocks. On reaching the seaside cliffs you will find secluded "private" nooks and the clearest of azure blue water. Moving along the rocks towards Agay, there is another nice beach in a small shallow bay, Plage de Camping-Long, but it is much closer to the road and unfortunately - a camping

There are not many houses on the coastline between La Napoule and St Raphäel, but the few that exist are considered to be among the the best on the Côte d'Azur

site. This fabulous walk from Dramont to Agay with its breathtaking views, isolated rocks and clear water will take about two hours, although it's not hard to spend an entire day here. Make sure to bring your own picnic - there are no restaurants !

AGAY

A newly constructed "vacation village," modelled on projects in Japan, sits across the road. It's centered around a couple of large swimming pools in a nicely landscaped garden with palm trees, lots of greenery, and an artificial *provençal* village. Cap d'Esterel is to be the most significant "Neo Tourist" complex in France, where everything is set up to replicate a traditional French, Mediterranean, or *provençal* village, except that there are no cars, almost like a perfect Hollywood set. There is a bit of St Tropez mixed with Marrakech and a touch of Spain - but just a little bit. The vacationer owning or renting an apartment also has a wide selection of activities connected with the "village" : golf, tennis, all kinds of water sports, and even a "circus school."

Agay itself is located in a wide bay, a favorite anchorage along the Esterel coastline, with a long sandy beach. There is one good restaurant to be mentioned, AUBERGE DE LA RADE, with a terrace on the beach. Although it is not the typical auberge and there are no rooms, the restaurant serves excellent food. Unfortunately, the easy access from the coastal road brings crowds of visitors into the bay, but it is still a far cry from the swarms of St Raphaël. Look-ing north, Agay is situated at the foot of the Esterel Mountains and has the only car road from the coast into the mountains. As an excursion, touring these mountains is an unbeatable experience, whether by car or mountain bike.

Get back on the MétrAzur in Agay and continue the trip along the coastline. The railroad is built on the rocks next to the sea and you can't get a better view of this magnificent coast - seated comfortably and relaxed - watch-ing the scenery pass by. The next station, Antheor-Cap Roux, is only 4 minutes away from the next area to be explored. The three red peaks of Cap Roux tower above the Esterel Mountains and the reddish, rocky coastline, all best seen from the observation point at the peak. Situated halfway between St Raphaël and La Napoule on the Cor-niche Esterel highway, Cap Roux is the least developed stretch along the coast, a wilderness of nature with quiet retreats even during peak season. It is reachable in only 15 minutes with the MétrAzur from St Raphaël and 18 min-utes from Cannes. By car, you're doing well if you make it one way in two hours! AUBERGE D'ANTHENOR, perched on a red rock over the sea, is a good place to stay and eat. Recently restored, it is equipped with a wonderful seaview and a pretty terrace, where on a hot summer's day you can cool off in the refreshing afternoon sea breeze and sit back listening to the breaking of the waves. The spacious rooms

all face the Mediterranean and have kitchenettes and some-times terraces which lead straight to the seawater swim-ming pool. The restaurant hangs over the rocks and a tiny private beach. The cliffs are great for a walk and for absorb-ing the magnificent scenery. An old road, closed to cars, leads up to Cap Roux, the second highest point in the Esterels at 440 m (1450 ft) above sea level. The 3-hour hike crosses a scrubland of sage and thyme as it weaves past monolithic red rock formations, always in full view of a glistening Mediterranean.

MIRAMAR

Next station is Le Trayas where you are back to the busy tourist life. The village itself, a former center for tuna fishing, is dominated by a the massive train bridge. There is a small beach and a bay with a few restaurants. Like in Agay, the combination of the crowded road and beach becomes a bit too much. If instead you stay on the train another couple of minutes, you will arrive at Theoule sur Mer, with its tiny beach occupied by the restaurant LA MARCO POLO, a place well worth a visit for lunch or a drink and a leisurely sit to look out at La Napoule and Cannes further on. Between Le Trayas and Theoule sur Mer, with no access by the railroad, there are fashionable neighborhoods with large seafront mansions, as well as the sophisticated resort, Miramar, which has its own yacht harbor and a protected beach with several private sunning areas and restaurants.

Next to the beach AUBERGE PERE PASCAL serves excellent food, especially seafood, on a very relaxed terrace, although prices are quite steep. HOTEL TOUR DE L'ESQUIL-LON has only 25 rooms, all built on the rock between the road and the sea with a rather unique feature : from the lobby at street level, a *téléphérique* provides access to the private beach and the restaurant at the foot of the rock. HOTEL CORNICHE D'OR, close to the Miramar, is built on the slopes facing west, looking out at the peaks of the Esterel Mountains, the sea, and spectacular fiery sunsets. The rooms are bright, spacious, and facing seaward ; the terrace is festooned with flowers and shaded by a large palm tree. Behind a semi-circular indoor terrace, the dining room boasts big windows and a panoramic view. With three stars, this restaurant is without competition between St Tropez and Cannes.

MASSIF DE L'ESTEREL - RIDING HIGH FOR A WALK ON THE WILD SIDE

All the way along this tour there are opportunities to escape civilization into the wilderness of the Esterels. Shortly after La Napoule/Mandelieu, heading for Fréjus on the N7, there will be a stable on your right CLUB HIPPIQUE that offers guided horse back tours into the Esterel Mountains or the mimosa forests of the Tanneron hills, all the way to the vineyards of Provence. In Valescure close to the golf course, there is another stable LES 3 FERS. Both offer white Camargue horses that are surefooted and eager to carry you to parts of the Esterel that other forms of transportation wouldn't reach. The riding has very little in common with the fussy rituals of German and British equestrian establishments. Here riding is western style, with large saddles, low stirrups, and single reins - easy armchair seating. And there are no hard hats, a cowboy hat will do to protect you from the strong sun as you travel through this primitive beauty. You can hire horses by the day or half-day and if arranged ahead, longer excursions are also available.

If you prefer to walk or drive, there are alternatives. Opposite the Club Hippique stables outside La Napoule/ Mandelieu, you'll find one of the two gateways by which to enter the wilderness of the Esterel Mountains in a car. A road sign indicates *Foret Domaniale de l'Esterel*. After about ten minutes of driving uphill, you'll come to a parking in front of a forest hut. Leave you car and follow signs to *Mont Vinaigre* - a half hour hike leads to the top.

Shortly after Valescure on the main road heading for the sea, you'll find the other "entrance" on the road that leads to the *Pic de l'Ours*, meaning the Bear's Peak, and continues through the entire Esterels. All along the road there are numerous possibilities of short walks on well prepared paths or longer hikes up to the red peaks. A short hike up to *Pointe l'Esquillon* offers fabulous views of the Lerins Islands and Cap d'Antibes, and from here you could continue up through the Col de la Cadiere to the Pic de l'Ours, the highest point of the Esterel Mountains at 496 m (1640 ft), a hike that will take 3 to 4 hours through wild aromatic scrubland.

The road skirts the south side of the Pic de l'Ours at an impressive almost vertical height of 323 m (1000 ft) above the rocky shoreline -with no protective roadside barriers ! before it turns inland and starts to wind its way down to La Napoule/Mandelieu.

Along the coast road there are no possibilities to enter the Esterel with a car, but several paths for walkers, hikers and mountain bikers. The most famous, Sentier des Balcons de la Côte d'Azur, starts in Le Trayas or in Theoule sur Mer, goes up to *Pic de l'Ours*, and then winds mostly in nature through Mandelieu, the Tanneron forests, the outskirts of Mougins, Valbonne, and Vence, all the way to Menton and the Italian border !

When you "discover" the Esterel, bring your own picnic. There are several well placed picnic areas arranged for comfortable seating while you look down on the white sails, casual fishing boats, and elegant yachts cruising between Cannes and St Tropez. But there are no restaurants, no hotels, and no campers !

St Tropez a truly magical place with entrancing pastel colors and a soft light

It's at the beach that St Tropez famous nightlife starts at lunch

ST TROPEZ

A magical place

aint Tropez is a jewel snuggled into its own gulf along the Côte d'Azur. It's the world's most famous and infamous seaside village, and quite possibly one of the world's "hottest spots." "A must" for anyone visiting the Riviera. St Tropez - the name rings with dreams of sunshine and beaches and resounds with tales of the naughty, of nudity, of the rich and famous, their lavish mansions and awesome yachts. Glamorous and gorgeous, St Tropez is still under the spell of its history, making it a truly magical place.

History tells us that a knight named Torpes, who was a steward at Nero's palace in Pisa, refused to renounce Christ and was, therefore sentenced to death. His head was cut off and thrown away. Much later, it was recovered by Christians who deposited it in the church of St Tropez, which still stands in Pisa. His body was placed in a boat with a cock and a dog, animals that symbolized parricide to the Romans. On May 17th in the year 68 AD, the boat,

driven east by the winds for several months, ran aground at Le Pilon. A Roman woman found the body of the Roman officer in full uniform, accompanied by the cock and the dog. The boat, its crew, and the holy martyr are depicted in polychrome carvings in the church of St Tropez.

IN ANCIENT TIMES, ST TROPEZ WAS COMMERCIALLY AN IMPORTANT PORT IN THE MEDITERRANEAN

The harbor coastline faces northeast! a rarity on the Côte d'Azur, providing protection from most winds. The harbor remains the central point of St Tropez, but today, several hundred years later, commerce is no longer merchandise from Africa and the Middle East, instead it is tourism, big yachts, wine, and the bounty of a few local fisherman!

For over a century St Tropez has enchanted artists, photographers, and vacationing visitors. The reason: its simplicity, pure beauty, pastel colors, and soft magic light. The bustle in its port and narrow streets contrast sharply

The harbor of St Tropez lined with pastel colored houses and traditional fishing boats, just like "it used to be"

with the quiet *provençal* countryside. But St Tropez has become a legend, and it's fashionable now to say:

"*Oh, you mean St Trop. It's nothing like it used to be - quiet with fishing boats and locals - before this crowd came. Just look at it now.*"

St Tropez, like every other popular place in the world, has gone public. But there are few, if any, of the world's "hot spots" that can compare to this peninsula. You will find no ugly high-rise or Belle Epoque hotels along the beach, no fast food chains in the village. The beachside restaurants are primarily charming shacks, and if you want to avoid the crowds, you can get up early and take a morning stroll around the port, when it is still as delightful as it ever has been.

Not until the late 19th century, long after "the discovery" of Cannes and Monaco, was the charm of St Tropez revealed. It took a novelist and a painter, both sailors, to realize the beauty, light, and serenity. The writer, Guy de Maupassant, sailed into St Tropez with his boat *Bel Ami* in 1887 and described almost instantly his enthusiasm for the region in his story, *Sur l'eau*:

"*It is one of those charming, simple daughters of the sea, one of those modest little towns that have grown in the water like a shellfish, fed on fish and the sea air, and which produces sailors. It smells of fish and burning tar, brine and boats. Sardine scales glisten like pearls on the cobblestones.*"

A few years later, in 1892, the young painter Signac cruised into the port on his boat "Olympia." His fascination with the village and the surrounding countryside enticed him to stay until World War I broke out in 1914. During that time he painted most of his masterpieces, inspired by the beauty of the region, still recognizable in his paintings. His enthusiasm brought many other artists of his generation, who were soon followed by younger ones.

In the late 1950s, St Tropez became the scene of the film "And God Created Woman" - a film that skyrocketed Brigitte Bardot and St Tropez to stardom. Though the film was rather innocent by today's standards, it stirred up a scandal at the time, leaving St Tropez an icon of iniquity and the bikini a fashion explosion, soon to be followed by the topless rage. Modern St Tropez was born.

Surprisingly, St Tropez has only 6000 inhabitants and is no larger than the children's playground in New

York's Central Park. But on certain summer days, as many as 100,000 visitors flock to explore the town and peninsula. Needless to say, it can get quite crowded. For two hectic summer months, St Tropez becomes a tourist trap, with soaring prices and declining service and quality. The only road in and out of town is usually at a standstill, smack full of foreign license plates from vacationing European countries. Despite this situation, St Tropez can be reached even during summer with the right strategy! Locals have their own short cuts, and there are several "secrets" to avoiding the traffic on the coastal highway: the fastest - regular helicopter service flies in and out unhampered; the "hottest" - a powerful offshore racer that will quickly bring you to hideaway coves along the coast; the smartest - a private yacht so you can relax in privacy and style, and watch the show!

SEASONS FILLED WITH CHARM AND TRANQUILLITY

OK, let's admit it, the two summer months are overcrowded, but it is unfair to claim that the village and countryside have lost their charm. The remaining 10 months are slow and hushed "like it used to be!" The autumn season is beautiful for beach lovers, with lot's of sun and fewer people. Shops and restaurants are still open, but prices are more reasonable. Spring and pre-summer are a nature lover's paradise, bursting with new-sprung flora, fauna, and the first blush of the region's distinctive light.

HOW TO ENJOY A SUMMER'S DAY TO ITS UTMOST

Don't get out of bed until 11 am. Have your breakfast in the harbor before boarding the yacht you invited yourself onto late last night. Enjoy a smooth cruise to the Pampelonne Beach while the first champagne glasses are raised. Once the yacht is anchored at a favorite spot, it's time for a little swim before the beach restaurant's tender comes to pick you up at the anchorage and brings you to the party! A rosé-filled lunch at the beach begins at 2 pm and by 4 you're ready for an hour's siesta in a comfortable beach chair, before it's time to join the party at the beach bar. By 6, the yacht cruises back to the harbor for some late afternoon shopping. Dinner is mostly at 11 pm and by 2 am it's time for a private party or some nightlife in the village. At around 5 am things tend to wind down. Arrangements for the next day should have been made and as you amble home through the darkened streets, you can buy freshly baked croissants at the bakery or sit down in the harbor for a last sip before preparing yourself for the next day - by grabbing a few hours sleep. No wonder why people complain about jet lag after a few day's vacation in St Trop, as the "in" crowd prefers to call it.

A unusual sight in St Tropez - no yachts. Only for a few hours once a year. The phenomena occurs when the participating sailboats rush out to the Gulf to race in the Nioulargue

Pampelonne Beach - *the miracle mile - the longest beach along the Côte d'Azur,*
stretches from Cap de St Tropez to Cap Camerat

For others, life in St Tropez starts when the party people go to bed. In the harbor fishermen come back with their catch-of-the-day, hand it over to their wives, and minutes later it's displayed in the fish market around the corner where locals make a choice among the colorful fish. Across the street, the mega-yachts are docked "stern to," squeezed into tiny spaces with their crews intensively polishing mahogany decks and shiny white sides. At the Place des Lices, little has changed over the centuries, dappled as always in sunshine and shaded by magnificent plane trees. Locals have their first pastis over an early game of boules, just as they have always done.

THE MIRACLE MILE - PAMPELONNE BEACH

Unlike so many other beaches on the Côte d'Azur, the Pampelonne has superbly soft sand and well-kept beaches, all differing in style. It's the longest beach along the Côte d'Azur, stretching three miles from Cap de St Tropez to Cap Camerat. The beach is only a five-minute drive from the village, and much longer if you cruise there by yacht. Walking along the beach, you'll find a section for every taste, every wallet, and every combination of sexes.

It all began with TAHITI PLAGE, when local fisherman Felix decided to open a restaurant on the beach in the late 1950s, inspired by Brigitte Bardot and Gunter Sachs. Today it's more than just a restaurant, it's become the playground of all their beautiful international friends, and includes a beach front hotel, a gym, boutiques, tennis, and a pool.

A little further down the beach, the chicest of the chic gather at MOOREA under parasols and matching beach mattresses of red and green, making it easy to locate. MOOREA is a meeting point for anyone who believes he is "somebody" in St Tropez. It has its own restaurant, featuring fashion shows at lunch with models who show the latest beachwear and hairstyles from the beach boutiques.

LA VOILE ROUGE is the meeting point for the "hot" people - the younger and topless generation! alongside the most beautiful women and the most divine playboys. Paul, the owner, knows everyone and everyone knows him. France's ever popular rock star Johnny Halliday, who survived the days of Elvis, hosts a party in one corner and Paul efficiently opens their champagne bottles the traditional way - with a sword - before he rushes over to join Luigi, the charismatic bartender who is dancing with Joan Collins. Here you can enjoy special beach drinks concocted by Luigi and his one man show, to the tune of rather loud music. This is where nightlife starts at lunch.

Continuing along the beach, there are some "public" beaches which tend to be extremely crowded until you reach LA LIBERTE, as in freedom, which begins the part of the beach where "it all hangs out" in every size and shape

*Showtime for Luigi, the charismatic bartender
at LA VOILE ROUGE beach*

imaginable, the nude beach, drawing primarily French and northern European sunbathers. This beach is linked to a huge camping area and there are both private sections with restaurants and public areas, always very crowded, very nude, and very indiscrete.

"I LEFT MY HEART IN ST TROPEZ AND I THINK IT WAS AT CLUB 55"

About half way down Pampelonne, the beach gets more civilized again. CLUB 55, a shaded oasis of flowers and greenery just off the beach, its soft light, created by groves of tamarisk trees, is restful and cooling after hours in the strong sun of the beach. This is "it" for sophisticated high society, mixed with French noblesse, and celebrities. The wealthiest, most beautiful clientele in the world that you're ever likely to find seated under one pine tree at the same time are here. This beach club is totally unpretentious and casual with tiny old tables spread with flowery cloths. Whether you are a celebrity or not, you will be greeted by a smile and words of welcome by owner *Monsieur* Patrice who has lived here on the beach since he was four years old.

If you manage to walk the entire beach, it will take about two hours from one end to the other, not including stops for refreshments or conversation along the way. The western end is more tranquil and harder to reach. The beach is still divided into private and public sections, very individual and some very gay.

The meeting point for the "hot" people - the younger and topless generation! alongside the most beautiful models and the most divine playboys

A LATE AFTERNOON RUSH TO THE PORT AND THE SUNSET

After beach hours, everyone rushes back to the village and to the port with its old harbor-front houses, each hosting a restaurant, a bar, or a boutique. Seat yourself at a waterfront café like SENEQUIER or the TABAC DU PORT, order a drink and let the scenery do the rest. Take in the sun as it slowly sets behind the Massif des Maures, creating a warmth of soft light as it reflects in the water in front of the pastel port facades. St Tropez is awake again as masses of people stroll the harbor: hot Harley Davidson types with head-to-toe leather gear, sun glasses and pony-tails; lightly dressed young girls pretty with their perfect all-over tans; distinguished elderly gentlemen in yachting outfits - all mingle with sunburned-red campers wearing shorts a bit too short, carrying plastic bags and accompanied by children sucking ice creams that drip onto their "I've been to St Tropez T-shirts." As if the people weren't entertainment enough, there is an ongoing carnival of street musicians, magicians, acrobats, and vendors, all competing for attention - and a few francs.

As the afternoon mellows out, the yachts start coming in from their daily excursion, jockeying for the best central dockage, while the red-nosed dock-master juggles a cigarette and a whistle in his mouth, trying to remember who gave him the best tip. And when, if ever, you've had enough of this spectacle, you can stroll any of the narrow streets behind the port where you'll find the hottest summer fashions available and more.

St Tropez might be crowded, but it's never boring.

DINING OUT

For many years, St Tropez tended to put gastronomy in the shade. The bacchanalia consisted of restaurants serving food at prices far exceeding quality and by nonchalant and spoiled waitresses, symbolizing a short-minded stupidity. Today the situation is changing, although you can still have unpleasant surprises. One morning when visiting a famous restaurant and bar at the very end of the beach, the bread - half a *baguette* - was served for breakfast at 40 times the price the same loaf of bread would have cost at a *boulangerie* around the corner. Responding to a complaint, the owner replied through the embarrassed waiter, *"That's how it is in St Tropez in the summer."* Unfortunately, incidents like that give St Tropez a bad reputation.

In recent years, there's a new luster to St Tropez' culinary reputation. A number of new restaurants have opened with excellent food at honest prices. If this tendency continues, St Tropez might very well become, in a few years, one of the better places along the Côte d'Azur for good food at good value, hopefully driving the expensive tourist traps out of business. Many of them are located in the harbor and frequented in the evenings by north-European

Beach vendors sell everything on Pampelonne Beach: T-shirts, toys, the latest swimsuits, and newspapers

campers, charmed to be in St Tropez, but still with little sense of what's good in life. But as always, you'll find exceptions. CHEZ VITAMINE is a newcomer that has moved to the front row after living in the shady back streets for many years. In an Oriental setting that contrasts to the rest of the *quai*, it offers an excellent five-course Thai/ Vietnamese dinner. You make your choice between fish or meat and they'll do the rest. Then there's LE GORILLE, always packed 24 hours a day and popular with locals who come in for a drink and the latest gossip, or just to look at pretty boys and girls. It's not a first choice for dinner, but it's a place where you can drop by to have a bite any-time. LE GORILLE is also a perfect stop for a late supper on your way home from a nightclub. Off-season when the beaches are closed, this is the place to choose for a casual lunch on its sunny terrace. The *moules marinières* are excellent, the *steak tartar* superb and the *French fries* are the best in St Tropez.

Moving uptown from the harbor, most of the narrow old streets lead up to La Ponche, the old fishing village. Every evening this area is transformed into an almost endless flow of dinner tables. CHEZ NANO, only one block up from the harbor, is a first choice that "has it all:" the food is excellent and the atmosphere is fun while prices are moderate. It's noisy and somewhat gay in every sense of the word, always crowded and a known *rendez-vous* for showbiz personalities.

Further up on the *boules* pitch, Place des Lices, few visitors or celebrities can pass up the opportunity of shooting a few *demi-portées* against the locals, followed by a pastis or two in LE CAFÉ DES ARTS, a classic institution, local and relaxed, far from the scene on the port. The café also has a restaurant hidden behind the bar and the kitchen with only a few tables sharing a tiny space. It's authentic, popular, and always full. Make a reservation and make sure to end up at the right place. It's easily mistaken for one of its neighbors, who will be happy to welcome you.

Between Place des Lices and the harbor, in one of the pedestrian streets, Chef Christian Leroy has opened his own gourmet bistro, LA TABLE DE MARCHE, after leaving his position as a Super Chef in one of the big hotels. The food is delicious and very inspired by the traditional *provençal* kitchen. It has been packed since the day it opened, lunch as well as dinner. Make your reservation and don't be surprised if there's a line of people waiting outside.

AND WHERE TO STAY

Many people prefer to stay outside of the village in the countryside with an easier access to the beach, and in the following chapter a selection of the best places will be given. This doesn't mean that there's nothing in St Tropez or that what exists is necessarily bad. It's just a matter of taste.

A palace opened its doors in the late 1960s thanks to an eccentric promoter of Lebanese origin, deeply fond of St Tropez and with a dream ... *".. in the shadow of the Citadel and a step away from the Place des Lices. It would be like a spacious and comfortable old house on a family estate. A village within a village. Palm trees, bougainvilleas, wisteria vines, olive trees. Immense gardens, little terraces and a sublime architecture covering each culture around the Mediterranean - if it was a hotel, it might be called BYBLOS."*

The dream came true. At BYBLOS you'll find Moroc-can vaulted archways, Arab-styled tearooms and flower gardens, Lebanese antiques, Italian tiles, fountains and terraces worthy of an Eastern pasha. Each room is unique and spectacularly decorated. Or you might prefer your own villa. BYBLOS offers two excellent restaurants, a pleasant bar, and the well known nightclub LE CAVE DU ROI.

Smaller and more romantic, LE YACA is a block away from the harbor and has only 24 rooms. Once a *provençal* house in the heart of town, it has been beautifully converted into a very comfortable hotel with an excellent restaurant. Disguised by its plain entrance, you will be pleasantly surprised by the inner courtyard, with trees and a swimming pool, around which the hotel is laid out. Make sure you get one of the rooms overlooking the pool.

For those who like "rock and roll," a slightly lower price range, and action, the picturesque LA SUBE is the place. Recently renovated, it is St Tropez' oldest hotel, located right in the middle of the port. Sip champagne while sitting on your own terrace, watching the sunset or the show in the harbor. LA SUBE is the only hotel mentioned which stays open year-round.

LA PINEDE, almost a private villa located on the seaside just before entering St Tropez, has its own beach facing the village and the harbor. Not only an oasis of privacy, comfort, and luxury, LA PINEDE is also famous for its excellent food, served under pine trees on a terrace by the sea. This Relais & Chateau, recently restored to perfection, has a private balcony for each room and apartment with postcard views through flowers and pines of the harbor and Gulf of St Tropez.

As the sun begins its westward dip the worlds biggest sailingyacht, racing in the Nioulargue will return to St Tropez

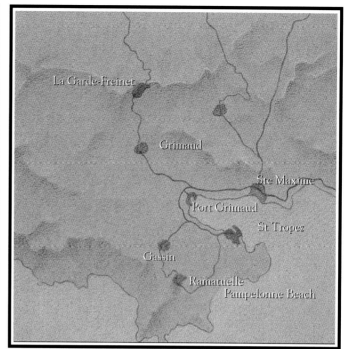

PRESQU'ILE DE ST TROPEZ

The quieter side

The peninsula Presqu'ile de St Tropez is bordered by the sea to the east, the Massif des Maures to the west and the Gulf of St Tropez to the north. One could easily picture the area as an isolated island within the greenery of Provence. Few know that St Tropez and its commune only cover about a quarter of the peninsula that bears its name. The nearby villages of Gassin and Ramatuelle administer the large majority of the surrounding land and beaches.

Many celebrities and people-in-the-know prefer to stay at an arm's length from the summer madness of St Tropez, in villages and a countryside that haven't changed much since medieval times. The beauty and peace of the pine and cork tree forests are perfect for outings in relative solitude to enjoy the scents of wild herbs or go horse back riding past the endless vineyards. This is the only segment of the entire Côte d'Azur that has been saved from the seafront railroad tracks. There is not even a coast road and in some areas the sea and the rocks can only be reached by long walks.

HOW TO TRAVEL THE BACK COUNTRY

To discover the beauty a car is not necessary, there are plenty

of long walks. The Pampelonne Beach, as described earlier, might be the nicest, even off-season, when the restaurants have closed and the tourists are gone. From the village of St Tropez to the Pampelonne Beach, there is a rather difficult 2-hour path along the rocky coast of Cap St Tropez - only reached by foot or boat - where one can catch a glimpse of magnificent private estates, including *La Madrague* belonging to Brigitte Bardot. However, the ultimate mode of transportation is on horseback. Private tours are arranged year-round, lasting from half a day to a week with wine tasting and nightly stays at auberges and in some cases even at the vineyards.

THE *MASSIF DES MAURES* AND THE COUNTY OF VAR

Further inland across the Maures Mountains a different landscape opens up, flat and bare. There are no longer any fancy summer homes or expensive green, manicured gardens. Instead you'll find farmhouses or old wine châteaux in endless fields of wine grapes. All the delights of the sea are close at hand, while the fields offer the stunning beauty of a cultivated countryside. Wander at your leisure, spend days wine tasting, sampling culinary delights, discovering hidden waterfalls, or exploring historical monuments like the Cistercian abbey at Thoronet.

TOURING THE VINEYARDS IN THE BACK COUNTRY OF ST TROPEZ

One of the great pleasures of travel is wine, and one of the great pleasures of wine is to drink it where it's grown and produced. If your wine tour is limited to the Presqu'ile de St Tropez it could be done in a day, even on a bike or horseback. If it's extended to the Maures Mountains, the cork forests of La Garde-Freinet, and parts of the lower Var Valley, it will take a minimum of 3 days.

ROUTE DU ROSÉ - THE NIOULARGUE

The Route du Rosé is an event that takes place in St Tropez every year in November and embraces traditions of the region. Horses with drays arrive from all over the area with coachmen and passengers who have traveled for three days collecting and tasting rosé wine from vineyards along the way. They reach the harbor of St Tropez piled high with barrels and cases of wine. In true *provençal* style, a troupe of wide-hatted and gaily dressed dancers lead the parade of wine and horses through town, followed by officials sporting the garb of the Chevaliers de Meduse, a joyous order created in 1660 by the French king's navy. The rosé is loaded onto tall sailing ships, some that gathered in St Tropez earlier for the international Nioulargue Regatta. Each ship will have its hold loaded with cases of wine from twelve different domaines and châteaux that make up the "Friends of the Route du Rosé." After a ceremony and some more wine tasting, they set sail for the West Indies and St Barthélemy, a chic little French possession in the Caribbean. Rumors insist that over 3000 bottles of *vin rosé* are consumed before the ships sail out of the Gulf of St Tropez.

Welcome to the Route du Rosé.

A narrow street in La Garde-Freinet

A countryside of vineyards and farmhouses

ROUTE DU ROSÉ

Touring the vineyards of the Var

When you leave St Tropez by the Route de Ste Anne heading towards the Ste Anne Chapel, you soon enter the soft *Tropézien* countryside, passing small bucolic vineyards mingled with quiet hotels and the gates of sumptious mansions. Ste Anne Chapel stands on the top of a rock spur in the shelter of majestic trees, just as it has since the 17th century, welcoming seafaring pilgrims.

The Route de Ste Anne runs through vineyards to the main Ramatuelle road. Once on the road, which runs parallel to Pampelonne Beach, you will be accosted by a series of signs enticing you down short rural roads to the various "private beaches:" Voile Rouge, Liberty, Club 55, Coco Beach, etc. After 5 km (3 miles) you will see the red tile rooftops of Ramatuelle, high above the vine fields on the slopes of the Maures Mountains.

This pretty medieval village embodies all the features you expect in Provence: narrow streets that uncoil from three tiny squares, arches, vaults, and tastefully restored houses huddled against an ancient town wall. On the main street try to find the sign for LA FARIGOULETTE hidden behind flowers on one of the tiny stone houses. It's a charming restaurant with only 10 tables, where light streams in through small openings in the roof. The terrace opens to a panorama of the *Presqu'ile* out to the sea.

The ambience of Ramatuelle is hushed and slow in comparison to St Tropez, but even so, in the summer every house along the main street seems to open up its door after dark and turn its living room and kitchen into a tiny restaurant. Located slightly outside of town, the HOTEL LE BAOU is comfortable and modern, but built in a traditional style with breathtaking views from all the bright and cheerfully furnished rooms, some of which have their own gardens. An elegant gastronomic restaurant flows across the roof terrace.

In between the beach and the village, the AUBERGE DE L'OUMED is a private house in the middle of a vineyard. The owners have converted one terrace into a restaurant with about 15 tables, serving only dinner. Their one menu

includes wine and goes for a reasonable price. This "private terrace" has quickly established itself as a very popular spot.

The Tropézien countryside, smooth hills, colorful vineyards, and small farmhouses

GASSIN - CENTER OF "*TROPÉZIEN*" WINE

Leave Ramatuelle by Route des Moulins de Paillas, which begins behind the main square and winds its way uphill. After several sharp curves you can take a last glance back to the Pampelonne Bay and the rooftops of Ramatuelle before the road turns inland through a pine and cork tree forest to *Col de Paillas*. At the top of the hill a spectacular panorama unfolds to the distant islands of Port Cros and Porquerolles to the west and the St Tropez peninsula to the east. Pass the ruins of three windmills as you wind your way through the enchanting, pine scented forest to the old village of Gassin, an important lookout point in former days. From the cafés and restaurant on the main square yet another vista unfolds over the Gulf of St Tropez, the vineyards, and the snow tipped Alps in the distant sky. Most of the famous wines from the region come from Gassin and as you head down towards the sea, you'll pass some of the best châteaux, all proud to let you taste their wines.

CHATEAU MINUTY is probably the most well known of the Côte de Provence wines and one of the few that has the noble title of *Cru Classé*, a privilege usually reserved for

The rooftops of Ramatuelle

only the finest Bordeaux wines. The title remains from the past, but carries a heavy responsibility to maintain high quality. Since 1955, after a decree by Baron de Rothschild, no other wines in France, except the Bordeaux and the Côtes de Provence, can obtain such a classification. The CHATEAU MINUTY rosé belongs to the legend of St Tropez, much like celebrities, yachts, and topless beaches. It's a wine of sunshine and enjoyment, and its traditional bottle, clear color, and smooth taste have made people laugh and relax under the warm sun for decades. The estate contains a château and a chapel built during the reign of Napoleon III. It stands in 42 hectares of vineyards, which have produced wine for hundreds of years. CHATEAU MINUTY has been owned by the same family since 1936, when Gabriel Farnet bought the estate and today, 3 generations later, Mr and Mme Matton, his daughter and son-in-law, and their son will greet you welcome. If you ask, you might be shown the chapel, which stands in a copse of trees and is still used on special occasions.

CHATEAU BARBEYROLLES

Next door the CHATEAU BARBEYROLLES is owned by a woman full of vitality, Mme Régine Sumeire. In St Tropez there are 2 Régines: one is the queen of nightclubs and responsible for St Tropez reputation of chic nightlife; the other has put the region's wines on the world map. Régine Sumeire is the daughter of a long tradition of vineyards, and at 26 she made the decision to buy her own. Etienne Matton of MINUTY helped her to purchase the neighboring Château Salesse, owned by an elderly British woman and completely in disrepair. With much patience, Mme Sumeire restored the old facilities and replanted the vines. Her first bottle arrived after 5 years of work. She then launched an international campaign with other vineyard owners to restore the reputation of *provençal* wines. The CHÂTEAU BARBEYROLLES wines are constantly improved and new varieties are created. In 1987, *Petale de Rosé*, a new rosé, light and feminine, was released. In 1988, Regine Sumeire inaugurated the Route du Rosé, when the world's largest private sailboats use rosé wine as ballast and race off to St Barthélemy in the Caribbean.

CHATEAU BELIEU - A DISCREET HIDEAWAY FOR THE RICH AND FAMOUS

Neighboring the CHATEAU BARBEYROLLES and CHATEAU MINUTY, you'll find the latest hideaway for the rich and discreet, CHATEAU BELIEU. This villa was for many years a favorite rental house for top jet-setters, until it was recently bought and converted into a very special hotel. Only a ten minute drive from St Tropez, it is located in a quiet off-the-main-road type of spot in the midst of its own vineyards, where another excellent Côte de Provence is produced. There are only a limited number of rooms and suites, all decorated individually and named in accordance to their styles : *Classique, Et Dieu A Crée La Femme, Art-Déco, Kamasutra*, etc. There are indoor and outdoor pools and a garden with a barbecue. The indoor restaurant is beautifully decorated in the traditional style, providing a warm and personal atmosphere. The health club (Centre Balneotherapie) has all the facilities you need to keep up with the hectic pace of St Tropez: sauna, jacuzzi, tennis, sunray bed (if the sun at the beach isn't enough), body building equipment, and massage. To avoid the heavy traffic on St Tropez access roads, CHATEAU BELIEU has its own private heliport... and best of all, the wine served is from its own backyard.

This very special villa creates a unique and private atmosphere. You hardly sense that you are among other guests or that you are actually staying in a hotel at all. As the manager in a slightly snobbish way explained the basics of this hotel: *"You must understand that the owner did not think of rentability on his investment when he created Château Belieu - he only thought of the comfort of his friends."*

GRIMAUD - PRETENDS TO BE A "MINI-VENICE"

Minutes away on the road towards Grimaud, you pass the DOMAINE DE BELIEU the hotel's "private" vineyard. The cave and the "showroom" where wine tasting takes place are in a pompous building with huge columns, a modern reminder of the Roman Empire, slightly misplaced in the middle of the wine fields. However, the wine is good and the owner is said to have one ambition - to make the best wine in Provence.

At the end of the Gulf of St Tropez, you have Port

A typical provençal mas in the countryside of Presqu'ile de St Tropez

Grinaud, rumored to be one of the world's most original and successful property developments, built like a modern Venice from an unwanted mosquito-infested swamp! All similarities with Venice must end there: canals, water, and fake gondolas. The mosquitos have turned into a mass invasion of tourists from all over Europe camping in the neighborhood, and the scent of the swamp has become an odor created by a mix of sweet pastry, cheap frying oil, and suntan lotion in the summer, while in the winter the little port takes on the air of a ghost town. "You can't fool the sea," as a wise man once said.

Slightly above Port Grimaud, the silhouette of castle ruins towering on a distant hilltop indicate the old village of Grimaud, a low-key haven for "older money." The village is named after the Grimaldi family, who once owned it. The narrow streets offer pleasant walks through arcades and past the doorways of restored medieval stone houses draped in flowers. There are a few good restaurants. LA BRETONNIÈRE is an unpretentious looking place with a beautiful and very warm interior. The owner, a character who is rotund and sometimes cheerful, looks like he is taking care of everything - which he is! The dinner menu of *la nouvelle cuisine* is set and you eat what you are served. The dessert tray is enormous and you won't be allowed out unless you have tried most of them. Nobody leaves this restaurant hungry. But the problem is not how to leave, but how to get in. The owner detests guides, will not let anyone in without a reservation, and has an antipathy for certain foreigners, so if you have an American accent make sure to polish a French touch to it.

LA SPAGHETTA is a small and very casual Italian restaurant serving a wide selection of delicious pasta dishes at reasonable prices. HOSTELLERIE DU COTEAU FLEURI is a stone country house hosting a gastronomic restaurant hidden amid flowers behind the church in the village center. From its terrace you look out across the vineyards in the valley below and to the Maures Mountains.

Slightly east of the village in the cork tree forest, there is a nice little *provençal* inn LE VERGER which offers the tranquility of the countryside. The brightly decorated rooms face the garden and pool, and a terrace serves delicious *al fresco* luncheons and dinners.

LA GARDE-FREINET

La Garde-Freinet is a kind of watershed which divides the coast from the mountain landscape further inland. You reach the village on the narrow D 558 which winds its way steeply upwards through a dark cork tree forest. The tiny village is known in history as the last stronghold of the Saracens and has otherwise gained renown for its cork industry and "whore house." Today only a minor part of the cork industry remains.

Along the way you'll see a miniature road sign pointing to Miremer. The track that runs uphill is dusty and can be conquered by a car, but it is nicer to walk and it will only

La Garde-Freinet as seen from the old Saracen stronghold

take 15 minutes. At the top, the small church of NOTRE DAME DE MIREMER stands shaded under enormous trees, looking out at the Gulf of St Tropez and an immense panorama of the surrounding countryside. For many years an eremite lived in this chapel, supposedly alone, until the church found out that she was fully enjoying life in La Garde-Freinet, where she could find gentle company to bring back home.

La Garde-Freinet is today the home of artists, sculptors, and potters, and has galleries and antique shops. In the village there is a restaurant called LA FOÜCADO which is one of the favorites in the entire region. You descend by a stairway through bushes and flowers and enter a gorgeous, shady terrace that abounds in pottery, flowers, cats, and dogs! The terrace serves as the summer restaurant. Further in, the winter room is decorated in the traditional style of a *provençal mas*: stone, beams, pottery, masses of dried flowers and herbs, natural honey colored wood, a huge open fireplace, cheery table cloths and more flowers, cats, and dogs. Then there's the food - huge portions of *foie gras, magret de canard,* and a superb fishsoup just to name a few. The owner, Jean Paul, will greet you welcome in his own way, depending on his mood. It's not a question of whether you like him or the place, but if he likes you! Behind the stage Jean Luis works in the kitchen and he welcomes anyone into his domain with comments on the food or a greeting and thanks for a delicious meal.

La Garde-Freinet's big excursion is to take a one hour hike up to the "cross," located on top of a rock, to look at the unique remains of the old Saracen stronghold. These remarkable people managed to survive, isolated and self-sufficient, for almost two hundred years before they died of incest. The ruins are well preserved and it's fascinating to study the outrageous skill and technique of building these people possessed 2000 years ago !

After La Garde-Freinet the road twists its way down the northern side of the mountain until it reaches the open fields of the valley below, where farmhouses are scattered in the patchwork of vineyards. "The land of wine" begins here and life tends to get much more relaxed than along the coast. When speaking with people you'll notice a more rural temperament - there will always be a tomorrow to rely on. Everywhere along the road small signposts bid you to the different châteaux and domains, promising *dégustation de vin,* wine tasting. By trying them all you surely won't travel very far. There is a big variety in quality between the wines, even though they are all neighbors and the earth seems to be the same. The wine of La Garde-Freinet at CHÂTEAU DE LAUNES is the first vineyard you'll come to when the road flattens out and cuts its way across the fields. It's worth a visit and the wine is an excellent *vin de table,* good value for money, especially the rosé and red.

The land of wine - the open fields north of the Maures Mountains, where farmhouses are scattered in a patchwork of vineyards and pine trees

THE ART OF LIVING GOLF

In the pine and cork forests surrounding La Garde-Freinet, Côte d'Azur's latest and biggest golf development was opened recently, LES DOMAINES DE VIDAUBAN, touted as the European Capital of Golf, where the art of living is golf. This is not golf for the lucky few or for the blue bloods who inherited memberships from the late Grand Duc Michel. This is golf as a facility for those addicted to playing the game. In the early eighties Robert Trent, Sr. discovered the sublime beauty of the Maures Mountains. He acquired 2500 acres of land and over the next 10 years worked to make his dream course come true. Apart from the three 18-hole golf courses open to everyone, there is a practice area of excep-

Hidden under large leafy trees at the edge of the water - AUBERGE DU LAC

tional size and also special facilities to allow the public to follow professional golf tournaments. But life on LES DOMAINES is not just golf. There are close to 40 tennis courts, 2 man-made lakes for water sports, walkways, a jogging path, and even a series of "authentic" new *provençal* villages, each with its own church, narrow streets, shady squares, art galleries, boutiques, hotels, and restaurants. Cars remain in the car parks and a shuttle service is provided by an electric funicular railway. LES DOMAINES DE VIDAUBAN promote a lifestyle built around three core values: liberty, conviviality, and freedom of choice.

DOMAINE DE LA BERNARDE AND DOMAINE PEYRASSOL

As you drive on you will pass the busy town of Le Luc, a main road, and a railroad intersection where you should join the N7 and continue west towards Flassans. Shortly after Le Luc a big white gateway on the left will announce DOMAINE DE LA BERNARDE. The present owner, Mr Roland Meulnart, used to be president of a successful precision tool company before he bought LA BERNARDE in 1974. Today he runs his vineyard with the same precision, producing a superb wine sold under 3 labels. The best, *Clos St-Germain*, makes up less than 10% of the entire production, only about 25,000 bottles a year! The rosé with a light feminine color is excellent and the red, which could easily be aged for 8 to 15 years, is among the best in the region - and also one of the most expensive.

Only 10 minutes away, down another sideroad that runs through the pretty countryside, you'll find DOMAINE PEYRASSOL, a huge *bastide* where wine has been produced for some 800 years! After centuries of cultivation, followed by a difficult period of stormy years or balmy seasons, PEYRASSOL awoke again in 1967 when new vines were planted. Françoise, *La Dame de Peyrassol*, today runs the vineyard with a passionate desire to put life back into the bastide. The "showroom" is an impressive cave with huge oak barrels, located underneath the old farm houses in vaulted cellars with walls made of handcut stones said to be over 4 meters (12 feet) thick. The wine is sold under 4 different labels. The great classic *Commanderie de Peyrassol* is a red that will be best after some years of ageing. The love child *Marie-Estelle* born in 1981 has a very limited production and each bottle of this red wine is numbered and dated. And two rosés... one a floral wine of inspiration, its label a painting by a local artist and the wine - the masterpiece.

Bump back down the dusty road and when you reach the main road continue heading west towards Flassans. You'll soon pass a sign LA GRILLADE AU FEU DE BOIS which points down another side track into the forest, to a small auberge with a pool, and an antique store situated in an old stone farmhouse. All the decoration and furniture belongs to the antique store, meaning that you can buy the chairs and table where you've just enjoyed a delicious dinner, if you like

Next page: Cabasse, a calm provençal style "wine village"

them as much as the food. At the far end of the restaurant an open fireplace grills the speciality of the house, barbecued steaks of all kinds.

DOMAINE GAVOTTY - *VIN DE MUSIC*

At Flassans turn right at the much smaller D 13 and continue north through endless vineyards. Shortly after you've passed under the autoroute, you will enter DOMAINE GAVOTTY bought by the Gavotty family in the early 19th century. Since that time six generations have succeeded one another at this beautiful *provençal* estate. Its late development into a high quality, prestige wine is thanks to Pierre and Bernard Gavotty, the latter a famous music critic of the "Figaro" newspaper under the well known pseudonym CLARENDON. In his honor and for its harmonious fruity taste, their best wine has been given his pen name as a *vin de music*. The label shows a woman playing a lute, symbolizing the marriage between wine and music.

Continuing north you will pass the calm little village of Cabasse, a charming *provençal* wine village. The 3-way intersection at the main square is where the village gossip is bandied about by farmers sitting on park benches in the shade of a few trees. Traditional French berets sit cockeyed on their heads and their noses seem a trifle big and red, but they discuss grapes, wine, and the weather while watching the instant traffic jams created on the narrow streets when two cars meet.

Not far from Cabasse, in a countryside that not long ago was vineyards, the vine fields have had to give way in favor of golf clubs. Another recent development, the BARBAROUX GOLF COURSE has been acknowledged as one of the best designed courses in Europe. This championship 18-hole course is nestled into the peaceful hills of Provence, in a wooded landscape interspersed by 6 huge lakes, which will cause trouble for even the most experienced golfer, or as they say in their colorful brochure, "All in the pure tradition of American golf."

THE QUIET LAKE OF CARCES AND THE CISTERCIAN ABBEY OF THORONET

Follow the signs for Lac de Carcés and within 15 minutes the landscape will change. The vineyards disappear and the country becomes a little rocky before you reach a small isolated lake settled into the green hillsides. A little house is hidden under large leafy trees at the edge of the water - AUBERGE DU LAC - which serves summer lunches and dinners *al fresco* on the shady terrace, where only a few fishermen might disturb the peace. The rest of the year the rustic dining room is warmed by an open fire and serves only at lunch. Three menus are proposed, ranging from the competitively priced 3 dishes to the more expensive 6-dish extravaganza.

The road skirts the lake for some miles with lots of opportunity for fishing until the lake ends abruptly and you're back into the vine fields. In this area plenty of signs will point the way to L'ABBEY THORONET, a short detour for an excursion. The abbey was built in the 12th century with austere simplicity by monks of the Cistercian Order. It sits in wooded hills, which were once very isolated, allowing the monks to maintain their strict orders. Today it's one of the most visited monuments in the region and in the summer it hosts important musical events. Wherever there have been monks there has also been wine and the Abbey Thoronet is no exception. Close to the abbey the monks grew grapes and olives, making their own wine and olive oil. In 1979, a Parisian named Franck Petit bought the land after he had made a fortune selling jeans on the coast. A lot of time and money have been spent since, and the slopes surrounding the *moulin à huile* have now been replanted with vines. The *moulin* has been beautifully restored and a chapel serves as a wine museum. A long tunnel leads to the enormous underground room which rises 10 meters (30 ft) to the roof. This spectacular room holds two big wooden olive presses and serves as a "showroom" for Mr Petit's excellent wine DOMAINE DE L'ABBEY. The white wine is among the best in the region and has won several awards.

Also in Thoronet, run on a much smaller scale, Douglas and Jenny Gibbon own the 25 acre DOMAINE BELLE VUE, which does not produce its own wine. All their grapes are delivered to the local wine cooperative. But their house, an authentic old *mas* in the middle of the vineyard, serves as a traditional English bed and breakfast where you will be most welcome to help with pruning, clipping, and harvesting of the grapes, or just to relax and learn a lot about wine. Douglas also arranges spectacular truffle hunting tours with a dog and a pig competing against each other or luncheon and dinner parties in the best vineyards.

ALONG THE BRESQUE CREEK

At this point you can either choose to cut your trip short and head back to the coast or continue deeper into the Var countryside. The village of Carcès, north of the lake, is a busy place that you will best discover by sitting down on the main square, Place Gabriel Peri, to have a drink at the bar CHEZ JACQUELINE. Locals congregate here to listen to bawling music from distant loudspeakers semi-hidden in the trees. From Carcès continue on D 31 and follow the signs for Entrecasteaux. This will take you along a road that runs next to the Bresque Creek through a natural landscape with lots of possibilities for horseback riding, marked hikes in the forest, or fishing.

Entrecasteaux comes next with its magnificent castle in a formal French garden that dates back to the 17th century, when it replaced an old fortress. In the early 1970s, it was bought and restored to perfection by an eccentric Scottish adventurer McGarvie-Munn. Since his death it has

When grape vines grow to the doorstep there is no room for manicured gardens

turned into a delightful combination of architectural monument, art gallery, concert hall, hotel, and private residence. Next to the castle there's a typical *provençal* restaurant in a stone house fronted by a terrace ablaze with flowers. LA FOURCHETTE faces the château and offers 3 menus, a delicious *terrine de canard* and a local speciality *feuillettes d'escargots au chévre persil*.

From here on, there are only a few vineyards and the road starts to twist its way uphill along the same woodlined creek to Salernes. You'll drive past more signs for nature excursions and sporting activities, including the ranch LES AMOURENES with a huge American flag waving above the roof - it is one of the best for horseback excursions in the area.

SALERNES - CITY OF TILES

Approaching Salernes you will see five tall pillars tiled in red on your left in front of a *provençal* building - the first sign that you have arrived at the center of tiles. This is ALAIN VAGH'S workshop and showroom for his artistic ceramic works: one among 15 others in Salerne. You will find traditional tiles in all colors, tiles inspired by *faience* and custom made tiles for any occasion - a car dressed in tiles, a cowboy boot dressed in tiles, etc. Salernes itself is busier, larger, more sprawling, and less pretty than most other villages in the area. Twice a week a popular market is held on the main square.

Close to the town center, the GRAND HOTEL ALLÉGRE has a cavernous dining room and a sitting area at the far end, where a log fire burns most winter days. Dark colors and a heavy interior mixed with wine-colored velvet chairs, waitresses of a "certain age" in white aprons, and tables set with crisp tablecloths give the room a slightly formal atmosphere rather misplaced in the middle of Provence. Cer-

La Cascade de Sillans, in an Amazon-like jungle water from the creek crashes down from 50m (165 ft) above

tainly the GRAND HOTEL is a place to choose for a dinner or lunch if you are looking for something different, but not a place to stay overnight.

A nice excursion from Salernes takes you west for 10 minutes on D 560 to the little village of Sillans la Cascade. It is a very charming, once fortified village with a throng of narrow dirt roads and a sunny square where two restaurants face the Bresque Creek. Next to the old chapel in front of the square, a handwritten wood sign easily missed reads *La Cascade*, the waterfall. A 30 minute hike crosses open fields before entering an Amazon-like tropical jungle. Led by the noise of falling water you will soon emerge at the small pool into which the water of the creek crashes from 50 meters (165 ft) above - an impressive sight and an unexpected milieu in the heart of Provence.

TOURTOUR - THE VILLAGE IN THE SKY

Take D 51 from Salernes and the tiny road will start to climb towards another picturesque village - Villecroze - from where you can see Tourtour high above, hanging majestically from the edge of a rock in the sky. Flanked by the ruins of two castles, the village is set above fields and green forests that spread to the horizon. It is the richest and best preserved village in the Var, a gastronomic center, world champion in egg throwing, and the inventor of a new type of *boules* - where you play with quadrangular balls instead of the round ones. It is centered around a main square with several nice bars that serve excellent food and a tabac. It's good to sit here to watch people and study how Rolls Royces and Ferraris manage to maneuver through the already narrow streets, made even smaller by the overflow of tables from the restaurants.

Tourtour is an irresistible combination of breathtaking views over the lower valleys of Provence, medieval vaulted passageways, and beautifully restored old stone houses. It's a village that has kept its appeal and charm but left mass-tourism out. Shortly before entering the village, look for the elegant restaurant LES CHÈNES VERTS which is situated in a private house with only a few tables. This type of restaurant you would expect to find in the business district of any major city, but not way out in the countryside of Provence. Its pricey gastronomic menu has lots of *fois gras* and *truffles*. Make sure you have a reservation and bring cash - credit cards are not accepted.

Behind the village church, screened by the forest, you'll find LA BASTIDE DE TOURTOUR - restful and luxurious with comfortable rooms facing south to a panoramic view from its castle-like building. The restaurant is excellent and for your leisure, there is a heated swimming pool, tennis court, whirlpool, a heliport, lovely walks in the forest, and a peaceful garden area where you can sit in comfy lounge chairs shaded by the pine trees. North of the village, in the countryside you'll find another treasure, AUBERGE SAINT PIERRE. It is an old country farm converted into a charming hotel on a huge property with lots of animals. The farm is still busy and provides the restaurant with most of its products. The family will arrange horseback excursions or long hikes in the forest, or you might like to spend a few relaxing hours fishing in their lake in the company of black and white swans.

CHEZ BRUNO AN ORGIE OF TRUFFELS

Form Tourtour the road winds its way downhill in the pine forest, and you should head for the coast via Lorgues. Shortly after Lorgues a sign to the right will read BRUNO and nothing else. Bruno is a writer and a well known person in French show business. This was Bruno's summer residence where he used to welcome all his famous friends from St Tropez and gave them excellent home cooked meals, until he one day decided to turn his home into a restaurant. Go there for lunch and make sure you're on the terrace. A reservation a few days in advance is "a must," since Bruno has to know how many he'll be cooking for. You'll receive a friendly welcome and maybe a hug and then Bruno will recount what you're going to eat, all while he cuts pieces of French truffles for you to taste. The food is superb and the bill a surprise, unless you've been impolite and asked for the price in advance. *Truffles* and *foie gras* are heaped into almost every dish and by the time coffee is served, you might start looking for slices of truffle instead of sugar.

Returning to the coast you'll pass the autoroute near the village of Vidauban and drive through the Maures Mountain by following the signs towards Plan de la Tour and Ste Maxime. The roads are narrow, but the forest is cheerful and filled with wild primroses and broom in the spring. You'll find isolated vineyards cleared between the woods, beautiful vistas and very few people - until you approach Ste Maxime on the Gulf of St Tropez.

Ste Maxime is a gateway to the popular beaches of the Gulf and all the cars and caravans coming off the autoroute stream into this seaside resort, once a very elegant spot. But in the wintertime it is peaceful and pleasant, with tranquil views of St Tropez in her mellow winter colors across the Gulf. At the traditional *boules* court where locals play, you will sometimes see a charming old man with a beret on his head, playing with the postman against other *varois* natives, as he has done for many years. He might be mistaken for a local, but his quiet ways hide the fact that he is the most celebrated inhabitant of Ste Maxime, His Royal Highness the Prince Bertil of Sweden.

In the countryside behind the coast and Presqu'ile de St Tropez you will discover more than provençal villages and vineyards. The lifestyle is laid back and there are potters, artist studios, beautiful nature, and the famous soft light

HOW TO FIND IT

87 major cities, towns and villages are listed in alphabetic order.
Under each you'll find "OUR TASTE," a selection of over 150 restaurants,
85 hotels and much more, all of them corresponding to each
of the previous stories and all.... worth a visit!

LES ADRETS
(Route de l'Esterel - page 203)
See also Mandelieu

AUBERGE
Auberge des Adrets ***
7 rooms, historical sight, pool, parking
RN 7
Tel: 94 40 36 24
Fax: 94 40 34 06

RESTAURANTS
Auberge des Adrets
Historical sight, terrace, parking
RN 7
Tel: 94 40 36 24

AGAY
(Route de l'Esterel - page 203)
See also Corniche d'Or and Cap Roux

RESTAURANTS
Auberge de la Rade
On the beach
Tel: 94 82 00 37

ANTHÉOR
(Route de l'Esterel - page 203)
See also Agay and Miramar

AUBERGE
Auberge d'Anthéor ***
Seaview, private terraces,
quiet, pool, parking
RN 98
Tel: 94 44 83 38
Fax: 94 44 84 20

RESTAURANTS
Auberge d'Anthéor
Seaview, terrace, rustic
interior, parking
RN 98
Tel: 94 44 83 89

ANTIBES
(Antibes - page 117)
See also Cap d'Antibes
and Juan-les-Pins

TOURIST INFORMATION: 93 33 95 64

AUBERGE
Auberge Provençale ***
Mr Martin
5 rooms, casual authentic auberge
with rustic decoration
Place National
Tel: 93 34 13 24

RESTAURANTS
Auberge Provençale *
Mr Martin
Terrace, provençal decor, open fire
Place National
Tel: 93 34 13 24

L'Oursin
Casual, oyster bar,
make a reservation
16, rue Republique
Tel: 93 34 13 46

Chez Paul le Pêcheur
Paul and Olga
Casual, fish & seafood direct
from Pauls fishingboat
42, Bd d'Aguillon
Tel: 93 34 59 42

Les Vieux Murs
Mr Georges Romano
Terrace, rustic decor, view, parking
Av. Admiral Grasse
Tel: 93 34 06 73

MUSEUM
Picasso Museum
Château Grimaldi, open every day
except Tuesdays and November
Place du Château
Tel: 92 90 54 20

HOUSE RENTING
Riviera Retreats
Private mansions at Cap d'Antibes
and apartments in Antibes
11, rue des Petit Ponts
Mougins-le-Haut
Tel: 93 64 86 40
Fax: 93 64 00 80

YACHT CHARTER AGENTS
Camper & Nicholsons
Mega Yachts for charter
12, av. de la Liberation
Tel: 92 31 29 12
Fax: 92 91 29 00

AURON
(Route des Neiges - page 81)
See also Isola 2000

SKIRESORT
Alt. 1600-2450 m (5200-6900 ft)
1 cable-car, 2 chair-lifts,
27 ski-lifts, 44 ski-runs
Snow information
Tel: 93 23 02 66
Fax: 93 23 07 39

HOTEL
Le Chastellares ***
32 rooms, mountainview
Place Téléphérique
Tel: 93 23 02 58
Fax: 93 23 01 54

Las Donnas ***
48 rooms, mountainview
Place Téléphérique
Tel: 93 23 00 03
Fax: 93 23 07 37

RESTAURANTS
Le Bataclan
In the ski slope, terrace
Tel: 93 23 31 20

La Grange d'Aur
For dinner, rustic interior
Place Téléphérique
Tel: 93 23 30 98

Le Pub - La Chaumière *
Only dinner, reservation a must
Place Téléphérique
Tel: 93 23 01 05

AFTER SKI
Le Sérac
Creperie, terrace
Place Téléphérique
Tel: 93 23 09 62

La Slalom
Bar/snack, terrace
Place Téléphérique
Tel: 93 23 00 13

BAGNOLS-EN-FORÊT
(Route de Provence - page 181)
See also St Paul-en-Forêt and Fayence

RESTAURANTS
Auberge Bagnolaise
Casual, terrace,
parking
Route de Fréjus
Tel: 94 40 60 24

L'Estable
Very small, very casual!
Place de l'Église
Tel: 94 40 61 53

BARGEMON
(Route de Provence - page 181)
See also Seillans and Pennafort

RESTAURANTS
Auberge des Arcades
Casual, parking
Av. Pasteur
Tel: 94 76 60 36

BEAULIEU-SUR-MER
(Cap Ferrat - page 45)
See also Cap Ferrat, Villefranche,
Èze and Éze-bord-du-Mer

HOTEL
La Réserve de Beaulieu **
3 suites, 37 rooms, seaview,
terrace, small private port,
pool, parking
5, bd Gal-Leclerc
Tel: 93 01 00 01
Fax: 93 01 28 99

Le Métropole **
3 suites, 50 rooms, seaview,
terrace, pool, parking
15, bd Gal- Leclerc
Tel: 93 01 00 08
Fax: 93 01 18 51

RESTAURANTS
La Réserve de Beaulieu *
Chef Denis Labonne
Seaview, terrace, parking,
small port for tenders
5, bd Gal-Leclerc
Tel: 93 01 00 01

BIOT
(Route d'Aventure - page 101)
See also Antibes and Valbonne

RESTAURANTS
Auberge du Jarrier **
In the old village, terrace,
rustic interior, boutique
30, passage Bourgade
Tel: 93 65 11 68

Les Terraillers **
Fulci & Jacques
Old pottery, stone vaulted
diningroom, terrace, parking
Route du Chemin-Neuf
Tel: 93 65 01 59

SIGHTS
Léger Museum
Open all year, closed Tuesday
Chemin du Val de Pome
Tel: 93 65 63 49

ART STUDIOS
Hans Hedberg, artist
Ceramics, pottery, sculptures,
visit only by appointment
15, Joseph Durbec
Tel: 93 65 00 30

Van Lith, artist
Glass, porcelain, ceramics,
visit only by appointment
44 bis, impasse St Sebastien
Tel: 93 65 13 47

La Verrerie de Biot
Hand-blown classic colored Biot glass
5, chemin Combes
Tel: 93 65 03 00

LA BOLLÈNE-VÉSUBIE
(Route Col de Turini - page 55)
See also Little Switzerland

HOTEL
Grand Hotel du Parc
42 rooms, private park, quiet, parking
D70
Tel: 93 03 01 01

BOULOURIS
(Route de l'Esterel - page 203)
See also Fréjus and Agay

HOTEL
Sol e Mar
47 rooms, very modern, seaview,
parking, open April to October
Le Dramont
Tel: 94 95 25 60
Fax: 94 83 83 61

CABASSE
(Route du Rosé - page 227)
See also Carcès and Thoronet

GOLF
Golf de Barbaroux
18 holes, a wooded landscape
interspersed with several lakes
Route de Cabasse
Tel: 94 59 26 01
Fax: 94 59 00 93

VINEYARDS
Domaine Gavoty
Bernard et Pierre Gavoty
Wine tasting all year, parking
Tel: 94 69 71 02
Fax: 94 59 64 04

CABRIS
(Route Napoleon - page 159)
See also Mougins

RESTAURANTS
Auberge le Petit Prince
Traditional provençal style, terrace
15, rue Fredric-Mistral
Tel: 93 60 51 40

Vieux Château
In the castle, terrace
Tel: 93 60 50 12

CALLAS
(Route de Provence - page 181)
See also Bargemon

HOTEL
Hostellerie Pennafort *
25 rooms, private park, very quiet,
pool, tennis, small lake, parking
Route de Pennafort, D25
Tel: 94 76 66 51
Fax: 94 76 67 23

RESTAURANTS
Hostellerie Pennafort
Very quiet, terrace, garden,
animals, parking
Route de Pennafort, D25
Tel: 94 76 66 51

CALLIAN
(Route de Provence - page 181)
See also Montauroux and Fayence

AUBERGE
Auberge du Puits Jaubert *
8 rooms, very quiet, old stone
"bergerie," parking
Route du Lac de Fondurane
Tel: 94 76 44 48

RESTAURANTS
Au Centenaire
Casual
Montée du Château
Tel: 94 47 70 84

Auberge du Puits Jaubert
Very quiet, terrace, open fire, stone
vaulted diningroom, parking
Route du Lac de Fondurane
Tel: 94 76 44 48

CANNES
(Cannes - page 143)
See also Mougins, Golfe-Juan
and Iles des Lérins

TOURIST INFORMATION: 93 39 01 01

HOTEL
Carlton **
28 suites, 298 rooms, beautiful view,
gym, pool, healthclub, private beach,
casino, parking
58, la Croisette
Tel: 93 68 91 68
Fax: 93 38 20 90

L'Horset Savoy **
5 suites, 101 rooms, modern,
pool on the roofterrace, parking
5, rue François Einessy
Tel: 92 99 72 00
Fax: 93 68 25 59

Majestic **
24 suites, 263 rooms, beautiful
view,pool, private beach, parking
14, la Croisette
Tel: 93 98 77 00
Fax: 93 38 97 90

Martinez **
14 suites, 416 rooms, beautiful view,
pool, tennis, private beach,
parking
73, la Croisette
Tel: 92 98 73 00
Fax: 93 39 67 82

Le Provence *
30 rooms, simple, quiet,
close to the beach, small garden
9, rue Molière
Tel: 93 38 44 35
Fax: 93 39 63 14

Splendid *
2 suites, 64 rooms, nice view
4, rue F. Faure
Tel: 93 99 53 11
Fax: 93 99 55 02

RESTAURANTS

Astoux et Brun
Casual, oyster bar, terrace
27, rue F. Faure
Tel: 93 39 21 87

Carlton beach *
Nice buffet, very "chic," parking
58, la Croisette
Tel: 93 68 91 68

La Cave *
Casual, reservation a must
9, bd de la République
Tel: 93 99 79 87

L'Embuscade
"Mike"
Old town,
10, rue St Antoine
Tel: 93 47 03 09

Le Maschou
Casual, old town, only dinner,
one menu, reservation a must
15, rue St Antoine
Tel: 93 39 62 21

La Palme d'Or ****
Hotel Martinez
Elegant, terrace
73, la Croisette
Tel: 92 98 74 14

Royal Bar
Good for watching people at lunch
41, la Croisette
Tel: 93 39 01 04

La Villa
Young, bar, music, only dinner
7, rue Marceau
Tel: 93 38 79 73

Le Voilier
On the beach, nice atmosphere
La Croisette
Tel: 93 94 25 46

Warner Café
For a quick lunch
3, rue Hélène Vagliano
Tel: 93 99 79 58

BEACH
Majestic Beach
Full service, bar, music, parking
Open May to October
14, La Croisette
Tel: 93 98 77 00

Lido Plage
Young & trendy, full service
restaurant open all year
La Croisette
Tel: 93 38 25 44

BAR/CAFÉ
La Chunga
Late night! Piano bar, restaurant
72, la Croisette
Tel: 93 94 11 29

Café Carlton
Nice view, afternoon tea, parking
58, la Croisette

Festival
Watch people after the beach
52, la Croisette

NIGHTLIFE
Carlton Casino Club
Casino, restaurant, bar, dressed up,
terrace, live music, parking
58, la Croisette
Tel: 93 68 00 33

Studio Circus
Fun, crazy, show, celebrities and
Arab princes, parking, open only
May, July and August (not June)
48, bd de la République
Tel: 93 38 32 98

EXCURSIONS
Iles de Lérins
Ile St Marguerite & Ile St Honorat
Historical sites, trails, restaurants
Gare Maritime
Tel: 93 99 62 01

GOLF
Golf Cannes-Mandelieu
18 + 9 holes, shaded by pinetrees.
Tel: 93 49 55 39

HOUSE RENTING
Riviera Retreats
Apartments & mansions, Cannes-
Californie, Mougins, Super-Cannes
11, rue des Petits Ponts
Mougins-le-Haut
Tel: 93 64 86 40
Fax: 93 64 00 80

YACHT CHARTER AGENTS
Figurehead
Sylvie Romain
Good selection of yachts for charter
14, rue Pasteur
Tel: 92 99 39 93
Fax: 92 99 39 99

HELICOPTER SERVICE
Heliair Monaco
Regular and private service
Tel: 93 05 00 50
Fax: 93 05 76 17

LUXURY CAR RENTALS
Monaco Auto Location
Chauffeur driven cars and limousine,
luxury cars, delivery and pick up
Monte-Carlo
Tel: 93 50 74 95 - 92 05 84 81
Fax: 93 25 78 38

CAP D'AIL
(Cap Ferrat - page 45)
See also Èze, Beaulieu and Monaco

RESTAURANTS
La Pinède
At the beach, relaxing, seaview
10, bd Mer
Tel: 93 78 37 10

CAP D'ANTIBES
(Antibes - page 117)
See also Antibes and Juan-les-Pins

HOTEL
Hotel du Cap ****
9 suites, 121 rooms, seaview, private
cabanas, big park, pool, tennis,
parking, NO Credit Cards
Bd Kennedy
Tel: 93 61 39 01
Fax: 93 67 76 04

Manoir Castel Garoup AXA ***
Mme Giraud and Mme Mammoliti
20 rooms, very quiet, pool, tennis,
parking, open April to November
959, bd la Garoupe
Tel: 93 61 36 51
Fax: 93 67 74 88

RESTAURANTS
Le Bacon **
Seaview, terrace, famous for
Bouillabaisse, parking
Bd Bacon
Tel: 93 61 50 02

César, Plage Keller
Mr Keller
At the beach, seaview, parking
Plage Garoupe
Tel: 93 61 33 74

Pavillion Eden Roc, Hotel du Cap
Seaview, terrace, parking,
NO Credit Cards
Bd Kennedy
Tel: 93 61 39 01

BEACH
Plage Keller
Private beach, full service
Plage Garoupe
Tel: 93 61 33 74

HOUSE RENTING
Riviera Retreats
Mansions & houses on the Cap
11, rue des Petits Ponts
Mougins-le-Haut
Tel: 93 64 86 40
Fax: 93 64 00 80

CAP FERRAT
(Cap Ferrat - page 45)
See also Villefranche, Beaulieu
and Èze)

TOURIST INFORMATION: 93 76 08 90

HOTEL
Bel Air Cap Ferrat ****
11 suites, 48 rooms,
seaview, big park, very quiet,
seawaterpool, tennis, parking
Bd Géneral de Gaulle
Tel: 93 76 00 21
Fax: 93 76 04 52

Brise Marine ***
16 rooms, seaview, garden,
quiet
Av. Jean Mermoz
Tel; 93 76 04 36
Fax: 93 76 11 49

Voile d'Or ****
5 suites, 45 rooms, seaview, terrace,
pool, parking, open March to Octobre
In the old harbor
Tel: 93 01 13 13
Fax: 93 76 11 17

RESTAURANTS
Le Cap, Hotel Bel Air ****
Chef Jean Claude Guillon
Seaview, terrace, quiet, parking
Bd General de Gaulle
Tel: 93 76 00 21

Club Dauphin, Hotel Bel Air
Poolclub, private cabanas, rocks,
seaview, only lunch and only
summertime, parking
Bd Géneral de Gaulle
Tel: 93 76 00 21

Le Provençal ***
View of port, terrace
Av. D. Semeria
Tel: 93 76 03 97

Paloma
Casual, on the beach, view of Èze
Route St Hospice
Tel: 93 01 64 71

Calablu
View of new port, terrace, best for fish
In the new harbor
Tel: 93 76 01 66

Voile d'Or ***
View of port and sea,
terrace, quiet, parking
In the old harbor
Tel: 93 01 13 13

SIGHTS
Ephrussi Rothschild Foundation
Beautiful gardens, art & antiques
collection, historical site, guided tours,
parking, closed November, December,
and Mondays
Tel: 93 01 33 39

CAP MARTIN
(Frontierland - page 35)
See also Monaco, Roquebrune and Menton

RESTAURANTS
Roque Martin
By the water, view of coastline, parking
42, av. Winston Churchill
Tel: 93 35 75 56

Le Pirate
Casual, wild, fun and expensive - don't bring a car
Promenade Cap Martin
Tel: 93 35 81 71

CAP ROUX
(Route de l'Esterel - page 203)
See also Agay and Miramar

AUBERGE
Auberge d'Antheor
Seaview, private terraces, quiet, pool, parking
RN98
Tel: 94 44 83 38
Fax: 94 44 84 20

RESTAURANTS
Auberge d'Antheor
Seaview, terrace, parking
RN98
Tel: 94 44 83 89

CARCÈS
(Route du Rosé - page 227)
See also Cabasse and Thoronet

RESTAURANTS
L'Auberge du Lac
Yannick Floury
View over lake, terrace, parking
Tel: 94 04 51 77

BAR/TABAC
Chez Jaqueline
Jaqueline
Place Gabriel Peri

CASTELLANE
(Route Napoleon - page 159)
See also Verdon and Trigance

AUBERGE
Ma Petite Auberge *
18 rooms, provençal style, parking
Tel: 92 83 62 06

Auberge du Teillon **
9 rooms, peaceful old "inn," parking
Route N 85 north of Castellane
Tel: 92 83 60 88

RESTAURANTS
Ma Petite Auberge
Provençal style, terrace, parking
Tel: 92 83 62 06

Auberge du Teillon
Peaceful old "inn," terrace, open fire, parking
Route N 85 north of Castellane
Tel: 92 83 60 88

CIPIÈRES
(Route d'Aventure - page 101)
See also Thorenc

HOTEL
Château de Cipières ***
6 spacious suites! Castle from 14th century, magnificent view, historical site, private park, gym, pool, parking
Tel: 93 59 98 00
Fax: 93 59 98 02

RESTAURANT
Château de Cipières *
As above
Only for overnight guests!

ADVENTURES
Aventure Evasion
Diving, canyoning, trial motorcycle, mountain bike, paragliding, climbing, hiking
Tel: 93 42 92 56
Fax: 93 42 93 83

CORNICHE D'OR
(Route de l'Esterel - page 203)
See also Fréjus and Agay

HOTEL
Sol e Mar
47 rooms, private terraces, seaview, very modern, parking
Le Dramont
Tel: 94 95 25 60
Fax: 94 83 83 61

ENTRECASTEAUX
(Route du Rosé - page 227)
See also Salernes

HOTEL
Châteaux d'Entrecasteaux *
1 suite, 2 rooms, historical site, pool, private park, parking
Tel: 94 04 43 95
Fax: 94 04 48 46

RESTAURANTS
La Fourchette
Traditional provençal, terrace, view of castle
Tel: 94 04 42 78

HORSE BACK RIDING
Club des Amourenes
Excursions
Tel: 94 67 54 91

ENTREVAUX
(Route des Neiges - page 81)
See also Puget-Théniers

RESTAURANTS
Vauban
View of fortress, parking
Pl. Louis Moreau
Tel: 93 05 42 40

ÈZE-VILLAGE
(Route Col de Turini - page 55)
See also Cap Ferrat, Beaulieu-sur-Mer, Monaco and Èze-bord-de-Mer

TOURIST INFORMATION: 93 41 26 00

HOTEL
Château de la Chèvre d'Or **
4 suites, 11 rooms, beautiful location dominating the coastline and the sea, small pool, picturesque decor, very quiet, only accessible by foot, parking, open March to November
Tel: 93 41 12 12
Fax: 93 41 06 72

Château EZA **
3 suites, 5 rooms, terrace with a magnificent view of coastline and sea, very quiet, only accessible by foot, parking, open from Easter to end of October
Tel: 93 41 12 24
Fax: 93 41 16 64

RESTAURANTS
La Bergerie
Old stone "mas" with rustic decor, parking
Grande Corniche
Tel: 93 41 03 67

Château de la Chèvre d'Or *
Beautiful view, picturesque decor, very quiet, only accessible by foot, parking, open March to November
Tel: 93 41 12 12

Château EZA *
beautiful view, terrace, very quiet, only accessible by foot, parking
Tel: 93 41 12 24

Auberge Troubadour
Picturesque decor, make reservation, only accessible by foot
Rue Brec
Tel: 93 41 19 03

ÈZE-BORD-DE-MER
(Cap Ferrat - 45)
See also Èze-Village, Cap Ferrat and Monaco

HOTEL
Cap Estel **
9 suites, 37 rooms, seaview, very private and quiet, park, pool, beach, tennis, parking
Basse Corniche
Tel: 93 01 50 44
Fax: 93 01 55 20

FAYENCE
(Route de Provence - page 181)
See also Callian and Montauroux

AUBERGE
Moulin de la Camandoule *
6 rooms, very quiet, parking
Ch. de Notre-Dame
Tel: 94 76 00 84
Fax: 94 76 10 40

RESTAURANTS

Moulin de la Camandoule
Terrace, old stone mill,
very quiet, parking
Ch. de Notre-Dame
Tel: 94 76 00 84

La France
Casual, terrace
1, grande rue du Château
Tel: 94 76 00 14

FRÉJUS
(Route de l'Esterel - page 203)
See also Cap Roux and St Raphaël

Tourist information: 94 51 54 14

HOTEL

Les Jardins de San Pedro *
28 room, private park, pool,
fitness- room, nice decor,
sauna, tennis, parking
Av. Colonel Brooke
Tel: 94 83 65 69
Fax: 94 40 57 20

RESTAURANTS

Lou Calen
Casual, provençal styled, old town
9, rue Desaugiers
Tel: 94 52 36 87

Les Jardins de San Pedro *
Private park, terrace,
nice decor, parking
Av. Colonel Brooke
Tel: 94 83 65 69

Le Vieux Four
"rustic interior," old town
57, rue Grissolle
Tel: 94 51 56 38

GOLF

Golf de Valescure
18 + 9 holes, golf academy
Av. du Golf
Tel: 94 82 42 42
Fax: 94 44 61 37

HORSE BACK RIDING

Les 3 Fers
Excursions in the Esterel massif
Domaine du Grenouillet
Tel: 94 82 75 28

LA GARDE
(Route Napoleon - page 159)
See also Castellane

AUBERGE

Auberge du Teillon **
9 rooms, peaceful old "inn," parking
Route N 85 (north of Castellane)
Tel: 92 83 60 88

RESTAURANTS

Auberge du Teillon
Peaceful old "inn," terrace, parking
Route N 85 (north of Castellane)
Tel: 92 83 60 88

LA GARDE-FREINET
(Route du Rosé - page 227)
See also Grimaud

RESTAURANTS

La Faücado
Jean Louis et Jean Paul
Provençal style, terrace,
open fire, dogs and cats
La Haute Perruche
Tel: 94 43 60 41

POTTERY

Les Vergers "Terre Cuite"
Henry-Biabaud
Tel: 94 43 62 18

VINEYARDS

Château des Launes
Open every day except Sunday
afternoon, parking
D558
Tel: 94 60 01 95
Fax: 94 60 01 43

GOLF

Robert Trent Jones
3 x 18 holes, hotel and restaurants,
tennis, pool, fishing, parking
Tel: 94 73 55 87
Fax: 94 73 55 89

GASSIN
(Route du Rosé - page 227)
See also Presqu'Ile de St Tropez

HOTEL

Villa Belieu **
5 suites, 13 rooms, all individually
decorated, very quiet, private
park, pool, tennis, gym, heliport,
parking
Tel: 94 56 40 56
Fax: 94 43 43 34

RESTAURANTS

Villa Belieu *
Terrace, tastefully decorated,
parking
Tel: 94 56 40 56

VINEYARDS

Château Barbeyrolles
Mme Régine Sumiere
Wine tasting all weekdays
Tel: 94 56 33 58
Fax: 94 56 33 49

Domaine de Bertaud-Belieu
Mlle Gourmelon
Wine tasting all weekdays
Tel: 94 56 16 83
Fax: 94 43 43 34

Château Minuty
Mr Matton-Farnet
Wine tasting, visit caves
all weekdays
Tel: 94 56 12 09
Fax: 94 56 18 38

GOLFE-JUAN
(Route Napoleon - page 159)
See also Cannes, Juan-les-Pins and
Vallauris

RESTAURANTS

Chez Christiane *
View of port, terrace,
fresh fish
In the harbor
Tel: 93 63 72 44

Chez Gigi
Antoine
Casual, view of port, terrace,
pizza, parking
Av. des Frères Rouston
Tel: 93 63 71 37

Nounou *
Seaview, terrace, "bouillabaisse,"
private beach, parking
On the beach
Tel: 93 63 71 73

Tetou **
Seaview, "bouillabaisse,"
private beach, parking,
No Credit Cards
À la plage
Tel: 93 63 71 16

CAFÉ

Café de l'Escale
View of port, terrace
Av. des Frères Rouston

ADVENTURES

Image Marin
Diving excursions,
31, av. des Frères Roustan
Tel: 93 63 22 37

GOURDON
(Route d'Aventure - page 101)
See also Opio and Valbonne

RESTAURANTS

Auberge de Gourdon
Casual, parking
Tel: 93 09 69 69

Le Nid d'Aigle
Beautiful view, rustic decor,
terrace, only accessible by foot
Tel: 93 09 68 52

GRÉOLIÈRES-LES-NEIGES
(Route d'Aventure - page 101)
See also Cipières and Thorenc

SKI RESORT
Alt.1450-1777m (4800-5850ft)
Closest ski-resort to the coast!
10 ski-lifts,
Snow information
Tel: 93 59 95 16

GRIMAUD
(Route du Rosé - page 227)
See also Presqu'Ile de St Tropez

HOTEL

La Boulangerie *
10 rooms, private garden, view,
pool, parking, open Easter
to mid October
D14
Tel: 94 43 23 16
Fax: 94 43 33 42

Coteau Fleuri *
14 rooms, view, quiet
parking,
Place des Penitents
Tel: 94 43 20 17
Fax: 94 43 33 42

RESTAURANTS

La Bretonnière *
Mr Rabud
Provençal style
Place des Pénitents
Tel: 94 43 25 26

Coteau Fleuri *
View, terrace,
parking
Place des Pénitents
Tel: 94 43 20 17

La Spaghetta
Mr Fabien de Paz
Casual, terrace
1, montée St Joseph
Tel: 94 43 28 59

HAUT-DE-CAGNES
(Route d'Aventure - page 101)
See also Vence, Biot and Antibes

HOTEL
Le Cagnard *
10 suites, 18 rooms, beautifully
decorated, old style, quiet and
peaceful, terraces, difficult access,
parking, closed Nov to mid December
Rue Pontis-Long
Tel: 93 20 73 21
Fax: 93 22 06 39

RESTAURANTS
Le Cagnard **
Beautifully decorated, old style, terrace
with view, open fire, quiet and
peaceful, difficult access, parking
Rue Pontis-Long
Tel: 93 20 73 21

ILES DE LÉRINS
(Cannes - page 143)
See also Cannes, Golfe-Juan
and Juan-les-Pins

ACCESS
Gare Maritime Cannes
In the old port, parking
Tel: 93 99 62 01

RESTAURANTS
L'Escale
Beautiful view of Cannes, terrace
Ile Ste Marguerite
Tel: 93 43 49 25

Frédéric
Close to monastery, shaded terrace
Ile St Honorat
Tel: 93 48 66 88

ISOLA 2000
(Route des Neiges - page 81)
Sea also Auron

SKIRESORT
Alt. 1800-2600 m (6000-8600 ft)
1 cable-car, 24 ski-lifts,
44 ski-runs, heliport
Snow information
Tel: 93 23 15 15
Fax: 93 23 14 25

HOTEL
Le Diva **
5 suites, 23 rooms, terrace, quiet,
beautiful mountainview, jacuzzi,
sauna, parking, open December to
May and end June to September
Tel: 93 23 17 71
Fax: 93 23 12 14

Le Chastillon **
54 rooms, nice once you're inside,
mountainview, close to skiing,
parking, open December to end April
Tel: 93 23 10 60
Fax: 93 23 17 66

RESTAURANTS
La Bergerie
Old stone "mas," in the skislopes,
terrace, barbecue, make reservation
Tel: 93 23 17 47

Le Diva *
Terrace, quiet, open fireplace,
beautiful mountainview, parking
Tel: 93 23 17 71

Edelweiss, at Chastillon
Terrace, open fireplace,
mountainview, parking
Tel: 93 23 10 60

AFTER SKI
The bar at Chastillon

Le Rendez-Vous
Lots of people, center of ski resort

ACTIVITIES
Ice Driving School
Tel: 93 23 14 43

3 Wheel Motor Bike Excursions
Tel: 93 23 14 43

Snow Scooter Excursions
Tel: 93 23 10 50

Horse back riding & sledges
In front of Résidence les Adrets
every day 2 - 6 PM

Dog sledge excursions
Monday, Wednesday and Friday
Tel: 93 23 15 15

JUAN-LES-PINS
(Antibes - page 117)
See also Antibes and Cap d'Antibes

HOTEL
Belles Rives **
4 suites, 40 rooms, beautiful seaview,
quiet, artdeco decor, private beach
and dock, parking, open Easter - Oct.
Bd du Littoral
Tel: 93 61 02 79
Fax: 93 67 43 51

Parc *
Quiet location, seaview, small pool,
parking, open March - October
Av. Guy Maupassant
Tel: 93 61 61 00
Fax: 93 67 92 42

RESTAURANTS
Belles Rives *
Beautiful sea view, terrace,
private beach and dock, parking
Bd du Littoral
Tel: 93 61 02 79

Bodega
Casual, streetlife
Av. Doctor Dautheville
Tel: 93 61 07 52

Moorea
Mr Djian
At the beach, trendy
Bd Charles Guillaumont
Tel: 93 61 58 68

Pousse Pousse
Liza and Maurice
Asian and Vegetarian food
Av. Doctor Dautheville
Tel: 93 61 41 99

Vesuvio
Casual, streetlife, terrace
Av. George Gallice
Tel: 93 61 21 47

BEACH
Belles Rives **
Beautiful view, private, terrace
for lunches, private dock, parking
Bd du Littoral
Tel: 93 61 02 79

Moorea
Mr Djian
Casual, trendy & young, fun, music
Bd Charles Guillaumont
Tel: 93 61 58 68

BAR/CAFÉ
Crystal
Streetlife, loud, large selection of beer
Av. George Gallice
Tel: 93 61 02 51

LIMONE
(Route des Neiges - page 81)

TOURIST INFORMATION: 0171- 92101

SKIRESORT
Alt. 1000-2100 m (3300-7000 ft.)
31 ski-lifts, 51 slopes,
cross-country skiing
Snow information
Tel: 39-0171-92 62 54

HOTEL
Principe Grand Hotel **
Facing slopes, very near ski-lifts, only
half board, pool, parking,
open December - April
Tel: 39-0171- 92 75 74
Fax: 39-0171- 92 70 70

Touring *
In the village, only half board,
parking, open Dec - April
4, via Roma
Tel: 39-0171-923 93
Fax: 39-0171-92 67 17

RESTAURANTS
Hosteria del Cartune
Younger people, stone vaulted
dining room, make reservation
16, via Roma
Tel: 39-0171-92 65 79

Mac Miche Ristorante *
Picturesque decor, elegant,
make reservation, avoid fish
12, via Roma
Tel: 39-0171-924 49

Il Bagatto Ristorante Osteria
Casual, make reservation
16, via XX Settembre
Tel: 39-0171-92 75 43

Trattoria del Salvatore
Casual & small, make reservation
2b, via Cap Centino
Tel: 39-0171-92 61 20

AFTER SKI
Cremeria Cäiri Gelati e Sorbeti
Selection of ice-creames,
pastery, and crepes
59, via Roma

Birreria de la Puncha
Beer-bar
54, via Roma

LITTLE SWITZERLAND
(Route Col de Turini - page 55)
See also Mercantour National Park,
St Martin-Vésubie,
St Dalmas-Valdeblore

AUBERGE
Auberge des Murès **
9 rooms, swiss style, mountainview,
quiet, parking, closed October to end
January and May
St Dalmas-Valdeblore
Tel: 93 02 80 11

Auberge St Pierre ***
20 rooms, Swiss style chalet, quiet,
parking, open mid May to mid Sep.
St Martin-Vésubie
Tel: 93 03 30 40

RESTAURANTS
Auberge des Murès
Swiss style, mountainview,
quiet, parking
St Dalmas-Valdeblore
Tel: 93 02 80 11

Auberge St Pierre
Terrace, open fire, rustic
wood decor, quiet, parking
St Martin-Vésubie
Tel: 93 03 30 40

HIKING
Guides Office
St Dalmas-Valdeblore
Tel: 93 02 84 59

Guides office
St Martin-Vésubie
Tel: 93 03 26 60

NORDIC SKIING
Borèon
25 km (15 miles) of tracks
Information
Tel: 93 03 21 28

SKI RESORT
La Colmiane
Alt. 1400-1800 m (4600 - 6000 ft)
1 chairlift, 9 skilifts, 21 runs
Snow information
Tel: 93 02 84 59

LORGUES
(Route du Rosé - page 227)

RESTAURANTS
Chez Bruno ***
Private atmosphere, quiet,
terrace, parking
Route de Vidauban
Tel: 94 73 92 19

VINEYARD
Château de Berne
Bill Muddyman
RN 7
Tel: 94 73 70 13

LE LUC
(Route du Rosé - page 227)
See also La Garde-Freinet, Cabasse

AUBERGE
Le Grillade au Feu de Bois ***
15 rooms, quiet, private park,
pool, parking
RN 7
Tel: 94 69 71 20
Fax: 94 59 66 11

RESTAURANTS
Le Grillade au Feu de Bois
Terrace, open fire, antiques, parking
RN 7
Tel: 94 69 71 20

VINEYARDS
Domaine de la Bernarde
Mr Meulnart
Wine tasting weekdays
RN 7
Tel: 94 60 71 31
Fax: 94 47 96 04

Commanderie de Peyrassol
Yves et Francoise Rigord
Wine tasting every day
RN 7
Tel: 94 69 71 02
Fax: 94 59 69 23

MANDELIEU
(Route de l'Esterel - page 203)
See also Théole, Adret, and Cannes

HOTEL
Le Domaine d'Olival ****
Apartments, private park, pool,
tennis, quiet, parking,
open mid January to mid October
778, av. de la Mer
Tel: 93 49 31 00
Fax: 92 97 69 28

RESTAURANTS
La Maison de Bruno et Judy
Terrace
Place du Château
Tel: 93 49 95 15

L'Oasis ****
Seaview, terrace, parking
Rue Jean Honore-Carle
Tel: 93 49 95 52

SIGHTS
Henry Clew Foundation
Medieval castle, art collection
2 daily guided tours March- October
Tel: 93 47 03 09

GOLF
Golf Club Cannes-Mandelieu
18 + 9 holes, seaside
Tel: 93 49 55 39

HORSE RIDING
Club Hippique-Centre Equestre
Excursions in the Esterel
RN 7 direction Fréjus
Tel: 93 49 42 39

MENTON
(Frontierland - page 35)
See also Roquebrune, Cap Martin and
Monaco

HOTEL
Ambassadeurs
12 suites, 42 rooms, open all year
3, rue Partouneaux
Tel: 93 28 75 75
Fax: 93 35 62 32

RESTAURANTS
L'Oursin
Casual, seaview, fresh fish!
3, rue Trenca
Tel: 93 28 33 62

MERCANTOUR
(Route Col de Turini - page 55)
See also Little Switzerland

NATURE ADVENTURES
Mercantour National Park
Information
23, rue d'Italie, 06006 Nice
Tel: 93 87 86 10 - 93 44 50 59
Fax: 93 86 01 06

MIRAMAR
(Route de l'Esterel - page 203)
See also Théole and Cap Roux

HOTEL
La Corniche d'Or
32 rooms, seaview, private park,
parking, open April to October
10, bd l'Esquillon
Tel: 93 75 40 12
Fax: 93 75 44 91

RESTAURANTS
Auberge Père Pascal
Seaview, terrace, parking
16, av. Trayas
Tel: 93 75 40 11 - 93 75 02 45

MONACO
(Monaco - page 23)
See also Èze, Roquebrune,
and Cap Martin

TOURIST INFORMATION: 92 16 61 16

HOTEL
Beach Plaza ****
9 suites, 304 rooms, private beach,
seaview, pool, terrace, parking
Av. Princesse Grace
Tel: 93 30 98 80
Fax: 93 50 23 14

Hermitage ****
22 suites, 220 rooms, view of port
and the rock, terrace, pool, parking
Square Beaumarchais
Tel: 92 16 40 00
Fax: 93 50 47 12

Hôtel de Paris ****
40 suites, 206 rooms, pool,
terrace, stylish decor, parking
Place Casino
Tel: 92 16 30 00
Fax: 93 25 59 17

Monte-Carlo Beach Hotel ****
46 rooms, private terraces, pool,
beach, parking, open mid May to
mid October
Av. Princesse Grace
Tel: 93 28 66 66
Fax: 93 78 14 18

RESTAURANTS
Café de Paris
Nice ambiance, terrace, casual,
Place Casino
Tel: 92 16 20 20

The Grill - Hotel de Paris ***
Rooftop, beautiful view, parking
Place Casino
Tel: 92 16 30 00

Louis XV - Hotel de Paris *****
Chef Alain Ducasse
Formal, stylish setting, parking
Place Casino
Tel: 92 16 30 01

Rampoldi
Classic Monte-Carlo
3, av. des Spélugues
Tel: 93 30 70 65

Texan
Casual, French TexMex, bar
4, rue Suffren Reymond
Tel: 93 30 34 54

Le Pinocchio
Casual, old town, small,
"terrace," reservation a must
30, rue Comte Félix Gastaldi
Tel: 93 30 96 20

Polpetta
The Guasco brothers
Casual, very Italian
2, rue Paradis
Tel: 93 50 67 84

Du Port
View of port, terrace, pasta
1, quai Albert
Tel: 93 50 77 21

Pulcinella
Casual, pasta, reservation a must
17, rue du Portier
Tel: 93 30 73 61

BEACH
Monte-Carlo Beach Hotel
Full service, pool, cabanas, parking
Av. Princesse Grace
Tel: 93 28 66 66

BAR/CAFÉ
Stars & Bars
Live music, casual, restaurant, fun
6, quai Antoine Ier
Tel: 93 50 95 95

SIGHTS
Museum of Oceanography
Open every day
Av. St-Martin
Tel: 93 15 36 00

GOLF
Monte-Carlo Golf Club
Magnificent view of coast & Monaco
La Turbie
Tel: 93 41 09 11

NIGHTLIFE
Sporting Club - Jimmy'z
Champagne - style and extravaganza,
show, dancing, terrace, garden,
parking
26, av. Princesse Grace
Tel; 92 16 27 77

HOUSE RENTING
Park Agence
Apartments & villas
25, av. de la Costa
Tel: 93 25 15 00
Fax: 93 25 35 33

YACHTING AGENT
Associated Yacht Brokers
Selection of large yachts for charter
26, bis bd Princesse Charlotte
Tel: 93 25 00 25
Fax: 93 25 83 10

HELICOPTER SERVICE
Heliair Monaco
Regular and private service
Tel: 92 05 00 50
Fax: 92 05 76 17

LUXURY CAR RENTALS
Monaco Auto Location
Chauffeur driven cars and limousines,
luxury cars, delivery and pick up
Tel: 93 50 74 95 - 92 05 84 81
Fax: 93 25 78 38

MONTAUROUX
(Route de Provence - page 181)
See also Callian and Fayence

RESTAURANT
Auberge la Marjolaine
Casual, provençal style
Face au Lavoir
Tel: 94 76 43 32

LA MOTTE
(Route de Provence - page 181)
See also Callas and Pennafort

RESTAURANTS
Les Pignatelles
Casual, terrace, open fire, parking
D 47
Tel: 94 70 25 70

VINEYARDS
Domaine du Jas d'Esclans
Mr René Lorgues
Wine tasting all week except Sunday
Route de Callas
Tel: 94 70 27 86
Fax: 94 84 30 45

Château Sainte Roseline
Domaines de Rasque de Laval
Wine tasting all week, chapel open
Sunday and Wednesday afternoon
Tel: 94 73 32 57

Château du Rouët
Mr Bernard Savatier
Wine tasting every day all week
D 47
Tel: 94 45 16 00
Fax: 94 45 17 42

MOUGINS
(Cannes - page 143)
See also Cannes and Valbonne

HOTEL
Mas Candille *
21 rooms, very quiet, provençal style,
pool, terrace, parking, closed
November to mid December
Bd Rebuffel
Tel: 93 90 00 85
Fax: 92 92 85 56

Manoir de l'Etang *
15 rooms, view over Mougins, private
park and olive grows, pool, parking,
closed mid November to mid December
and February
Allée de Manoir
Tel: 93 90 01 07
Fax: 92 92 20 70

RESTAURANTS
L'Armendier de Mougins **
Roger Vergé,
Old stone mill, terrace
Au village
Tel: 93 90 00 91

Le Bistro de Mougins
Casual,
Au village, place de la Mairie
Tel: 93 75 78 34

Ferme de Mougins *
Old "mas," nice setting in private
park, terrace, open fire, parking
St Basile
Tel: 93 90 03 74

Feu Follet
Casual, terrace
Au village, place de la Mairie
Tel: 93 90 15 78

Mas Candille *
Very quiet, provençal style,
open fire, terrace, parking
Bd Rebuffel
Tel: 93 90 00 85

Manoir de l'Etang *
Terrace with view over Mougins,
quiet, parking
Allée de Manoir
Tel: 93 90 01 07

Moulin de Mougins ***
Roger Vergé
Temple of haute cuisine, terrace, art
collection, beautiful decor, parking,
closed February and March
Route Valbonne, D3
Tel: 93 75 78 24

COOK SCHOOL
Roger Vergé
À la carte lessons, food week, training
course, professionals or beginners
Place du Commandant Lamy
Tel: 93 75 35 70
Fax: 93 90 18 55

GOLF
Country Club de Cannes-Mougins
18 holes
175, av. du Golf
Tel: 93 75 79 13

MOUSTIERS-STE-MARIE
(Route Napoleon - page 159)
See also Verdon

RESTAURANTS
Les Santons *
Provençal style, picturesque decor,
reservation is recommended
Place Église
Tel: 92 74 66 48

LE MUY
(Route de Provence - page 181)
See also Pennafort

RESTAURANTS
Les Pignatelles
Casual, terrace, open fire,
parking
D 47
Tel: 94 70 25 70

VINEYARDS
Domaine du Jas d'Esclans
Mr René Lorgues
Wine tasting all week except Sunday
Route de Callas
Tel: 94 70 27 86

Château Sainte Roseline
Domaines de Rasque de Laval
Wine tasting, visit of caves all week,
chapel open Sunday and Wednesday
afternoon
Tel: 94 73 32 57
Fax: 94 47 53 06

Château du Rouët
Mr Bernard Savatier
Wine tasting every day all week,
parking
D 47
Tel: 94 45 16 00
Fax: 94 45 17 42

LA NAPOULE
(Route de l'Esterel - page 203)
See also Théole, Adrets, Cannes

HOTEL
Le Domain d'Olival
*Apartments, private park, quiet,
tennis, pool, parking, closed
November to mid January*
778, av. de la Mer
Tel: 93 49 31 00
Fax: 92 97 69 28

RESTAURANTS
La Maison de Bruno et Judy
Terrace, facing the castle
Place de Château
Tel: 93 49 95 15

L'Oasis **
*Seaview, terrace, elegant,
parking*
Rue Jean Honore-Carle
Tel: 93 49 95 52

SIGHTS
Henry Clew Foundation
*Medieval castle, home to
Henry Clew and his art collection,
2 daily guided tours March- October*
Tel: 93 47 03 09

GOLF
Golf Club Cannes-Mandelieu
*18 + 9 holes, seaside, shaded
by pinetrees*
Route du Golf
Tel: 93 49 55 39

HORSE RIDING
Club Hippique-Centre Equestre
Excursions in the Esterel Mountains
RN 7 direction Fréjus
Tel: 93 49 42 39

NICE
(Nice - page 67)
See also Villefranche and Cap Ferrat

HOTEL
Beau Rivage **
*12 suites, 106 rooms, sea and
mountainview, private beach,*
24, rue St-François-de-Paule
Tel: 93 80 80 70
Fax: 93 80 55 77

Palais Maeterlinck **
*6 suites. 20 rooms, magnificent view
of sea and coast, pool, private garden,
private dock, parking, closed January
to mid February*
30, bd M. Maeterlinck
Tel: 92 00 72 00
Fax: 92 00 72 10

Négresco **
*20 suites, 150 rooms, seaview, beach,
impressive art & antique collection,
historical site*
37, promenade des Anglais
Tel: 93 88 39 51
Fax: 93 88 35 68

La Perouse **
*65 rooms, beautiful view of coastline
and sea, close to old town, pool*
11, quai Rauba-Capeu
Tel: 93 62 34 63
Fax: 93 62 59 41

RESTAURANTS
Barale
*Mme Barale
Casual, cuisine niçoise*
39, rue Beaumont
Tel: 93 89 17 94

Brasserie Flo
*Casual, art deco,
Sunday brunch!*
4, rue S-Guitry
Tel: 93 80 70 10

Chantecler ***
*Chef Dominique Le Stanc
Formal, incredible cuisine*
37, promenade des Anglais
Tel: 93 88 39 51

Les Dents de la Mer
*Close to the market,
good for fish*
2, rue St François-de-Paule
Tel: 93 80 99 16

Frog
*American TexMex, casual,
dinner only, music*
3, rue Milton Robbins
Tel: 93 85 85 65

La Merenda **
Cuisine niçoise, no reservation
4, rue du Terrasse
Tel: No telephone!

Le Safari
*At the market place, terrace,
the young Niçoise*
1, cours Saleya
Tel: 93 80 18 44

Spaghettissimo
*Fredric Gollong
At the market place, terrace,
casual, pasta!*
3, cours Saleya
Tel: 93 80 95 07

BEACH
Beau Rivage
Wood deck, full service
Promenades des Anglais
Tel: 93 80 80 70

BAR/CAFÉ
Café Turin
Café, oyster bar, casual
Place Garibaldi

NIGHTLIFE
Le Comptoir
Casual, bar, restaurant
22, rue St François-de-Paule
Tel: 93 92 08 80

SIGHTS
Marc Chagall Museum
*Open all day early June to late Sep.
rest of the year morning and after-
noon, closed Tuesdays*
Av. Dr. Ménard
Tel: 93 81 75 75

Museum of Modern Art
Closed Thursdays and holidays
Promenade des Art
Tel: 93 62 61 62

Russian Cathedral
Closed Sunday morning
Av. Nicolas II
Tel: 93 96 88 02

VINEYARDS
Château de Bellet
*Count Ghilain de Charnacé
Visit only by appointment*
Route de Saquier
Tel: 93 37 81 57

Château de Cremat
*Mr Bagnis
Visit only by appointment*
442, chemin de Cremat
Tel: 93 37 80 30

GALLERIES
Galerie Ferrero
Arman, Cécar
2, rue de Congres
Tel: 93 88 34 44

SPECIAL SHOPS
Moulin d'Huile d'Olive Alziari
Olive oil, olives & local products
14, rue St François-de-Paule

HELICOPTER SERVICE
Heliair Monaco
Regular and private service
Tel: 92 05 00 50
Fax: 92 05 76 17

LUXURY CAR RENTALS
Monaco Auto Location
*Chauffeur driven cars and limousines,
de luxee cars, delivery and pick up*
Monte-Carlo
Tel: 93507495 - 92058481
Fax: 93 25 78 38

OPIO
(Route d'Aventure - page 101)
See also Valbonne

RESTAURANTS
Mas des Géraniums
*Nice view from terrace over
olivegrews, good for lunch,
parking*
D 7, San Peyre
Tel: 93 77 23 23

SPECIAL SHOPS
Moulin a Huile Michel
*Special regional products including
olives and "home"made olive oil,
parking*
2, route de Châteauneuf
Tel: 93 44 45 12

LA PEILLE
(Route Col de Turini - page 55)
*See also Ste-Agnès, La Peillon,
and La Turbie*

BAR/CAFÉ
Auberge Belverde
Terrace with beautiful view

LA PEILLON
(Route Col de Turini - page 55)
*See also La Peille, Ste-Agnès
and La Turbie*

AUBERGE
Auberge de la Madone
*3 suites, 17 rooms, terrace with view,
small park, quiet, tennis, pool,
parking, closed mid October to mid
December*
La Peillon
Tel: 93 79 91 17
Fax: 93 79 99 36

RESTAURANTS
Auberge de la Madone
*Terrace , quiet, lots of charm,
parking*
La Peillon
Tel: 93 79 91 17

PENNAFORT

(Route de Provence - page 181)
*See also Bargemon, Le Muy,
and La Motte*

HOTEL
Hostellerie Pennafort *
*25 rooms, very quiet, private garden,
lake, pool, barbecue, parking*
Route de Pennafort, D 25
Tel: 94 76 66 51
Fax: 94 76 67 23

RESTAURANTS
Hostellerie Pennafort
Very quiet, terrace, garden, parking
Route de Pennafort, D 25
Tel: 94 76 66 51
Fax: 94 76 67 23

PONT-DU-LOUP

(Route d'Aventure - page 101)
*See also Tourettes-sur-Loup, and
Cipières*

HOTEL
La Reserve *
*15 rooms, view over river
and mountain, quiet, private
park, pool, parking*
Tel: 93 59 40 00

RESTAURANT
La Reserve
View over river and mountain
Tel: 93 59 40 00

ADVENTURES
Aventure Evasion
*Canyoning, trial motorcycle,
mountain bike, paragliding,
climbing, hiking*
Tel: 93 42 92 56
Fax: 93 42 93 83

PRÉ-DU-LAC

(Route d'Aventure - page 101)
See also Gourdon

BAR/CAFÉ
La Pergola
*Meeting point for most
adventures and excursions*

ADVENTURES
Aventure Evasion
*Diving, canyoning, trial motorcycle,
mountain bike, paragliding,
climbing, hiking*
Tel: 93 42 92 56
Fax: 93 42 93 83

PRESQU'ILE DE ST TROPEZ

(Route du Rosé - page 227)
*See also Gassin, Grimaud,
Ramatuelle, and St Tropez*

TOURIST INFORMATION: 94 97 41 21

HOTEL
Byblos **
*37 suites, 70 rooms, quiet, each room
individually decorated, pool, parking,
open March to end October*
Av Paul Signac
St Tropez
Tel: 94 97 00 04
Fax: 94 97 40 52

Résidence de la Pinède **
*6 suites, 35 rooms, private beach,
beautiful view over bay and port,
quiet, pool, parking,
open April to mid October*
Plage de la Bouillabaisse
St Tropez
Tel: 94 97 04 21
Fax: 94 97 73 64

La Sube *
*Mme A. Bollore
32 rooms, view over port, noisy,
balconies facing port*
Quai Suffren
St Tropez
Tel: 94 97 30 04
Fax: 94 54 89 08

Le Yaca **
*22 rooms, in the village, quiet, small
garden, pool, open April to mid Oct.*
1, bd Aumale
St Tropez
Tel; 94 97 11 79
Fax: 94 97 58 50

Auberge des Vieux Moulins *
*5 rooms, charming old "mas,"
warm decor, parking, open
April to mid October*
Route de la Plage
Pampelonne
Tel: 94 97 17 22
Fax: 94 97 70 72

Tahiti *
*Felix Palmari
20 rooms, at the beach, pool,
tennis, gym, workout, parking,
open May to mid October*
Tahiti Plage
Pampelonne
Tel: 94 97 18 02
Fax: 94 54 86 66

Villa de Belieu **
*15 suites, 13 rooms, all different,
very quiet, private park, pool,
tennis, heliport, parking,
open March to January*
Gassin
Tel: 94 56 40 56
Fax: 94 43 43 34

La Boulangerie *
*10 rooms, private garden, view,
pool, parking, open Easter to mid
October*
D14
Grimaud
Tel: 94 43 23 16
Fax: 94 43 33 42

Coteau Fleuri *
14 rooms, view, quiet, parking
Place des Penitents
Grimaud
Tel: 94 43 20 17
Fax: 94 43 33 42

Le Baou *
*31 room, beautiful view, terrace, pool,
parking, open March to mid November*
Rue Gustav Etienne
Ramatuelle
Tel: 94 79 20 48
Fax: 94 79 28 36

RESTAURANTS
Café des Arts
*Mme Yvette Bains
Terrace, bar, view of place de Lices*
Place des Lices
St Tropez
Tel: 94 97 02 25

Le Gorille
Casual, streetlife, terrace facing port
Quai Suffren
St Tropez
Tel: 94 97 03 93

Chez Nano
Trendy, terrace, "gay"
Place Hotel de Ville
St Tropez
Tel. 94 97 01 66

La Table du Marché **
*Christophe Leroy
Reservation a must*
38, rue G. Clémenceau
St Tropez
Tel: 94 97 85 20

Terrace de la Pinède *
*Private beach, quiet, terrace,
parking*
Plage de la Bouillabaisse
St Tropez
Tel: 94 97 04 21

Chez Vitamine *
One menu, Asian food
Quai Suffren
St Tropez
Tel: 94 97 88 22

Club 55
*Mr Patrice
Casual "chic," shaded terrace,
beach, parking*
Plage de la Pampelonne
Tel: 94 79 80 14

Mooréa
*Good lunch at the beach,
parking*
Plage de Pampelonne
Tel: 94 97 18 17

Villa de Belieu **
*Terrace, very tastefully decorated,
heliport, parking*
Gassin
Tel: 94 56 40 56

La Bretonière *
*Mr Rabud
Provençal styled*
Place des Penitents
Grimaud
Tel: 94 43 25 26

Coteau Fleuri *
*View, terrace,
parking*
Place des Penitents
Grimaud
Tel: 94 43 20 17

La Spaghetta
*Mr Fabien de Paz
Casual, terrace*
1, montée St Joseph
Grimaud
Tel: 94 43 28 59

L'Auberge de l'Oumède
*Mr et Mme Fresia
Terrace, view over sea and vineyards,
dinner, one menu,
parking*
Chemin de l'Oumède
Ramatuelle
Tel: 94 79 81 24

La Terrasse du Baou
*Beautiful view over sea and vineyards,
terrace, parking*
Rue Gustav Etienne
Ramatuelle
Tel: 94 79 20 48

La Farigoulette
*Old style "mas," terrace, only dinner,
No Credit Cards*
Rue Victor Leon, Ramatuelle
Tel: 94 79 20 49

BAR/CAFÉ
Café des Arts
View over place de Lices
Place des Lices, St Tropez

Le Gorille
*View over the port, terrace, streetlife,
24 hours a day summertime*
Quai Suffren
St Tropez

La Sube
Mme A. Bollore
View over the port, balcony
Quai Suffren
St Tropez

Tabac du Port
View over the port, terrace,
streetlife, loud
Quai Suffren
St Tropez

BEACH
Club 55
Private beach, full service,
style: distinguished "bourgeois,"
parking,
Plage de Pampelonne
Tel: 94 79 80 14

Mooréa
Private beach, full service, boutiques,
hairdresser, style: "chic," parking,
open only summer
Plage de Pampelonne
Tel: 94 97 18 17

Voile Rouge
Paul and Luigi
Private beach, full service, style:
"young & beautiful," fun, music,
trendy, parking, open only summer
Plage de Pampelonne
Tel: 94 79 84 34

VINEYARDS
Château Barbeyrolles
Mme Régine Sumiere
Wine tasting, visit the caves, parking,
open every day
Gassin
Tel: 94 56 33 58
Fax: 94 56 33 49

Domaine de Bertaud-Belieu
Mlle Gourmelon
Wine tasting, visit the caves, parking,
open every day
Gassin
Tel: 94 56 16 83
Fax: 94 43 43 34

Château Minuty
Mr Matton-Farnet
Wine tasting, visit the caves, parking,
open every day
Gassin
Tel: 94 56 12 09
Fax: 94 56 18 38

HOUSE RENTING
Immobilier Champs Elysées
Villas & apartments
Passage du Port, St Tropez
Tel: 94 54 87 88
Fax: 94 54 87 89

HORSE BACK RIDING
Les Ecuries de Pampelonne
Excursions
Route de Plage
Tel: 94 79 83 84

BICYCLE & MOTORCYCLE RENTING
Holiday Bikes
Route de Tamaris
Tel: 94 79 87 75

HELICOPTER SERVICE
Heliair Monaco
Regular and private service
Tel: 93 05 00 50
Fax: 93 05 76 17

LUXURY CAR RENTALS
Monaco Auto Location
Chauffeur driven cars and limousines,
luxury cars, delivery and pick up
Monte-Carlo
Tel: 93 50 74 95 - 92 05 84 81
Fax: 93 25 78 38

PUGET-THENIERS
(Route des Neiges - page 81)
See also Touët-sur-Var and Entrevaux

RESTAURANT
Les Acacias
Nice "road inn," terrace, parking
RN 202
Tel: 93 05 05 25

RAMATUELLE
(Route du Rosé - page 227)
See also Presqu'Ile de St Tropez

TOURIST INFORMATION: 94 79 26 04

HOTEL
Le Baou *
41 room, beautiful view, terrace, pool,
parking, open March to November
Rue Gustave Etienne, Ramatuelle
Tel: 94 79 20 48
Fax: 94 79 28 36

Auberge des Vieux Moulins *
5 rooms, charming old "mas,"
warm decor, parking, open April to
October
Route de la Plage, Pampelonne
Tel: 94 97 17 22
Fax: 94 97 70 72

Tahiti *
Felix Palmari
20 rooms, at the beach, pool, tennis,
gym, workout, parking, open May to
mid October
Plage Pampelonne
Tel: 94 97 18 02
Fax: 94 54 86 66

RESTAURANTS
Auberge de l'Oumède
Mr et Mme Fresia
Terrace, view over sea and
vineyards, dinner, one menu, parking
Chemin de l'Oumède
Tel: 94 79 81 24

La Terrasse du Baou
Beautiful view over sea and vineyards,
terrace, parking
Rue Gustave Etienne
Tel: 94 79 20 48

La Farigoulette
Old style "mas," terrace, only dinner,
No Credit Cards
Rue Victor Leon
Tel: 94 79 20 49

BEACH
Club 55
Private beach, full service,
style: distinguished "bourgeois,"
parking
Plage de Pampelonne
Tel: 94 79 80 14

Mooréa
Private beach, full service, boutiques,
hairdresser, style: "chic," parking,
open only summer
Plage de Pampelonne
Tel: 94 97 18 17

Voile Rouge
Paul and Luigi
Private beach, full service,
style: "young & beautiful," fun,
music, trendy, parking, open only
summer
Plage de Pampelonne
Tel: 94 79 84 34

HOUSE RENTING
Immobilier Champs Elysées
Villas & apartments
Passage du Port
St Tropez
Tel: 94 54 87 88
Fax: 94 54 87 89

HORSE BACK RIDING
Les Ecuries de Pampelonne
Excursions
Route de la Plage
Tel: 94 79 83 84

BICYCLE & MOTORCYCLE RENTING
Holiday Bikes
Route de Tamaris
Tel: 94 79 87 75

ROQUEBRUNE VILLAGE
(Frontierland - page 35)
See also Monaco and Cap Martin

HOTEL
Deux Frères *
10 rooms, view of Monaco, terrace,
closed November to mid December
Place Deux Frères
Tel: 93 28 99 00
Fax: 93 28 99 10

RESTAURANTS
Dame Jean
Vaulted cellar, rustic, view
1, chemin de Sainte Lucie
Tel: 93 35 10 20

Piccolo Mondo
Tony Minetti
Casual, small and very Italian,
"terrace," make reservation
15, rue Grimaldi
Tel: 93 35 19 93

ROQUEFORT-LES-PINS
(Route d'Aventure - page 101)
See also Valbonne, Biot, Haute-de-Cagnes

AUBERGE
Auberge du Colombier *
20 rooms, view, private garden,
quiet, tennis, pool, parking, closed
January to mid February
Route de Grasse, D 2085
Tel: 93 77 10 27
Fax: 93 77 07 03

RESTAURANTS
Auberge du Colombier *
View, terrace,
parking
Route de Grasse, D 2085
Tel: 93 77 10 27

STE-AGNÈS
(Route Col de Turini - page 55)
See also La Peille, Peillon
and Menton

RESTAURANTS
La Vielle Auberge
Casual, nice view, terrace, open fire
16, rue Comtes Leotardi
Tel: 93 35 92 02

ST DALMAS-VALDEBLORE
(Route Col de Turini - page 55)
See also Little Switzerland

AUBERGE
Auberge des Murès
10 rooms, swiss style, view of mountain, quiet, parking, closed October to end January and May
Tel: 93 02 80 11

RESTAURANTS
Auberge des Murès
Mountainview, quiet, parking
Tel: 93 02 80 11

HIKING
Guides Office
Tel: 93 02 84 59

NORDIC SKIING
Boréon,
25 km (15 miles) of tracks
Information Tel: 93 03 21 28

SKI RESORT
La Colmiane
1400-1800 meter (4600 - 6000 feet)
1 chairlift, 9 skilifts, 21 runs
Snow information
Tel: 93 02 84 59

ST MARTIN-DU-VAR
(Route Col de Turini - page 55)
See also Nice

RESTAURANTS
Auberge de la Belle Route *
Jean-François Issautier
Only for the food, parking
RN 202
Tel: 93 08 10 65

ST-MARTIN-VÉSUBIE
(Route Col de Turini - page 55)
See also Little Switzerland

AUBERGE
Auberge St Pierre
20 rooms, swiss style chalet, quiet,
Tel: 93 03 30 40

RESTAURANTS
Auberge St Pierre
Terrace, open fire, rustic wood decor
Tel: 93 03 30 40

HIKING
Guides office
Tel: 93 03 26 60

ST PAUL-DE-VENCE
(Route d'Aventure - page 101)
See also Haute-de-Cagnes, Biot, and Roquefort-les-Pins

HOTEL
La Colombe d'Or *
Mme Roux and family
10 suites, 15 rooms, view, terrace, provençal decor, unique art collection, private atmosphere, pool, small park, parking, closed November to mid December
Entrance of village
Tel: 93 32 80 02
Fax: 93 32 77 78

Mas d'Artigny **
3 villas, 29 suites, 53 rooms, private park, very quiet, private pools, pool, tennis, heliport, parking
Route des Hauts de St Paul
Tel: 93 32 84 54
Fax: 93 32 95 36

RESTAURANTS
La Colombe d'Or *
Mme Roux and family
View, terrace, provençal decor, unique art collection, private atmosphere, parking
Entrance of village
Tel: 93 32 80 02

Mas d'Artigny *
Terrace with view, very quiet, heliport, parking
Route des Hauts de St Paul
Tel: 93 32 84 54

CAFÉ/TABAC
Café de la Place
Bar, snack
Place de Gaulle

SIGHTS
Fondation Maeght
Contemporary art, open July to September all day, rest of the year only business hours
Tel: 93 32 81 63

Galleries
Gault
Miniature provençal architecture
41, place Grande Fontaine
Tel: 93 32 50 54

Gallerie C. Issert
Contemporary art
Rond point St Claire
Tel: 93 32 96 62

ST PAUL-EN-FORÊT
(Côte de Provence)
See also Bagnol-en-Forêt and Fayence

RESTAURANTS
Chez Annie
Casual
Place de l'Eglise
Tel: 94 76 30 71

ST TROPEZ
(St Tropez - page 213)
See also Presqu'ile de St Tropez)

TOURIST INFORMATION: 94 97 41 21

HOTEL
Byblos **
37 suites, 70 rooms, quiet, each room individually decorated, pool, parking, open Easter to October
Av. Paul Signac
Tel: 94 97 00 04
Fax: 94 97 40 52

Résidence de la Pinède **
6 suites, 35 rooms, private beach, beautiful view, pool, parking, open April to mid October
Plage de la Bouillabaisse
Tel: 94 97 04 21
Fax: 94 97 73 64

La Sube *
Mme A. Bollore
32 rooms, view over port!
Quai Suffren
Tel: 94 97 30 04
Fax: 94 54 89 08

Le Yaca **
22 rooms, in the village, quiet, small garden, pool, open April to mid October
1, Bd Aumale
Tel; 94 97 11 79
Fax: 94 97 58 50

Auberge des Vieux Moulins *
5 rooms, charming old "mas," warm decor, parking, open April to mid October
Route de la Plage, Pampelonne
Tel: 94 97 17 22
Fax: 94 97 70 72

Tahiti *
Felix Palmari
20 rooms, at the beach, pool, tennis, gym, workout, parking, open May to mid October
Tahiti Plage, Pampelonne
Tel: 94 97 18 02
Fax: 94 54 86 66

RESTAURANTS
Café des Arts
Mme Yvette Bains
Terrace, bar, view of Place des Lices
Place des Lices
Tel: 94 97 02 25

Club 55
Mr Patrice
Casual "chic," shaded terrace, beach, parking
Plage de Pampelonne
Tel: 94 79 80 14

Le Gorille
Mr Guerin
Casual, streetlife,terrace facing port, lunch or late night, open 24 hours during summer
Quai Suffren
Tel: 94 97 03 93

Mooréa
Good lunch at the beach, parking
Plage de Pampelonne
Tel: 94 97 18 17

Chez Nano
Trendy, terrace, "gay"
Place Hotel de Ville
Tel. 94 97 01 66

Terrace de la Pinède *
Private beach, quiet, terrace, parking
Plage de la Bouillabaisse
Tel: 94 97 04 21

**La Table du Marché **
Christophe Leroy
Reservation a must
38, rue G. Clemenceau
Tel: 94 97 85 20

Chez Vitamine *
One menu, Asian food
Quai Suffren
Tel: 94 97 88 22

BEACH
Club 55
Mr Patrice
Private beach, full service, style: distinguished "bourgeois," parking
Plage de Pampelonne
Tel: 94 79 80 14

Mooréa
Private beach, full service, boutiques, hairdresser, style: "chic," parking
Plage de Pampelonne
Tel: 94 97 18 17

Voile Rouge
Paul and Luigi
Private beach, full service, style: "young & beautiful," fun, music, trendy, parking
Plage de Pampelonne
Tel: 94 79 84 34

BAR/CAFÉ
Café des Arts
View over Place de Lices
Place des Lices

Le Gorille
View over the port, terrace, streetlife
24 hours a day!
Quai Suffren

La Sube
View over the port, terrace
overlooking port
Quai Suffren

Tabac du Port
View over the port, terrace, streetlife
Quai Suffren

NIGHTLIFE
Cave du Roi
Hotel Byblos
"chic" and elegant, open summer
season only
Av. Paul Signac
Tel: 94 97 00 04

Le Papagayo
Résidence du Port
Tel: 94 54 88 18

HOUSE RENTING
Immobilier Champs Elysées
Apartments & villas
Passage du Port
Tel: 94 54 87 88
Fax: 94 54 87 89

HORSE BACK RIDING
Les Ecuries de Pampelonne
Excursions
Route de la Plage
Tel: 94 79 83 84

**BICYCLE & MOTORCYCLE
RENTING**
Holiday Bikes
Route de Tamaris
Tel: 94 79 87 75

HELICOPTER SERVICE
Heliair Monaco
Regular and private service
Tel: 92 05 00 50
Fax: 92 05 76 17

LUXURY CAR RENTALS
Monaco Auto Location
Chauffeur driven cars and limousines,
luxury cars, delivery and pick up
Monte-Carlo
Tel: 93 50 74 95 - 92 05 84 81
Fax: 93 25 78 38

SALERNES
(Route du Rosé - page 227)
See also Sillans and Tourtour

RESTAURANTS
Grand Hotel Allègre
Route St Jaques Rousseau
Tel: 94 70 60 30

ART
Alain Vagh's
Artistic tiles, full show room
Route d'Entrecasteaux
Tel: 94 70 61 85
Fax: 94 67 52 78

SEILLANS
(Route de Provence - page 181)
See also Fayence and Bargemon

HOTEL
France et restaurant Clariond *
20 rooms, parking
Place du Thouron
Tel: 94 76 96 10
Fax: 94 76 89 20

RESTAURANTS
Auberge Mestre Cornille
Provençal style, terrace
Tel: 94 76 87 31

France et restaurant Clariond
Casual, terrace, quiet, parking
Place du Thouron
Tel: 94 76 96 10

SERANON
(Route Napoleon - page 159)
See also Cabris, Castellane

RESTAURANTS
Chez Marius
Countryside "inn," parking
Tel: 93 60 30 17

BAR
Auberge Napoléon
View, snacks

SILLANS-LA-CASCADE
(Route du Rosé - page 227)
See also Sillans and Tourtour

HOTEL
Les Pins *
20 rooms
Tel: 94 04 63 26
Fax: 94 04 72 71

RESTAURANTS
Les Pins
Casual, terrace, open fire, parking
Tel: 94 04 63 26

SOSPEL
(Route Col de Turini - page 55)
See also Turin

RESTAURANTS
La Taverne Toscane
Casual, old chapel
Av. Jean Médecin
Tel: 93 04 00 40

EXCURSIONS
Aventure Voyage
4x4 wheel trips, any day all year by
arrangement, one day or week-end
Tel: 93 04 04 72

THÉOULE-SUR-MER
(Route de l'Esterel - page 203)
See also Miramar and Mandelieu

RESTAURANTS
Marco Polo
Seaview, terrace, parking
Route Lerrins
Tel: 93 49 96 59

BEACH
Marco Polo
Restaurant and bar, parking
Route Lerrins
Tel: 93 49 96 59

THORENC
(Route d'Aventure - page 101)
See also Cipières

RESTAURANTS
Auberge des Voyageurs
Casual, quiet, terrace, parking
Tel: 93 60 00 18

ADVENTURES
Aventure Evasion
Diving, canyoning, trial motorcycle,
mountain bike, paragliding,
climbing, hiking
Tel: 93 42 92 56
Fax: 93 42 93 83

THORONET
(Route du Rosé - page 227)
See also Cabasse and Carcès

BED & BREAKFAST
Domaine de Belle Vue *
Douglas and Jenny Gibbon
Casual, located in a vineyard, parking
Tel: 94 73 88 41
Fax: 94 60 12 01

VINEYARDS
Domaine de Belle Vue
Douglas and Jenny Gibbon
Tel: 94 73 88 41
Fax: 94 60 12 01

Domaine de L'Abbaye
Mr Franc Petit
Abbey, winemuseum, parking, wine
tasting, open all year
Tel: 94 73 87 36
Fax: 94 60 11 62

ADVENTURES
Domaine de Belle Vue
Douglas and Jenny Gibbon
Truffelhunting, wine tasting etc.
Tel: 94 73 88 41
Fax: 94 60 12 01

TOUËT-SUR-VAR
(Route des Neiges - page 81)
See also Valberg and Puget-Théniers

RESTAURANTS
Auberge des Chasseurs *
Nice "by the road inn," terrace,
good for lunch
RN 202
Tel: 93 05 71 11

TOURETTE-SUR-LOUP
(Route d'Aventure - page 101)
See also Vence and St Paul

HOTEL
Résidence des Chevaliers *
12 rooms, view, nice garden,
pool, parking, open April to October
Tel: 93 59 31 97

RESTAURANTS
Petit Manoir
Provençal style, only access by foot,
make reservation
21, grande rue
Tel: 93 24 19 19

TOURTOUR
(Route du Rosé - page 227)
See also Salerne and Sillans

HOTEL
La Bastide de Tourtour **
Mr et Mme Laurent
25 rooms, quiet, private park, view,
terrace, pool, tennis, heliport, parking,
open March to end October
Route Draguignan
Tel: 94 70 57 30
Fax: 94 70 54 90

Auberge St Pierre *
18 rooms, countryside, animals,
private park and lake, pool, tennis,
parking, open April to mid October
D 51
Tel: 94 70 57 17

RESTAURANTS
La Bastide de Tourtour *
Mr et Mme Laurent
Quiet, private park, view
terrace, parking
Tel: 94 70 57 30

Les Chênes Verts *
Terrace, view, "truffles," parking
Route Villecroze
Tel: 94 70 55 06

VINEYARDS
Château Thuerry
Mr et Mme Piolet
Wine tasting open every day
Villecroze
Tel: 94 70 63 02
Fax: 94 70 67 03

TRIGANCE
(Route Napoleon - page 159)
See also Verdon

HOTEL
Château de Trigance **
10 rooms, old stone castle, magnificent
restored, beautiful view, parking,
open end of March to mid November
Tel: 94 76 91 18
Fax: 94 47 58 99

Ma Petite Auberge
12 rooms, view, pool, parking,
open February to December
Tel: 94 76 92 92
Fax: 94 47 58 65

RESTAURANTS
Château de Trigance *
Stone vaulted dining room,
open fire, parking
Tel: 94 76 91 18

LA TURBIE
(Route Col de Turini - page 55)
See also Èze-Village, Monaco,
and Roquebrune

RESTAURANTS
Ferme de la Gorra
Old farm house, family atmosphere,
only reservation, parking
D 53, north of La Turbie
Tel: 93 41 15 58

GOLF
Monte-Carlo Golf Club
Magnificent view of
coast and Monaco
Tel: 93 41 09 11

TURINI PASS
(Route Col de Turini - page 55)
See also La Bollène and Sospel

AUBERGE
Trois Vallées
20 rooms, view, quiet, parking
Tel: 93 91 57 21
Fax: 93 79 53 62

RESTAURANT
Trois Vallées
Terrace, open fire, view,
quiet, parking
Tel: 93 91 57 21

UTELLE
(Route Col de Turini - page 55)
See also Little Switzerland,
and St Martin-du-Var

AUBERGE
Le Bellevue **
Chez Martinon
15 rooms, nice mountainview,
pool, parking
Tel: 93 03 17 19

RESTAURANTS
Le Bellevue
Chez Martinon
Terrace, nice mountainview, parking
Tel: 93 03 17 19

VALBERG
(Route des Neiges - page 81)
See also Touët-sur-Var

SKIRESORT
Alt. 1400-2000 m (4700-6900 Ft)
6 chair-lifts, 21 ski-lifts, 57 ski-runs
Snow information
Tel: 93 02 52 77
Fax: 93 02 52 27

VALLAURIS
(Route Napoleon - page 159)
See also Golfe-Juan, and Mougins

RESTAURANTS
Le Manuscrit
"old brewery," terrace, small
garden, parking
224, ch. Lintier
Tel: 93 64 56 56

GALLERIES
Madoura
Alain Ramie
Picasso replicas
Quart. Plan
Tel: 93 64 66 39

Moulins des Pugets
Pottery, antiques
58, av. Georges Clemenceau
Tel: 93 63 99 94

VALBONNE
(Route d'Aventure - page 101)
See also Mougins, and Biot

HOTEL
Armoiries *
Newly refurbished, opened 1992
Place des Arcades
Tel: 93 12 90 90
Fax: 93 12 90 91

Château de la Bégude *
Golf de Valbonne
Old stone "mas," pool, tennis,
golf, parking
Route de Roquefort-les-Pins
Tel: 93 12 21 05
Fax: 93 12 29 95

RESTAURANTS
Golf de Valbonne
Terrace, best for lunch,
parking
Route de Roquefort-les-Pins
Tel: 93 12 27 01

Le Mas de Valbonne *
Old mill, open fire,
shaded terrace, parking
Route de Cannes
Tel: 93 42 00 30

Moulin des Moines
Old mill next to church, parking
Place Eglise
Tel: 93 42 03 41

La Table Gourmande
"Old town," rustic decor
1, faubourg St-Esprit
Tel: 93 40 24 25

GOLF
Golf de Valbonne
18 holes, hotel, tennis,
pool, restaurant, parking
Route de Roquefort-les-Pins
Tel: 93 12 00 08
Fax: 93 12 26 00

VENCE
(Route d'Aventure - page 101)
See also St Paul, Haut-de-Cagnes,
and Tourette

TOURIST INFORMATION: 93 58 06 38

HOTEL
Château St-Martin **
10 suites, 15 rooms, view of
coast and mountain, private park,
private villas, very quiet, pool, tennis,
parking, open mid March to mid
November
Route de Coursegoules
Tel: 93 58 02 02
Fax: 93 24 08 91

RESTAURANTS
Auberge des Seigneurs
Historical site, rustic decor, open fire
Place Frêne
Tel: 93 58 04 24

Château St-Martin **
View of coast and mountain,
terrace, very quiet, parking
Route de Coursegoules
Tel: 93 58 02 02

Le Pécheur du Soleil
A choise of 300 pizzas!, "old town"
1, place Godeau
Tel: 93 58 32 56

SIGHTS
Chapelle du Rosaire
The Matisse Chapel, guided tours
Tuesdays and Thursdays or by
appointment
466, av. H. Matisse
Tel: 93 58 03 26

VENTIMIGLIA
(Frontierland - page 35)
See also Menton

HOTEL
Baia Beniamin
*6 rooms, on the beach, tropical setting,
parking*
Coastal road just after boarder (S1)
Tel: 39- 184- 380 02
Fax: 39- 184- 380 27

Riserva
*Beautiful view, 350 m (1200 ft.),
terrace, pool tennis, parking,
open April to October*
Above the old town
Tel: 39-229-533 352 181

RESTAURANTS
Baia Beniamin *
*On the beach, tropical setting,
romantic, terrace, beach,
parking*
Coastal road just after boarder (S1)
Tel: 39- 184- 380 02

Balzi Rossi **
*Giuseppina Beglia
Terrace with beautiful view,
parking*
Tel: 39-184-380 02

Marco Polo
Casual, on the beach
Passeggiata Cavalotti
Tel: 39-184- 35 26 78

VERDON, GORGE DU
(Route Napoleon - page 159)
*Castellane, Trigance, and
Moustiers-Ste-Marie*

AUBERGE
Ma Petite Auberge **
18 rooms, provençal style, parking
Castellane
Tel: 92 83 62 06

Auberge du Teillon **
9 rooms, peaceful old "inn," parking
Castellane
Route N 85 north of Castellane
Tel: 92 83 60 88

Château de Trigance **
*10 rooms, old stone castle, magnificent
restored, beautiful view, parking,
open end of March to mid November*
Tel: 94 76 91 18
Tel: 94 47 58 99

Ma Petite Auberge
*12 rooms, view, pool, parking, open
mid Feb. to end November*
Trigance
Tel: 94 76 92 92
Fax: 94 47 58 65

RESTAURANTS
Ma Petite Auberge
Provençal style, terrace, parking
Castellane
Tel: 92 83 62 06

Auberge du Teillon
Peaceful old "inn," terrace, parking
Route N 85 north of Castellane
Tel: 92 83 60 88

Château de Trigance *
Stone vaulted dining room, parking
Tel: 94 76 91 18

Les Santons *
*Provençal style, picturesque decor,
reservation is recommended*
Place Église
Moustiers-Ste-Marie
Tel: 92 74 66 48

ADVENTURES
Alp Rafting
Riverrafting
Tel: 92 83 62 02
Fax: 92 83 73 80

VILLEFRANCHE
(Cap Ferrat - page 45)
*See also Nice, Cap Ferrat, and
Beaulieu*

HOTEL
Welcome Hotel *
In the port, seaview, terrace
1, quai Courbet
Tel: 93 76 76 93
Fax: 93 01 88 81

RESTAURANTS
St. Pierre
In the port, seaview, terrace
1, quai Courbet
Tel: 93 76 76 93

BAR/TABAC
Les Palmiers
Place du Marché

SOME FINAL WORDS

All photos has been taken with a Nikon F4, a Contax RTL, and a Asahi Pentax 6 x 7 with standard
zoom lenses ranging from 24 mm to 500 mm using only Velvia Fujichrome film. They are all
"snapshots," no arrangements has been made, no set-ups and no artificial light.
They are all available in original signed prints, any size. Please write to:
TopSpoT Production, TexBarter AG, Zugerstrasse 45, CH-6330 CHAM, Switzerland

AND SOME VERY SPECIAL THANKS TO:

My parents,

My family;
Ann, Aprilia, Joen
and the dogs

Gunnar

Jean Pierre Cohen
New Riviera

Eloise & John Paul
for buying the first books